INDIGENOUS ENVIRONMENTAL
JUSTICE

Indigenous Justice

MARIANNE O. NIELSEN AND KAREN JARRATT-SNIDER
Series Editors

EDITED BY
KAREN JARRATT-SNIDER AND
MARIANNE O. NIELSEN

INDIGENOUS

ENVIRONMENTAL

JUSTICE

THE UNIVERSITY OF
ARIZONA PRESS

TUCSON

The University of Arizona Press
www.uapress.arizona.edu

ISBN-13: 978-0-8165-4083-9 (paper)

Cover design by Leigh McDonald
Cover art by Lomayumtewa K. Ishii

Library of Congress Cataloging-in-Publication Data
Names: Jarratt-Snider, Karen, editor. | Nielsen, Marianne O., editor.
Title: Indigenous environmental justice / Karen L. Jarratt-Snider and Marianne O. Nielsen
   (editors).
Description: Tucson : The University of Arizona Press, 2020. | Series: Indigenous justice |
   Includes bibliographical references and index.
Identifiers: LCCN 2019046953 | ISBN 9780816540839 (paperback)
Subjects: LCSH: Environmental justice—North America. | Indians of North America—
   Government relations. | Environmental policy—North America.
Classification: LCC GE240.N7 I64 2020 | DDC 363.70089/97—dc23
LC record available at https://lccn.loc.gov/2019046953

Printed in the United States of America
♾ This paper meets the requirements of ANSI/NISO Z39.48-1992 (Permanence of Paper).

This book is dedicated to the Indigenous scholars who are doing such necessary and innovative research for Indigenous communities, to John and Ciana for their love and support (Karen), and to Dr. Chester Cunningham, a mentor for generations of Canadian Aboriginal and non-Aboriginal community leaders and scholars, including me (Marianne).

CONTENTS

Acknowledgments   *ix*

Introduction   3

KAREN JARRATT-SNIDER AND MARIANNE O. NIELSEN

PART I.
PERSPECTIVES ON INDIGENOUS ENVIRONMENTALISM
AND INDIGENOUS ENVIRONMENTAL JUSTICE   17

1. Powerful Parallels: Deep Ecology and the Writings of
   Vine Deloria Jr.   21

   RICHARD M. WHEELOCK

2. Environmental Injustice, Land, and American Indian
   Religious Freedom   36

   KAREN JARRATT-SNIDER

3. Environmental Injustices and State-Corporate Crime
   on Navajo and Hopi Lands   59

   LINDA M. ROBYN

4. Environmental Racism: Contaminated Water in Indigenous
   and Minority Communities   92

   LINDA M. ROBYN

PART II.
INDIGENOUS COMMUNITY RESPONSES   115

5. Two Cases of Navigating Legal Complexity:
    Environmental Justice in Barrow and Tar Creek   119
    KAREN JARRATT-SNIDER

6. The Water–Energy Nexus and Environmental Justice:
    The Missing Link Between Water Rights and Energy
    Production on Tribal Lands   136
    MIA MONTOYA HAMMERSLEY

7. Not in Our Lands: A Canadian Comparative Case Study
    of Indigenous Resistance Strategies to Natural Resource
    Development in British Columbia and the Arctic   160
    T. TIMOTHY CASEY

8. Urban Native American Women as Environmental Justice
    Leaders   179
    ANNE LUNA-GORDINIER

    Conclusion   203
    KAREN JARRATT-SNIDER AND MARIANNE O. NIELSEN

    Contributors   *211*
    Index   *215*

ACKNOWLEDGMENTS

WE WOULD like to express our gratitude to the authors and illustrator who contributed to this third book in the series. It took a while to get it into print and we appreciate your willingness to stick with the project and continue to trust that we would get your work out there. We particularly want to thank Delsey Benally for her support and gentle patience in helping get this project done. We would like to acknowledge Northern Arizona University for its commitment to Native American students and communities and for encouraging projects such as this. We are particularly grateful to the anonymous reviewers who provided excellent suggestions on how to make this a stronger book. Finally, we want to say thank you to the good people at the University of Arizona Press who believed in this project to the point of being willing to publish three (and maybe more) books in the series.

INDIGENOUS
ENVIRONMENTAL
JUSTICE

INTRODUCTION

KAREN JARRATT-SNIDER AND
MARIANNE O. NIELSEN

OPEN-PIT URANIUM mines; contaminated water from uranium, lead, zinc, and cadmium; cancer clusters; and the denial of the right to protect and have access to one's sacred places: these are topics that, if they occurred in predominantly wealthy, white communities would garner immediate media attention and public demands for emergency cleanup actions. Unfortunately, these are common stories among Native American tribal nations and communities, and for the most part, there is no sustained media or public outcry, no daily national news reports until the problems are corrected. They are all examples of environmental justice, or rather injustice, and while some issues end in successful outcomes for Indigenous people, many do not.

But what exactly is environmental justice? When asked, many people look puzzled for a moment and then offer some vague answer about preserving beautiful environmental landscapes. "Being an environmentalist" some people answer, including students in the Indigenous environmental justice course taught by one of the authors. When it is announced on the first day of class that environmental justice is about protecting people—not just the environment—and that the course is not a course on environmentalism, typically several students immediately leave and drop the class. A colleague once also offered his guess about what environmental justice means. After pondering the question for the moment, he answered, "Justice by the environment is swift and unforgiving. Don't mess with

Mother Nature." It was an amusing response, but once again an essential element was missing, the part that connects people with justice.

There is no single definition of environmental justice. The Environmental Protection Agency (EPA) defines environmental justice thus:

> Environmental justice is the fair treatment and meaningful involvement of all people, regardless of race, color, national origin, or income with respect to the development, implementation, and enforcement of environmental regulation and policies. . . . [The] EPA has this goal for all communities and persons across the nation. It will be achieved when everyone enjoys: the same degree of protection from environmental health hazards, and equal access to the decision-making process to have a healthy environment in which to live, work, and learn. (EPA 2019)

Environmental justice (EJ), then, is about fairness in environmental decision-making. It is a relatively new term, less than thirty years old. It was preceded by the term "environmental racism" and is in part a critique of the environmental movement. While the relationship between Indigenous Peoples and the environment has existed since time immemorial, the emphasis on justice, again, is relatively new. Illegal dumping on Indigenous lands and harms from resource extraction (mostly without the consent of Native peoples) are just some of the reasons that Indigenous Peoples found it necessary to ally with the EJ movement (and is also why others in the EJ movement allied with Native peoples).

HISTORY OF THE ENVIRONMENTAL JUSTICE MOVEMENT

By the 1970s the environmentalism movement was well underway in the United States. The National Environmental Policy Act of 1969 was the first sweeping national legislation creating mandates for environmental review of proposed actions by federal agencies. Other major environmental legislation soon followed, including the Clean Air Act (CAA) in 1970, the Clean Water Act (CWA) of 1972, and the Safe Drinking Water Act (SDWA) of 1974. The environmental movement's focus was, unsurprisingly, on protecting the environment, including forests and wilderness areas, especially on public lands. The movement was composed primarily of middle- or upper-middle-class whites (Peña and Mondragon-Valdez 1998; Taylor 2002; Rechtschaffen, Gauna, and O'Neill 2009; Sandler and Pezzulo 2007). People of color, low-income communities, and Native Americans were missing from the picture, and their concerns were different from those of the environmentalists. Cole and Foster (2001) discuss those groups involved in early efforts for EJ, including grassroots efforts, civil rights activists, the antitoxics groups, labor groups, and Native Americans. As in this volume, Cole and Foster (2001) approach the subject from an interdisciplinary perspective. While some scholars use the terms "environmental racism" and "environmental justice" interchangeably, we do not, because environmental justice is broader than environmental issues of racism alone. It also includes low-income communities. In this volume we address issues of Indigenous environmental (in)justice, and as is discussed later in this chapter, Indigenous Nations are political entities, not racial ones.

In 1987 a national study by the United Church of Christ's Commission for Racial Justice found a correlation between the siting of commercial hazardous waste facilities, race, and uncontrolled toxic waste sites (Rechtschafffen, Gauna, and O'Neill 2009). The study garnered national attention, with Reverend Ben Chavis of the commission noting that "race is a major factor in the siting of hazardous waste facilities" (quoted in Bullard 1990, 15).

Then in 1990 Robert Bullard published *Dumping in Dixie: Race, Class and Environmental Quality*, a book about environmental inequity and social injustice in five African American communities. *Dumping in Dixie* illustrated the intersection of the civil rights movement and activists with unfairness in environmental decision-making, resulting in issues of environmental racism. As even more evidence of environmental discrimination surfaced, the movement for EJ began to grow. Bullard has since authored many articles and books on the subject of EJ. In 1991 the First National People of Color Environmental Summit in Washington, D.C., culminated in producing the seventeen "Principles of Environmental Justice" (reprinted in Rechtschaffen, Gauna, and O'Neill 2009). Three of the principles particularly relate to EJ for Native Peoples: Principle Number 5 states, "Environmental Justice affirms the fundamental right to political, economic, cultural, and environmental self-determination of all peoples";

Number 10 reads "Environmental justice considers governmental acts of environmental injustice a violation of international law, the Universal Declaration on Human Rights, and the United Nations Convention on Genocide"; and finally, Principle Number 11 states, "Environmental justice must recognize a special legal and natural relationship of Native Peoples to the U.S. government through treaties, agreements, compacts and covenants affirming sovereignty and self-determination." Principle Numbers 10 and 11 especially resonate with several articles in the U.N. Declaration on the Rights of Indigenous Peoples (2007), which are also basic human rights—a point discussed by some of the authors later in this volume.

The summit, along with the growing movement for EJ, finally made it to the national policy agenda, and in 1994 President Bill Clinton issued Executive Order 12898 on Environmental Justice. The order instructed all federal agencies to make achieving EJ part of their mission. The executive order requires federal agencies to identify and address "disproportionately high and adverse human health and environmental effects" of agency actions on low-income and minority populations. Section 6–606 of the order states that the requirements also apply to Native American programs as a protected populations (Executive Order 12898). Another requirement under Executive Order 12898 that is particularly important for some Native American communities is section 4–4, requiring federal agencies to collect data and analyze the risk of consumption of fish or wildlife to communities who depend primarily on subsistence and eat levels of fish or wildlife at levels beyond what is considered in standard risk assessments. Section 4–4 requires agencies to notify communities about the risk related to their particular consumption of these foods (Executive Order 12898). The order also established an Inter-Agency Working Group (IWG) on Environmental Justice. Within the IWG, a special task force was established in 1999 on Native American Issues. James Grijalva (2008) describes how the EPA worked early on, prior to and during the start of the EJ movement, to find a way to recognize the sovereignty of tribal nations in environmental regulation within their lands by finding a solution for tribal nations to administer federal environmental laws on their lands, just as states did. Tribal nations, unlike states, were not mentioned in NEPA, the CAA, the CWA, or the SDWA. This is not surprising, considering that many of those environmental laws were enacted just prior to the era of American Indian Self-Determination Policy. Grijalva

(2008) details how the EPA worked to create the Treatment as States policy, setting up a process where qualifying tribal nations could, like states, administer those major federal environmental laws, setting standards for clean air and clean and safe drinking water, and significantly, also providing tribes with the ability to set more strict standards than the minimum required under those federal laws. This process is sometimes overlooked in the EJ literature, but as Grijalva notes, it recognizes the sovereignty of tribal nations—Principle Number 11 in the Principles of Environmental Justice.

WAYS OF UNDERSTANDING ENVIRONMENTAL JUSTICE: KUEHN'S TAXONOMY

Robert R. Kuehn's "A Taxonomy of Environmental Justice" offers us four categories or ways of viewing EJ issues in the context of this book: EJ as distributive justice, EJ as corrective justice, EJ as social justice, and EJ as procedural justice. EJ as distributive justice, Kuehn emphasizes, is not redistribution. Distributive justice is about "equal protection for all and the elimination of environmental hazards and the need to place environmental hazards in any community. It's about the lowering of risks, not the shifting of risks" (Kuehn 2009, 8). EJ as corrective justice focuses on the way damages are addressed and the "duty to repair the losses for which one is responsible" (11). Corrective justice also includes fairness in punishment for polluters and fixing responsibility, regardless of legal liability. This is the "polluter pays" principle (11). EJ as social justice includes fairness in the economic and cultural effects of environmental decisions. It is the broadest of the four categories of EJ, but important. It focuses on fairness in meeting basic needs of those in every community (Kuehn 2009). This concept is explained in clear, bottom-line terms in an article by Ernest Atencio, describing a conversation he had with someone about EJ: "An anthropologist at a recent conference I attended suggested that there will soon be no nature to protect unless we address social justice issues to share the world's resources more equitably" (Atencio 2000, 17). The fourth category Kuehn discusses is procedural justice. According to Kuehn it has been defined as "the right to be treated as an equal" (2009, 9). In short, procedural justice is about fairness in the environmental decision-making process, from the beginning to the end. To ensure fairness it requires opportunities for *meaningful* participation from low-income or minority communities or American Indian tribes. Meaningful participation, as opposed to simply participation, requires effort and outreach by federal agencies to ensure they provide opportunities for participation that EJ populations can feasibly participate in. For example, meetings held during the middle of the week and middle of the day likely will not garner many attendees from working-class or poor communities. Likewise, meetings held in churches may make some from other faiths not feel welcome to participate. Sending written documents for comments to Indian tribes via courier to tribal governments in very rural places without addresses, or at the bottom of canyons, are examples of opportunities for participation that are such in name only. They do not offer meaningful participation for EJ communities. Recently Powys Whyte (2017) addressed the lack of meaningful participation opportunities for the people of Standing Rock Sioux tribe in the Dakota Access Pipeline environmental review.

The EJ movement has grown over the years. It is no longer just the anti-toxics movement, as some described the early movement (Rechtschaffen, Gauna, and O'Neill 2009; Mutz, Bryner, and Kenney 2001). For example, Bullard's *The Quest for Environmental Justice* (2005) looks at EJ through the lens of human rights (as do some of the authors in this volume). Other scholars have broadened the field by bringing together literature in political ecology, ecofeminism, critical race theory, and theory on anarchism into a perspective labeled critical environmental justice studies (Pellow 2016). Most recently, Estes (2019) has described the fight of water protectors in the #NoDAPL movement and compares the resistance of those in the current movement to Indigenous resistance of the past, including the 1970's occupation of Wounded Knee. Gilio-Whitaker (2019) discusses the #NoDAPL movement along with other IEJ issues, including connections among American Indian health and the environment, Indigenous women, feminism and EJ, and sacred sites. Gilio-Whitaker also discusses issues of land-based identity of Indigenous Peoples and difficulties in protecting their culturally significant sites, as does Jocks (2020) and Jarratt-Snider in chapter 2 of this volume. Finally, Gilio-Whitaker (2019) notes the differences between Indigenous issues of EJ and mainstream EJ theory, as do we in this chapter.

INDIGENOUS ENVIRONMENTAL JUSTICE

While all Indigenous environmental justice (IEJ) issues are EJ issues, not all EJ issues are IEJ issues. There are three factors that make IEJ distinct from EJ issues for non-Indigenous communities:

(1) *Native American tribes are governments, not ethnic minorities.* Individual Indians are part of ethnic minorities, but Native nations are government entities. Evidence includes treaties between tribes and European nations predating the United States, as well as hundreds of treaties made between the United States and tribal nations. While Congress ended treaty-making in 1871, existing treaties are still valid and lawful. The unique legal and political status of tribal nations is that they are "distinct political communities. . . . with the right of self-government" whose sovereignty can be limited by the United States (*Worchester v. Georgia* 1832). They are in a unique category within the American political system, domestic dependent nations (*Cherokee v. Georgia* 1831). The sovereignty of tribal nations has been affirmed again and again by a host of federal laws, policies, and executive orders (see generally Getches, Wilkinson, Williams Jr. 1993; Wilkins and Lomawaima 2001). It bears repeating that the U.S. Supreme Court has noted that the term "Indian," relating to tribal nations, is a political designation—not a racial one (*Worcester v. Georgia* 1832). The unique legal and political status of federally recognized tribal nations in the United States sets up a special legal relationship between tribes and the federal government, known as the Trust Doctrine. This aspect of IEJ is a significant difference. The EJ movement's early works linking environmentalism to civil rights is at odds with the legal and political status of Native nations. Civil rights accrue to individuals, as they would to individual American Indians like all others, but Native nations are governmental entities, as noted above. The relationship between Native nations and the United States is one like no other in the U.S. political system. The Trust Doctrine means that the United States has an obligation to protect the interests of Indian tribes.

(2) *Connections to traditional homelands.* This component of IEJ is often at the center of environmental injustices over protection of or access to sacred sites that are within traditional homelands of Indian Peo-

ples but are now legally public lands managed by a federal agency. Connection to homelands is the heart of identity for Native people: Spokane identity is tied to their Native homelands, as is the case of the Diné, Hopi, Choctaw, Nez Perce, Apache and all Native peoples (Deloria 1994). Indigenous spirituality and religions are, then, place-based, in contrast to Eurocentric, particularly Judeo-Christian, religious traditions (Deloria 1994). Winona LaDuke's (1999, 2005) work on the importance of Native lands to Native identity and cultural survival offers further compelling discussions and examples of this point.

(3) *The continuing effects of colonization.* This includes dispossession of homelands (related to the second unique factor of IEJ discussed above) but can also involve loss of subsistence rights, lack of access to clean water, and impacts from federal Indian policies that lead to environmental contamination from mining and other extractive industries. Settler colonial states see Indigenous people as dispensable (Veracini 2010), and therefore the consequences of environmental devastation and degradation of Indigenous lands and peoples are of little consequence unless they have an impact on non-Indigenous communities or priorities. As Wolfe (2006, n.p.) writes:

> Settler-colonization is at base a winner-takes-all project whose dominant feature is not exploitation but replacement. The logic of this project, a sustained institutional tendency to eliminate the Indigenous population, informs a range of historical practices that otherwise might appear distinct—invasion is a structure not an event.

These three distinct characteristics of IEJ provide the context for the discussions of Indigenous Environmental injustice issues and resolutions by such Native American scholars as Gedicks (2005) and LaDuke (1999, 2005), as well as for the chapters of this book. Before discussing particular themes and chapters though, it is important to include one final thought: The common statement among EJ scholars and activists is that EJ issues are found where we live, work, go to school, and play. For Indigenous Peoples, IEJ issues occur where we live, work, go to school, and play, and where we pray.

THEMES OF THE BOOK

Although each chapter offers different examples of and perspectives on IEJ, several themes emerge throughout this volume. Richard Wheelock's chapter sets the tone for understanding how Indigenous values about land and, in turn, the environment, differ greatly from the values of those who create environmental injustice. This theme of *Indigenous values* related to traditional homelands is reflected throughout the book. The theme of the *continuing impacts of the colonization* on Indigenous Peoples is also evident in all chapters. Such impacts include the loss not only of land, resources, and lives but of religious freedom and the traditional leadership roles of women. *Human rights* is also a theme that cuts across all chapters in the volume. The UN Declaration on the Rights of Indigenous Peoples (2007) is a particularly important document in discussions of IEJ since it sets an international benchmark for the achievement of Indigenous rights, and is referred to by several authors. Another theme is IEJ issues on *public lands* that were once traditional homelands and still contain sacred sites. Because of the lack of understanding and respect for Native land-based spirituality practices, American Indians continue to fight to protect sacred places. See, in particular, Karen Jarratt-Snider's chapter on sacred sites. Anne Luna-Gordinier's chapter of the role of *Indigenous women in IEJ* reminds us that Indigenous women have been and continue to be leaders in IEJ.

Corporate greed for Indigenous land and resources, a driving force of colonization that continues today, contributes to IEJ issues. This is exemplified by the effects of *mining* on or adjacent to Native lands and the environmental and human health effects of waste left on Indian lands, as found in chapters by Linda Robyn on water and uranium mining and by Jarratt-Snider on legal complexities. The impact of corporate lust for *water* is also an IEJ issue discussed by Mia Hammersley (chapter 6), Robyn (chapter 4), Jarratt-Snider (chapter 5), and Timothy Casey (chapter 7). Robyn in both of her chapters explains how *social harms*, even though they may not technically be crimes, intersect with IEJ issues of water contamination and uranium mining.

There are, fortunately, some positive themes in the book as well. *Community resilience* is alive and well and exemplified in chapters by Casey, Hammersley, Jarratt-Snider, and Luna-Gordinier. This relates closely to *de facto sovereignty and self-determination* that also play important roles in

IEJ. As we wrote in *Crime and Social Justice in Indian Country*, de facto sovereignty occurs when "Native nations are not waiting for the law to return authority to them" (Nielsen and Jarratt-Snider 2018, 191). De facto sovereignty differs from the legal definition of sovereignty and it differs from international law's definition of self-determination. De facto sovereignty occurs when tribal nations take the initiative and assume authority to act. In cases where this occurs, Indian people move toward de facto self-determination. "De facto self-determination is the practice of Indigenous nations and communities asserting authority by developing programs and services that address some of the many social justice areas" (191). In the case of IEJ, de facto self-determination may offer EJ solutions for more tribal nations. Indigenous resilience can be seen in the exercise of de facto sovereignty as evident in Casey's discussion of Indigenous resistance strategies against natural resource extraction, Luna-Gordinier's discussion of Indian women's EJ leadership in urban areas, and Jarratt-Snider's discussion of the cleanup efforts of the Native villages of Barrow and Tar Creek.

THE BOOK

This book considers EJ and (in)justices affecting Indigenous Peoples through an Indigenous lens—that is to say, one that embraces the unique factors of IEJ described above. The book offers examples of scholarship in IEJ using examples from various regions of North America and a variety of types of IEJ issues, such as mining, legal and cooperative approaches to obtaining IEJ, toxic substances, and religious freedom, which involve different Indigenous nations and communities. EJ activism has been a foundational piece of the EJ movement and led to the summit that produced the very Principles of Environmental Justice, as noted above. Often discussions of EJ or IEJ focuses on activism by those using direct action to effect change (see, for example, Estes 2019; Estes and Dhillon 2019 on #NoDAPL activism). Indigenous people and scholars often refer to activism and direct action by another term—resistance—as Estes's (2019) recent work on the #NoDAPL issue. Many of the chapters here examine legal and policy challenges and solutions to achieving IEJ.

This book is the third in the Indigenous Justice series. The first is *Crime and Social Justice in Indian Country* (2018), which looks at aspects of crimes

such as hate crimes and involuntary sterilization and aspects of social justice such as lack of protections for state-recognized tribes, the struggle to
address juvenile justice, sovereignty through athletics, and finally, community responses to these issues. The second book in the series is *Traditional,
National, and International Law and Indigenous Communities* (2020). The
book engages such topics as the history and future of traditional law; the
impact of national law on religious freedoms, child welfare, and Indigenous
women; international comparative views on the recognition of Indigenous
justice, and the contributions of Indigenous justice programs on Indigenous
human rights. This current book examines a small variety of the many IEJ,
or injustice, cases that exist in the United States and Canada. More than
one of the chapters focuses on issues within the Navajo Nation. The inclu-
sion of more than one issue involving the Navajo Nation and Diné people
is due in part to many of the authors being from the southwestern United
States, where we are next door to the Navajo Nation. With over three
hundred thousand citizens living on and off the reservation (Yurth 2012),
and a vast geographical territory, the Navajo Nation is the largest federally
recognized Native nation in the United States and, as Robyn points out,
the involuntary host of more than one Superfund site. Additionally, the
harms and potential harm from uranium mining still pose an enormous
environmental threat to the Diné people.

Unfortunately, since there is no shortage of IEJ issues, we could fill
many volumes. What we offer here are different lenses with which to
consider IEJ, including perspectives from criminology, EJ, and Indigenous
studies. We use cases that are different from each other but representative
of many types of ongoing IEJ issues. This book contains only a small sampling intended to engage readers with recent and continuing Indigenous
environmental justice and injustice issues.

REFERENCES

Atencio, Ernest. 2000. Environmental Justice and Public Lands Ranching in
    Northern New Mexico. *Quivara Coalition* 4 (1): 17–22.
Bullard, Robert D. 1990. *Dumping in Dixie: Race, Class and Environmental Qual-
    ity*. Boulder, Colo.: Westview Press.
Bullard, Robert D., ed. 2005. *The Quest for Environmental Justice: Human Rights
    and the Politics of Pollution*. Berkeley, Calif.: Counterpoint.

Cole, Luke W., and Sheila R. Foster. 2001. *From the Ground Up: Environmental Racism and the Rise of the Environmental Justice Movement.* New York: New York University Press.

Deloria, Vine, Jr. 1994. *God Is Red: A Native View of Religion.* Golden, Colo.: Fulcrum.

EPA (Environmental Protection Agency). 2019. "Environmental Justice." www .epa.gov/environmentaljustice.

Estes, Nick. 2019. *Our History Is the Future: Standing Rock Versus the Dakota Access Pipeline and the Long Tradition of Indigenous Resistance.* New York: Verso.

Estes, Nick, and Jaskiran Dhillon, eds. 2019. *Standing with Standing Rock: Voices from the #NO DAPL Movement.* Minneapolis: University of Minnesota Press.

Gedicks, Al. 2005. "Resource Wars Against Native Peoples." In *The Quest for Environmental Justice: Human Rights and the Politics of Pollution,* edited by Robert D. Bullard, 168–87. Berkeley, Calif.: Counterpoint.

Getches, David H., Charles F. Wilkinson, and Robert A. Williams Jr. 1993. *Federal Indian Law: Cases and Materials.* 3rd ed. St. Paul, Minn.: West.

Gilio-Whitaker, Dina. 2019. *As Long as Grass Grows: The Indigenous Fight for Environmental Justice from Colonization to Standing Rock.* Boston, Mass.: Beacon.

Grijalva, James M. 2008. *Closing the Circle: Environmental Justice in Indian Country.* Durham, N.C.: Carolina Academic Press.

Kuehn, Robert R. 2009. "A Taxonomy of Environmental Justice." In *Environmental Justice: Law, Policy, and Regulation,* edited by Clifford Rechtschaffen, Eileen Gauna, and Catherine O'Neill, 6–13. Durham, N.C.: Carolina Academic Press.

LaDuke, Winona. 1999. *All Our Relations: Native Struggles for Land and Life.* Cambridge, Mass.: South End Press.

LaDuke, Winona. 2005. *Recovering the Sacred: The Power of Naming and Claiming.* Cambridge, Mass.: South End Press.

Mutz, Kathryn, Gary Bryner, and Douglas Kenney, eds. 2001. *Justice and Natural Resources: Concepts, Strategies, and Applications.* Washington, D.C.: Island Press.

Nielsen, Marianne O., and Karen Jarratt-Snider, eds. 2018. *Crime and Social Justice in Indian Country.* Tucson: University of Arizona Press.

Nielsen, Marianne O., and Karen Jarratt-Snider, eds. 2020. *Traditional, National, and International Law and Indigenous Communities.* Tucson: University of Arizona Press.

Pellow, David N. 2016. "Toward a Critical Environmental Justice Studies: Black Lives Matter as an Environmental Justice Challenge." *Du Bois Review–Social Science Research on Race* (13) 2: 1–16.

Peña, Devon, and Maria Mondragon Valdez. 1998. "The 'Brown' and the 'Green' Revisited: Chicanos and Environmental Politics in the Upper Rio Grande." In *The Struggle for Economic Democracy: Environmental Justice Movements in the United States,* edited by Daniel Faber, 264–85. New York: Guilford.

Powys Whyte, Kyle. 2017. "The Dakota Access Pipeline, Environmental Justice, and US Colonialism." *Red Ink* 19 (1): 154–69.

Rechtschaffen, Clifford, Eileen Gauna, and Catherine O'Neill. 2009. *Environmental Justice: Law, Policy, and Regulation*. Durham, N.C.: Carolina Academic Press.

Sandler, Ronald, and Phaedra C. Pezzulo. 2007. *Environmental Justice and Environmentalism: The Social Justice Challenge to the Environmental Movement (Urban and Industrial Environments)*. Cambridge, Mass.: MIT Press.

Taylor, Dorceta, E. 2002. *Race, Class, Gender, and American Environmentalism*. General Technical Report # PNW-GTR-534. Portland, Ore.: USDA Forest Service, Pacific Northwest Research Station.

Veracini, Lorenzo. 2010. *Settler-Colonialism: A Theoretical Overview*. Houndmills, UK: Palgrave Macmillan.

Wilkins, David E., and K. Tsianina Lomawaima. 2001. *Uneven Ground: American Indian Sovereignty and Federal Law*. Norman: University of Oklahoma Press.

Wolfe, Patrick. 2006. Settler-Colonialism and the Elimination of the Native. *Journal of Genocide Research* 8 (4): 387–409. https://www.tandfonline.com/doi/full/10.1080/14623520601056240.

Yurth, Cindy. 2012. "Census: Native Count Jumps by 27 Percent." *Navajo Times*. January 26, 2012. navajotimes.com/news/2012/0112/012612census.php.

LEGAL RESOURCES

Cherokee Nation v. Georgia. 39 U.S. 1 (1831)

Clean Air Act. 42 U.S.C. § 7401 et seq. (1970)

Clean Water Act. PL 92–500 (1972)

Executive Order 12898. "Environmental Justice" (1994)

National Environmental Policy Act of 1969. PL 91–190, U.S.C 4321–4327 (1970)

———. Amendment. PL 94–52 (1975)

———. Amendment. PL 97–258 (1982)

Safe Drinking Water Act. 42 U.S.C. § 300f et seq. (1974)

UN Declaration on the Rights of Indigenous Peoples (2007)

Worcester v. Georgia. 31 U.S. (6 Pet.) 515 (1832)

PART I

PERSPECTIVES ON INDIGENOUS ENVIRONMENTALISM AND INDIGENOUS ENVIRONMENTAL JUSTICE

INTRODUCTION BY MARIANNE O. NIELSEN AND KAREN JARRATT-SNIDER

THE INDIGENOUS environmental justice issues in this first part of the book provide examples of the social harms that result from the confluence of corporate and/or state disregard of Indigenous relations to and presence on the land, corporate and/or state disregard of the sovereign rights of Indigenous Peoples, and colonial ideologies that are now evidenced in racist attitudes and discrimination toward the rights of Indigenous Peoples.

The opening chapter by Wheelock is very different from the others that follow. He provides a philosophical context for Indigenous values and understandings of the natural world. He provides an interpretation of renowned Indigenous scholar Vine Deloria Jr.'s description of the relationship between Indigenous Peoples and the rest of creation (see Deloria 1999). Wheelock compares Deloria's understandings to the closest Western concept, which is deep ecology. If Deloria's view became the guidepost for environmental decision-making affecting Indigenous Peoples, there would be no such concept as Indigenous environmental injustice.

The chapters that follow focus on issues of Indigenous environmental injustice that seem to be the inevitable consequence of colonization. The main characteristics of Indigenous environmental justice that differentiate it from environmental justice, as described in the introduction to this volume, include the trust relationship that American Indian peoples have with the federal governments of both Canada and the United States (though these differ due to historical events and legal history). These trust relations have been ignored from the beginning of colonial contacts as evidenced by the treaties that were broken repeatedly and knowingly by colonial governments (see Nielsen and Robyn 2019). The Doctrine of Discovery was one of the earliest legal tenets that laid the groundwork for discriminatory colonial laws used to exploit Indigenous Peoples and their environments worldwide. Under the Doctrine of Discovery, the acquisition of Indigenous lands was justified in international law by the current occupancy and actual possession of the land. This meant that "lands not put to the highest agricultural use (as defined by Europeans) were essentially 'vacant' or in a state of 'waste,' subject to European discovery and occupation" (Pommersheim 2009, 95). This eliminated any rights of Indigenous Peoples to their own traditional lands since they used agricultural practices appropriate to their environments (Nielsen and Robyn 2019).

Indigenous environmental injustice increased exponentially (and continues to do so) when resource extraction interests become intertwined with federal Indian policy, as was the case as far back as 1877 with the Lakota Sioux, which is just one early example. In their original treaty with the United States, the 1868 Treaty of Ft. Laramie, the sacred Black Hills remained under Sioux control, but when gold was discovered, legislation was passed that took the land away from the Sioux and opened it for gold mining and thereby serious environmental degradation (Hopkins 2014). This exemplifies another aspect of Indigenous environmental injustice— the continuing effects of colonization, including loss of connection to traditional lands, and consequently the inability to protect them, and the loss of identity that comes with such alienation. The chapters by Robyn on uranium mining and water clearly demonstrate the impacts of the failure of such trust obligations and the use of law and policy to alienate Navajo individuals and communities from their land. The chapter by Jarratt-Snider on American Indian religious freedom focuses on how ineffective trust relations can be in preserving access to traditional lands.

In addition to clearly illustrating the unique nature of Indigenous environmental justice issues, the chapters also reflect many of the main themes of the book. All of them refer back to the continuing impacts of colonization, including loss of land and resources, as well as human rights. Robyn's two chapters focus particularly on land and water degradation resulting from corporate greed in mining and the social harms that follow. Jarratt-Snider's chapter focuses on the social harms that arise from the loss of religious freedoms and the resulting lack of human rights, as discussed in the introduction to this volume.

REFERENCES

Deloria, Vine, Jr. 1999. *Spirit and Reason: The Vine Deloria, Jr., Reader.* Golden, Colo.: Fulcrum.

Hopkins, Ruth. 2014. "Reclaiming the Sacred Black Hills." *Indian Country Today.* June 28, 2014. https://newsmaven.io/indiancountrytoday/archive/reclaiming -the-sacred-black-hills-ueqUBTSDuUK2nq8VzF4Rdg/.

Nielsen, Marianne O., and Linda M. Robyn. 2019. *Colonialism Is Crime.* New Brunswick, N.J.: Rutgers University Press.

Pommersheim, Frank. 2009. *Broken Landscape: Indians, Indian Tribes, and the Constitution.* New York: Oxford University Press.

1

POWERFUL PARALLELS

Deep Ecology and the Writings of Vine Deloria Jr.

RICHARD M. WHEELOCK

V INE DELORIA Jr. would probably argue that his understandings of
tribal traditions about the relationships between specific peoples
and specific homelands are a far cry from those championed by
today's "deep ecology" movement. His writings, though, reveal some of
the most useful discussions of the intellectual and cultural dimensions
of the human relationship to the natural world that might, if considered
in our time of rapidly dwindling energy resources and global climate
changes, yield a valuable conceptual framework for future policies, especially where Indigenous Peoples are themselves involved in development
decisions.

A number of Indigenous scholars have noted that much of the thinking in many fields of scholarship and even in the popular culture seems to
be slowly moving closer to what many traditional peoples have believed
about the universe all along (Pierotti 2010; Gomez-Baggethun, Corbera,
and Reyes-Garcia 2013). Some of the positions taken by environmentalists
seem to reflect this paradigm shift in thought. Much of Deloria's writing
reveals his own belief that traditional tribal thought has been wrongly
dismissed by the Western intellectual tradition, obviating tribal ideas from
the discussion of many areas of human development, including current
environmental affairs (Deloria [1979] 2012; 1970, 186). As debates continue
about the deteriorating health of the world's natural environment, Deloria's views of tribal traditional "relatedness" to the many natural entities

of a specific homeland can provide a powerful intellectual basis for development of viable alternatives to the present flawed global land ethic (see, for example, Wildcat 2009).

Deloria rarely wrote entire articles devoted solely to the tribal traditions concerning human relationships with nature. Most often he mentions those traditions as part of a larger discussion designed to extol the legitimacy and practicality of tribal traditions as a part of his critiques of modern science (Deloria 1997), religion (Deloria 1999, 339; [1973] 2003; 2010) or politics (Deloria and Lytle 1984). In so doing, he often made rather sweeping statements about the sense of relatedness people of the tribes of North America feel or once felt for the sentient entities in their homelands. One of the recent collections of his writings provides many such cases. In the book *Spirit and Reason*, Deloria's comments are characteristically direct, as he states:

> This idea that everything in the universe is alive, and that the universe itself is alive, is knowledge as useful as anything that Western science has discovered or hypothesized. When understood and made operative by serious and sensitive individuals, it is as reliable a means of making predictions as anything suggested by mathematical formulas or projected by computer programs. There are, however, substantial differences in the manner in which predictions are made. Because the universe is alive, there is choice for all things and the future is always indeterminate. Consequently, predictions are based on the knowledge of the "character" of an entity. Statements about how an entity will behave have almost the same probabilities as the educated speculations made at the subatomic level in physics. (Deloria 1999, 50)

Deloria's assertion that the universe is a living being, made up of many other living and sentient beings, parallels the concept of "deep ecology," a relatively recent conceptual creation of Western science and philosophy, which has some roots in the consideration of tribal traditions, including pagan traditions of Europe, long ago dismissed in the religious, philosophical, and scientific developments of today's mass society. Deep ecology's proponents champion a concept of "inherent value" in nature, beyond any value humans may otherwise ascribe to it (FDE 2012a). It is a revolutionary idea, bringing such thinkers as George Sessions and Arne

Naess to the brink of acknowledging an animistic universe (Sessions 1995; Naess 2008).

As these ecologists began to look for ways to improve the relationships between mass society and the natural world in the 1980s, it quickly became clear that the worldview of most Americans and other people of the developed world provided few models upon which to base public policy initiatives, unless that policy was to be rapid exploitation. As environmental collapse loomed on a global scale, lifestyles of traditional Indigenous Peoples stood in stark contrast to those of the people of modern postindustrial nations. It seemed a natural development for thinkers and writers in the environmental movement to draw upon tribal models and advocate selected portions of those lifeways in the search for solutions to the seemingly overwhelming impacts of global corporate development. A sense of human separation and dominance over nature emerged from Western religion and philosophy, a cultural orientation that leads to frequent disregard for impacts upon nature other than the possible economic disadvantages that might result, unless statutes arising from other value systems are enacted to secure protections for natural processes.

Today, national and global development schemes, supported by a mentality of denial of many of these impacts, have forced environmentalists to reach for arguments that will reenergize their movement that was so compelling in public policy circles only a decade or two ago. As a result of the ruminations of people like Naess and Sessions, two radical strategies have been advocated by today's ecologists: deep ecology and bioregionalism, each with strong parallels to the perceived values of traditional tribal peoples in North America. Though not all environmentalists adhere to the values of these two concepts, the philosophical framework for environmental policy-making has been greatly affected by both of them. Bioregionalism, which is outside the scope of this chapter, is "an environment movement and social movement and social philosophy that envisions decentralized community self-rule within political boundaries redrawn to reflect the natural contours of differing ecosystem types," and has similarities to Indigenous Peoples' relationships to the beings believed to be present in a particular landscape (Taylor 2000, 50).

Deep ecology is based upon the realization that nature has a value of its own, beyond the human, anthropocentric patterns of today's mass society. Essential to the deep ecology movement, James Lovelock's writings on the Gaia concept of the self-regulating, living earth, demonstrate that even in the early development of Western culture, spiritual connections with natural "beings" were once a crucial part of the "pagan" heritage of many peoples (Lovelock 1979). Today's writers in this movement sometimes refer to that heritage and parallel it with the tribal traditions of the Indigenous Peoples of North America and elsewhere and to traditional ecological knowledge (Gomez-Baggethun Corbera, and Reyes-Garcia 2013). The sense of connectedness that arises from this contemplation compels deep ecologists to recognize the essential spiritual demeanor demanded as humans interact with natural forces. The kind of spiritual solitude that comes from direct, intimate contemplation of nature's wonders is an immediate and inherent experience that many ecologists feel only in what is called "wilderness" today. See Leopold (1949) for what was a revolutionary call at the time for a land ethic and wilderness designations. That sort of reasoning, combined with a certain irreverence toward Western innovations that have created a "mass society" (Casty 1973; Wheelock 1998), was crucial to the emergence of deep ecology.

The "Deep Ecology Platform" was formulated by Naess and Sessions while camping in Death Valley in 1984. The simple, straightforward statement reads like a creed:

(1) The well-being and flourishing of human and nonhuman life on
    Earth have value in themselves (synonyms: inherent worth; intrinsic
    value; inherent value). These values are independent of the usefulness
    of the nonhuman world for human purposes.
(2) Richness and diversity of life forms contribute to the realization of
    these values and are also values in themselves.
(3) Humans have no right to reduce this richness and diversity except to
    satisfy vital needs.
(4) Present human interference with the nonhuman world is excessive,
    and the situation is rapidly worsening.
(5) The flourishing of human life and cultures is compatible with a
    substantial decrease of the human population. The flourishing of
    nonhuman life requires such a decrease.
(6) Policies must therefore be changed. The changes in policies affect
    basic economic, technological structures. The resulting state of affairs
    will be deeply different from the present.

(7) The ideological change is mainly that of appreciating life quality
(dwelling in situations of inherent worth) rather than adhering to
an increasingly higher standard of living. There will be a profound
awareness of the difference between big and great.

(8) Those who subscribe to the foregoing points have an obligation
directly or indirectly to participate in the attempt to implement the
necessary changes. (Naess and Sessions, cited in FDE 2012b, n.p.)

Naess and Sessions's platform has become the basis of a major intellectual dialogue. Long treatises continue to appear elucidating or attacking
each of the eight elements of the platform, and continuing discussions of
the implications of such a far-reaching intellectual and spiritual quest are
certain. Yet the platform is often attacked as not only impractical but anti-
human in its implications, especially by those who are convinced by their
faith or economic demands that humans are manifestly dominant over
nature. For some it is seen as an attack upon nearly all Western values. It
seems clear to this author that the threat of attack on deep ecologists by
the religious Right and by corporate America in U.S. politics has forced
ecologists to carefully define their perception of the proper relationship
with nature (see, for example, Rosier 2017; Tashman 2013).

The continuing public debate has sometimes included the use of perceived tribal understandings by both ecologists and their critics, often
inaccurately. Tribal traditions have been mischaracterized and even desecrated in a number of cases, and non-Indian environmentalists have
been accused of interference in tribal economic development and religious
practices. Of course, those committed to unbridled development under
corporate power have sometimes attacked the environmental movement
by targeting what they perceive as inaccurate and romantic portrayals
of tribal connectedness with the natural world. Apologists for Western
intellectual development, like Shepard Krech (1999), have targeted Deloria's writings in poorly supported attacks on tribal traditions in a hostile
attempt to discredit tribal traditions as possible models for the modern
ecology movement (22, 42–43, 214). These unforeseen consequences of
environmental advocacy have often stymied the possibility of coordinated
actions on environmental degradation between today's Native peoples and
the mass society that surrounds them. Yet the development of concepts of
deep ecology have revealed some powerful parallels with Indigenous tribal

traditions that warrant further consideration if the search for a more harmonious relationship between humans and the rest of the natural world
is to be accomplished (Pierotti and Wildcat 2000).

TRIBAL CONCEPTS IN TODAY'S PUBLIC DEBATE ON THE ENVIRONMENT

At the extreme levels of the public debate over the environment, both
sides of the controversy have had to rely upon a rather abstract set of
notions about the human connection to nature. Right-wing prodevel-
opment advocates have been able to frighten voters with the specter of
economic collapse and loss of private property while espousing a relationship with nature that relies upon their perception of biblical imperatives
(Scherer 2004; Burke 2005). Deep ecologists have had to imagine and
advocate a worldview far removed from the experiences of most Americans as they warn of imminent environmental catastrophe and are forced
to find alternatives to present development models (Sessions 1995; FDE
2012a). Both groups reach deeply into the psyche of the American public,
into areas of faith, philosophy and worldview.

It is a public policy argument of epic proportions, of course, one in
which tribal traditions are both championed and denigrated, even though
tribal people themselves are rarely recognized as proponents in the debate.
Nonetheless, Indian people have taken on some impressive environmental
projects of their own, frequently outside the scrutiny of the raging public
debate, as we shall see.

Deloria's approach is to focus upon the concept of "relatedness." Thus
he avoids the separation of humans from nature. Tribal traditions, especially those of the Teton Sioux he is familiar with, require humans to
experience and interact with other entities in a very personal, subjective,
experiential way. Humans are not separated from the cosmos, he claims,
but are essential participants in a network, a web, of interacting entities. He has gone so far as to trace the Western concepts of separation
from and dominance of nature to their religious and philosophical roots,
including Greek philosophy, as he tries to explain the distinction of tribal
relatedness (Deloria 1999, 1997). As dedicated readers of his works know,
Deloria has produced a legion of articles and chapters of books that deal

with the distinctions between the basic orientations to the universe of Western and tribal conceptions (Deloria 1999, 225). Among the many areas of contention he has revealed, two are of great importance in the discussion of modern concepts of deep ecology.

First, Deloria has documented the tribal concepts of a living, sentient universe, one in which many entities strive together toward maturity and completeness. Though not all of these entities are in harmony with each other's quest at all times, the shared processes involved are the main causal framework of the experiences they and we all have. Such an orientation requires mutual respect and an ethic of participation in the processes of the living universe (Deloria 1999, 50). He has characterized the human participation as "extreme subjectivity" as he contrasts the concept with the "extreme objectivity" of modern science (47). Humans, then, are not separate from or dominant over nature. Instead, their responsibilities lie in their ongoing commitment to conscious, purposeful efforts to maintain communication and even reciprocal spiritual relationships with other entities.

Second, Deloria reminds us that the tribal relationships with other living entities are personal and specific, sometimes not easily delineated from our relationships with other humans. His idea that humans and other entities actually create "covenants" in the visionary, spiritual realm helps to explain the destiny that the people share with other entities in the universe (51). In such a conception, it is hard to imagine the role of "stewardship" over nature for humans, a major part of the justification for environmental groups before the advent of deep ecology. In tribal traditions though, stewardship plays a role in only the most mundane levels of interaction with natural forces. Humans communicate with other entities in the obvious direct ways provided by daily experience and through prayers, ceremony, vision, dreams, and in insightful moments. These resulting relationships are evidenced in naming, spirit helpers, and many other very direct, personal relationships. In that conception, humans and other natural entities intervene regularly in each other's lives, creating a basis for continuing mutual interdependence that reaches far beyond the material needs of humans as a web of other beings are acknowledged and compensated.

As a result of just these two conceptual points, Deloria uncovers the vast differences in orientation to the universe between traditional tribal people and Western mass society. In contrast to what Western thinkers call ecology, Deloria (228) states that, for Indigenous Peoples,

> it is a relationship of specific responsibilities, specific insights, specific knowledge, and a specific task in the world. It is never a community of human beings who go out and "embrace nature." In this situation, what is nature? Nature is too generalized a concept to deal with.

In the same writing, he continues to place the challenge on Western thinkers, encouraging them to look back on the development of their cultural worldview:

> Why did people six thousand or seven thousand years ago determine that heaven is good and "down here" is bad? Why did they decide to go out and conquer things? Then why did the Greeks later make that other division between history and nature? And why, after Newton and Darwin, did you grab that one quadrant [the portion of experience that could be called "science"] and say that is what the world is about? (229)

Deloria's challenge to today's environmentalists in these writings illustrates the difficulty of finding a new land ethic for the modern mass society. He points out that scientists fear a subjective relationship with the natural world, since they have the experience of repression of their discipline by Western religious dogmas that see science as a challenge to the biblical version of creation. Those same religious leaders fear the tribal viewpoints as heresy, because they arise from peoples they see as heathens and infidels, whom they have always suppressed. Since Western thought is so bound up in religious, philosophical, and economic patterns that have emerged from its formative development, truly revolutionary processes would be necessary to change its conceptions of "nature," still so widely separated from humans (Williams 1990; Getches 1993, 42–47). Thus, crucial areas of divergence remain between the modern ecological thought and tribal traditions. As vast as that paradigm shift may seem, though, in its effort to acknowledge the intrinsic value of natural beings, the deep ecology movement has come a long way toward recognizing the interrelated, sentient characteristics of the universe described by Deloria (1999, 33–34).

When one considers the void between deep ecologists and the forces of development in mass society today, then, deep ecology seems the appropriate domain of philosophers and poets, not that of pragmatic policy-makers. Present global neoliberal economic development schemes championed by the World Trade Organization and funded by the World Bank clearly are headed in the opposite direction (Menotti 2006, 59–68). Local bioregions, often considered the proper regional focus for deep ecology initiatives, are not a part of present global economic policies, which instead seem aimed at creating a single, vast marketplace where imports and exports are the only practical products. Any local sustainability in such an economy would depend on the ability of local planners to create products for that marketplace and would rely upon imports from elsewhere to meet even the most basic needs of once diverse, self-sufficient tribal economies. In that milieu the eight elements of the Deep Ecology Platform would seem increasingly obsolete as time passes.

At the present time, the consideration of deep ecology at the global policy-making level is clearly blocked by other values. Yet in tribal economics, some interesting alternatives have arisen that rely to greater or lesser degrees upon tribal traditions like those Deloria has described. In writings from a book he coauthored with Clifford Lytle, entitled *The Nations Within: The Past and Future of American Indian Sovereignty*, Deloria urges tribes to

> develop programs that are perceived by the people as natural extensions of the things they are already doing. A natural economy maximizes the use of the land in as constructive a manner as possible, almost becoming a modern version of hunting and gathering in the sense that people have the assurance that this kind of activity will always be available to them. (1984, 259)

As tribes are forced to consider the finite resources on tribal lands, they have the opportunity to find sustainable economic devices that build upon their own values, adapting their plans to meet modern economic needs. Whether these adaptations violate the traditional values Deloria describes is, of course, a matter for those tribes to decide for themselves. Today's demands for pragmatic consideration of strategies in a climate of desperate economic conditions have forced tribes to follow very destructive corporate models such as the mining of energy resources or the always controversial strategy of gaming as they struggle for survival in an increasingly commodified economic environment.

EXAMPLES OF TRIBAL ECONOMIC INITIATIVES THAT BUILD UPON TRIBAL TRADITIONAL VALUES

There are a number of economic strategies that tribes have discovered in their struggle to maintain what was called "Fourth World" development strategies in the 1970's (Manuel and Posluns 1974, 214–66). If one remembers that the first two "worlds" are comprised of capitalism as expressed by the United States and its major allies and communism as expressed by the USSR and its allies, one will recall that the discussion of global economics was once couched in terms of the Cold War economic environment. When one recalls that the "Third World" referred to those countries being developed economically and militarily under the economic umbrella of one of the first two worlds, that Cold War analysis becomes clear.

The Fourth World, though, is a concept that lingers in discussions among those most involved in Indigenous affairs in the global context, most visible in the nongovernmental organization of the UN's International Labor Organization. The United Nations resolution on the Rights of Indigenous Peoples (2007) is the basis of a unique pattern of political, cultural, social, and, for the purposes of this paper, economic reality among Indigenous Peoples of the world, and remains the most important recognition of Indigenous Peoples' rights on the global stage. For many, the global implications of the resolution are a bit disconcerting, since tribes themselves live in such intimate, local social environments. Nonetheless, the Indigenous Fourth World concept provides a useful framework for tribally controlled, sustainable economic plans that rely mainly upon tribal traditions and tribal direction. While the deep ecology movement is presently stymied by present economic policies in the United States, a remarkable number of tribal initiatives have relied upon the sovereign and Aboriginal status of tribes in the United States and Canada as they develop culturally appropriate economic strategies that arise from the experiences of Indigenous Peoples.

One such strategy has evolved in Canada. Because so much of the public lands of that nation, the so-called Crown lands, retain an unresolved

Aboriginal claim, some tribal groups have recently found ways to foster their own development strategies, shielding themselves from some of the usual exploitive relationships of corporate and government development plans. Though tribes are not recognized in the same ways as U.S. tribes, with protections of sovereign status over specified reservation lands, the tribal interests in those unceded public lands provide leverage for the continuation of their long-standing economic uses there (see Monchalin 2016). Among some major Aboriginal victories, including modern "treaties" and even the creation of Nunavut out of the northern part of the Northwest Territories, the Barriere Lake Algonkins in northern Ontario and Quebec have championed a trilateral agreement between the tribal peoples, the province of Ontario, and the Canadian government. Of greatest importance from the tribal peoples' perspective is the preservation of a way of life based upon subsistence economics in the lands they have always relied upon. Their way of life is to be preserved in an integrated resource-management plan that recognizes their subsistence economy. Traditional relationships with the many entities in the region are specifically addressed in the then-pending agreement (Notzke 1993, 5). Unfortunately, political changes (see Monchalin 2016) have dampened the Canadian government's commitment to the agreement, causing Indigenous and Northern Affairs Canada to end supplemental funding for the negotiations in 2001 (Indigenous and Northern Affairs Canada 2016). Russell Diabo (2006), one of the major technical advisors for the Algonquins, remains hopeful that the arrangement will eventually be fully implemented, since it shares management of the area among many groups who have interests there yet preserves the most substantial of Algonquin traditional uses in ways that ensure their continued efficacy.

In the United States, another economic strategy has emerged, based upon the traditional understandings that Deloria advances. The White Earth Land Recovery Project has provided an economic strategy for the tribe that is deeply linked to tribal traditions. It is a sustainable development project that features tribal tradition yet makes use of the most modern marketing practices of the mass society (White Earth 2006). The online website emphasizes the priority of regaining economic self-sufficiency for tribal peoples and regaining control of wild rice resources in the region, while it helps market traditional arts and crafts of the White Earth Chippewas/Ojibwes. The amazing work of the director of the White Earth Land Recovery Project, Winona LaDuke, an economist, innovator, and activist in Indian Country, leaves no doubt about the ultimate "Fourth World" approaches involved (1999, 126–29). The White Earth Land Recovery Project has helped the tribe regain crucial lands on the reservation and secured the passage of tribal laws that forbid genetically modified organisms there. She has framed her work in the traditional tribal beliefs that recognize wild rice and other "entities" on Ojibwe lands as crucial to any economic plans.

Modern economic plans that reveal a commitment to traditional beliefs include: initiatives among Northwest fishing and maritime tribes, like the Lummi and Makah of Washington; Western and Plains tribes who continue their traditions in their plans for economies partially based upon their relationships with buffalo; and continued agricultural plans among tribes as disparate in traditions as the Oneidas of Wisconsin and the pueblo groups of the Southwest. It is a "growth industry," one that recognizes the kinds of values Vine Deloria has expressed in his philosophical discussions of tribal traditions of "relatedness."

Those in the deep ecology movement should be watching closely as concepts parallel to their own ideas about bioregionalism and the inherent value in natural entities is demonstrated daily across Indian country. Though those tribally appropriate development projects still face many challenges, their concern with maintaining the traditions of interaction and interdependence with the other entities in the universe are immensely instructive. It can be hoped that deep ecologists will feel encouraged in their efforts to transform the economies of destruction that have so long characterized Western mass society.

Without a massive cultural change in today's global economics, though, no initiatives in Indian Country are likely to be enough to stem the tide of environmental collapse augured by present global corporate development. It may seem unlikely at this moment that any environmental movement can establish massive change in the underpinnings of the worldview of developers, but that is exactly what deep ecologists must do. A new generation of Indigenous scholars, activists, and community leaders within Indigenous communities is meeting a new generation of environmentalists. With great good luck, perhaps alliances between traditional Indigenous people and the deep ecology movement will yet be forged. Vine Deloria Jr.'s writings have helped bridge the gaps in understanding between Indigenous Peoples and the colonial mass society in so many areas of human development. One can hope that the influence he has had on the discussions about environmental values will continue to generate dialogues between traditional Indigenous Peoples and a global mass society seemingly dancing on the edge of catastrophe.

REFERENCES

Burke, William Kevin. 2005. "The Wise Use Movement: Right-Wing Environmentalism." *PublicEye.Org*. July 17, 2005. http://www.publiceye.org/magazine/v07n2/wiseuse.html.

Casty, Alan. 1973. *Mass Media and Mass Man*. 2nd ed. New York: Holt, Reinhart and Winston.

Deloria, Vine, Jr. 1970. *We Talk, You Listen: New Tribes, New Turf*. New York: Macmillan.

Deloria, Vine, Jr. (1973) 2003. *God Is Red: A Native View of Religion*. Golden, Colo.: Fulcrum.

Deloria, Vine, Jr. (1979) 2012. *The Metaphysics of Modern Existence*. Golden, Colo.: Fulcrum.

Delora, Vine, Jr. 1997. *Red Earth, White Lies: Native Americans and the Myth of Scientific Fact*. Golden, Colo.: Fulcrum.

Deloria, Vine, Jr. 1999. *Spirit and Reason: The Vine Deloria, Jr., Reader*. Edited by Wilma Mankiller. Golden, Colo.: Fulcrum.

Deloria, Vine, Jr. 2010. *The World We Used to Live In: Remembering the Powers of the Medicine Men*. Golden, Colo.: Fulcrum.

Deloria, Vine, Jr., and Clifford Lytle. 1984. *The Nations Within: The Past and Future of American Indian Sovereignty*. New York: Pantheon.

Diabo, Russell. 2006. Personal interview conducted by the author during the Indigenous People's Convening on Bio-Piracy. Sandia Resort, February 18, 2006.

FDE (Foundation for Deep Ecology). 2012a. "Our Mission." http://www.deepecology.org/mission.htm.

FDE. 2012b. "The Deep Ecology Platform." http://www.deepecology.org/platform.htm.

Getches, David H., Charles F. Wilkinson, and Robert A. Williams, Jr. 1993. *Federal Indian Law: Cases and Materials*. 3rd ed. St. Paul, Minn.: West.

Gomez-Baggethun, Erik, Esteve Corbera, and Victor Reyes-Garcia. 2013. "Traditional Ecological Knowledge and Global Environmental Change: Research Findings and Policy Implications." *Ecology and Society* 18 (4): 72–79.

Indigenous and Northern Affairs Canada. 2016. "Algonquins of Barriere Lake: The 1991 Trilateral Agreement." https://www.aadnc-aandc.gc.ca/eng/1100100016352/1100100016353.

Krech, Shepard, III. 1999. *Myth and History: The Ecological Indian.* New York: W. W. Norton.

LaDuke, Winona 1999. *All Our Relations: Native Struggles for Land and Life.* Cambridge, Mass.: South End Press.

Leopold, Aldo. 1949. *Sand County Almanac.* Oxford: Oxford University Press.

Lovelock, James. 1979. *Gaia: A New Look at Life on Earth.* Oxford: Oxford University Press.

Manuel, George, and Michael Posluns. 1974. *The Fourth World: An Indian Reality.* New York: Free Press.

Menotti, Victor. 2006. "How the World Trade Organization Diminishes Tribal Sovereignty." In *Paradigm Wars: Indigenous Peoples' Resistance to Globalization,* edited by Jerry Mander and Victoria Tauli-Corpuz, 59–68. San Francisco: Sierra Club Books.

Monchalin, Lisa. 2016. *The Colonial Problem: An Indigenous Perspective on Crime and Injustice in Canada.* Toronto, Ont.: University of Toronto Press.

Naess, Arne. 2008. *Ecology of Wisdom: Writings by Arne Naess.* Edited by Alan Drenson and Bill Devall. Berkeley, Calif.: Counterpoint.

Native Harvest. "White Earth Land Recovery Project and Native Harvest Online Catalog." 2006. http://www.nativeharvest.com/index1.asp.

Notzke, Claudia. 1993. *The Barriere Lake Trilateral Agreement.* Lethbridge, Ab.: University of Lethbridge, November, 1993. http://data2.archives.ca/rcap/pdf/rcap-141.pdf.

Pierotti, Raymond. 2010. *Indigenous Knowledge, Ecology and Evolutionary Biology.* New York: Routledge.

Pierotti, Raymond, and Daniel Wildcat. 2000. "Traditional Ecological Knowledge: The Third Alternative" (Commentary). *Ecological Applications* 10 (5): 1333–40.

Rosier, Paul C. 2017. "The Long War on Environmentalism." *Hindsights.* October 13, 2017. https://medium.com/hindsights/the-long-war-on-environmentalism-376f2f0d16ca.

Scherer, Glen. 2004. "The Godly Must Be Crazy: Christian-Right Views Are Swaying Politicians and Threatening the Environment." *Grist Magazine.* October 27, 2004. http://www.grist.org/news/maindish/20/04/10/27/scherer-christian/.

Sessions, George, ed. 1995. *Deep Ecology for the 21st Century: Readings on the Philosophy and Practice of the New Environmentalism.* Boston, Mass.: Shambhala.

Tashman, Brian. 2013. "Robertson Lashes Out at 'Doctrinaire' Environmental 'Fanatics.'" *Right Wing Watch*. March 5, 2013. http://www.rightwingwatch.org/post/robertson-lashes-out-at-doctrinaire-environmentalist-fanatics/.

Taylor, Bron. 2000. "Bioregionalism: An Ethics of Loyalty to Place." *Landscape Journal* 19 (1–2): 50–72.

Wheelock, Richard M. 1998. "The 'Ideal Tribe' and 'Mass Society' in Tribal Communications Research." In *A Good Cherokee, A Good Anthropologist: Papers in Honor of Robert K. Thomas*, edited by Steve Pavlik, 127–48. Los Angeles: American Indian Studies Center, UCLA.

Wildcat, Daniel R. 2009. "Indigenizing the Future." In *Destroying Dogma: Vine Deloria, Jr., and His Influence on American Society*, edited by Steve Pavlik and Daniel R. Wildcat, 131–56. Golden, Colo.: Fulcrum.

Williams, Robert A, Jr. 1990. *The American Indian in Western Legal Thought: The Discourse of Conquest*. New York: Oxford University Press.

LEGAL RESOURCES

United Nations Declaration on the Rights of Indigenous Peoples (2007)

2

ENVIRONMENTAL INJUSTICE, LAND, AND AMERICAN INDIAN RELIGIOUS FREEDOM

KAREN JARRATT-SNIDER

TO SAY that the First Amendment to the U.S. Constitution guarantees various freedoms that American society values is a vast understatement.[1] Almost every day the news carries stories of a protest against something, or a march for it. Everyone from members of the Black Lives Matters movement, to immigration rights activists, to those for and those against gun control, are able to assemble in protest (as long as it remains peaceful) because the First Amendment gives them the right to do so. Freedom of the press, another guarantee of the First Amendment, is vital to the democratic society of the United States, as it lends transparency to the actions of government.

The second clause of the First Amendment—one that American society deems critical for our democracy, is the freedom of religion clause: "Congress shall make no law respecting an establishment of religion, or prohibiting the free exercise thereof" (United States Constitution 1791). There are actually two closely related clauses in that piece. The second clause is the free exercise clause. The first is what is known as the "establishment clause," which is intended to preclude the government from establishing a state religion, which in turn, would prevent free exercise of religion. But while the free exercise clause is considered a fundamental right by many, the courts as well as the federal government have at times rationalized, dismissed, and ignored altogether the free exercise clause when it comes to American Indian religions and religious practices (Getches, Wilkinson, and Williams Jr. 1993). This is particularly true when the issue involves the protection of or access by Indians to a sacred site. These traditional sites, which are important to the practice and protection of American Indian religions, are now legally designated public lands. The nexus of American Indian religious practices and their traditional homelands that are now public lands are Indigenous environmental justice (IEJ) issues. This chapter offers a brief history of unequal protection of religious freedom rights—those for non-Indians and those for Native Americans; a discussion of environmental justice (EJ) and how it is interwoven with protection of and access to Native American culturally significant sites; an examination of some current IEJ culturally significant sites issues; and examples of success stories with respect to some Native American culturally significant, or sacred, sites.

AMERICAN INDIANS AND FREE EXERCISE OF RELIGION

The relationship between American Indians and settler colonists has become more complicated since the assimilationist federal Indian policies of the 1800s. Missionaries had been prevalent in North America since colonization to convert the Indian "heathens" to Christianity, but assimilation efforts intensified as the United States shifted from the Indian removal policy of the 1830s, to the reservation policies of the 1860s and 1870s, and then to the allotment and assimilation policy era of the 1880s (see, generally, Getches Wilkinson, and Williams Jr. 1993, 45–72, 167–214; Deloria and Wilkins 1999).

President Grant's peace policy (1869–77), for example, sought to assure peace between Indians and settlers by creating Indian reservations, providing food supplies—rations—and sending missionaries to convert Native peoples to Christianity (Keller 1967; Levine 1985; Heise 2017). While these actions clearly violated the no establishment of religion clause of the First Amendment, the policy went forward unimpeded by law. As American Indians were considered heathens, perhaps the thought of violating their civil rights did not bother those crafting or implementing the policy. While American Indians as a whole did not become citizens until much later—1924—it is well-established law that civil rights under the U.S. Constitution apply to noncitizens in the United States (*U.S. v Wong Van Ark* 1898). This decision came nearly thirty years after the start of the Peace Policy but serves to illustrate how the United States viewed Indians at the time: as a population less than deserving of basic constitutional rights. While tribal nations are government entities to whom the individual freedoms guaranteed in the Bill of Rights do not apply, their members, as individuals living in the United States, were and are entitled to those protections, and they were clearly violated under the no establishment clause. Under the peace policy, reservations were divided up according to Christian denomination (Imoda and Weber 1969; Heise 2017), and today on Indian reservations it is often the case that one particular denomination is dominant. In other words, one reservation may have mostly Lutheran churches, while others may have primarily Baptist churches, and another will have mostly Methodist churches. In *Grant's Peace Policy: A Catholic Dissenter*, J. C. Imoda and Francis Weber (1969, 57) discuss the Catholic Church's complaint that they did not receive their fair share of Indian reservations on which to practice conversion:

> There was considerable displeasure, for example, about the government's lopsided distribution system. Only eight of the 38 nominations to which they were entitled were given to the Catholic missionaries, though the number of Natives evangelized under Catholic auspices was about 100,000 as opposed to 15,000 for the Protestants. With the assignment of the other agencies to the spiritual and temporal control of the various Protestant denominations—most of them Methodist—80,000 Catholic Indians suddenly found themselves isolated from the church to which they professed spiritual allegiance.
>
> The 'Catholic Commissioner of Indian Affairs' noted the intended impact of the policy, saying that if it had been "properly administered, it would have brought 'real and lasting peace and prosperity to the Indians' and would have 'given to their missions *more power* than any Christian church has had in modern times *in its efforts to evangelize heathen nations.*'" (emphasis added)

In almost every instance, Native religious traditions and practices were viewed by the federal government and those sent to convert American Indians as being antagonistic to Christianity. In fact, from the mid-1880s (the allotment and assimilation era) until 1934, Native spiritual practices were suppressed either through the secretary of the Interior or BIA—who had the authority to do so without an act of Congress—or sometimes

simply outlawed by a presidential order. Religious movements such as the
Sun Dance and Ghost Dance are two examples of Native religious practices that were outlawed (The Pluralism Project n.d.; Gubi 2008). These
actions and the quotation above epitomize the past and present struggle
of Native American peoples in the United States (as well as Indigenous
people in other colonized countries) for the religious freedom to practice
their traditional religions and protect and maintain access to their sacred,
or culturally significant, sites.

From the beginning of colonization, Native peoples were considered
uncivilized by virtue of the fact that they were not Christians, a key component of the Doctrine of Discovery (Getches, Wilkinson, and Williams Jr.
1993, 48–54). The ideas of Indians as heathens compared to civilized Christian peoples carried over into decisions about Indian lands (55–82)—some
of which still impact Indian lands today. The categorization of Indians as
"heathens" became institutionalized into federal Indian policy and at times
federal Indian law, from the birth of the United States until at least the start
of the American Indian Self-Determination era in federal Indian policy
(see, for example, *Johnson v. M'Intosh* 1823 for one of the earliest cases). Some
would argue that it still exists in American society, if not in black-letter
government policy. This view of American Indians, coupled with Indian
religious practices being place-based and site specific, are both key factors
in difficulties American Indians face in their religious freedom rights being
protected (Gordon 1985; Gubi 2008). It seems to be difficult for some non-
Indians to understand how a place without a structure can be holy ground
for Native peoples, instead seeing only raw land or perhaps a beautiful landscape, but not some place that should be protected for Indians (McLeod
2001). The following are current and recent examples seen through an EJ
lens of culturally significant places Native peoples are fighting to protect and
preserve their access to in order to keep their traditions intact.

ENVIRONMENTAL JUSTICE, NATIVE AMERICANS
AND RELIGIOUS FREEDOM

EJ, simply put, is fairness in environmental decision-making, regardless
of race, socioeconomic status, or status as a federally recognized American Indian tribal nation. The Environmental Protection Agency (EPA)
defines EJ as

the fair treatment and meaningful involvement of all people regardless of race, color, national origin, or income with respect to the development, implementation, and enforcement of environmental laws, regulations, and policies. . . . [The] EPA has this goal for all communities and persons. Environmental justice will be achieved when everyone enjoys the same degree of protection from environmental and health hazards, and equal access to the decision-making process to heave a healthy environment in which to live, learn, and work (EPA n.d.-a).

On February 11, 1994, President Bill Clinton signed Executive Order 12898, entitled "Federal Actions to Address Environmental Justice in Minority and Low-Income Populations." The order required all federal agencies to make EJ part of their missions "by identifying and addressing, as appropriate, disproportionately high and adverse human health or environmental effects of its program, policies, and activities on minority populations and its territories and possessions[,]" including Puerto Rico, the Mariana Islands, and the District of Columbia (Executive Order 12898 1994). Section 6–606 of the order states that all federal responsibilities included in the order "shall apply equally to Native American Programs" and that the secretary of the Interior should consult with tribal leaders and coordinate with the working group of federal agencies established under the order, known as the Inter-Agency Working Group (IAWG), and "shall coordinate steps to be taken pursuant to this order that address federally-recognized Indian tribes" (Executive Order 12898 1994). Section 5–5 places the onus upon the federal agencies—not the protected populations identified in the order—with respect to "public participation and access to information." Clearly this section sends a message that fairness in the process of environmental decision-making requires opportunities for *meaningful* participation by the very people the order seeks to protect from environmental discrimination. The order also, as noted in the introduction to this book, requires agencies, "wherever practicable and appropriate," to engage in data collection, research, and analysis with respect to EJ. Particularly of note, the order instructs agencies to specifically include diverse populations in research, data collection, and analysis to consider potential effects of multiple exposures and cumulative effects to potentially affected populations. Another requirement under Executive Order 12898 that is particularly important for some Native American communities is section 4–4, requiring federal agencies to collect data and analyze the risk of consumption of fish or wildlife to communities who depend primarily on subsistence and eat levels of fish or wildlife at levels beyond what is considered in standard risk assessments. Section 4–4 requires agencies to notify communities about the risk related to their particular consumption of these foods (Executive Order 12898 1994). Within the working group, the EPA has taken the lead among the now more than seventeen federal agencies in achieving EJ (EPA n.d.-b).

UNIQUE FACTORS OF INDIGENOUS ENVIRONMENTAL JUSTICE

For Native Americans and Indigenous Peoples there are three unique factors of EJ: tribal sovereignty, connections to traditional homelands (including culturally significant—or sacred—sites), and the continuing effects of colonization. These factors are also noted in the introduction to this book.

Tribal sovereignty, which in the United States applies to all federally recognized American Indian tribal nations, is an integral piece of IEJ. As noted earlier in this book, tribal nations are governments and therefore fall into a different category than low-income or minority populations. Section 6–606 of Executive Order 12898 on EJ recognizes this by stating that everything in the order "applies equally" to federally recognized Native American tribes. The tribal nations have a government-to-government relationship with the United States, who also has a trust responsibility to protect the interests of federally recognized tribal nations.

Indigenous Peoples, including Native Americans, define their identity from their traditional homelands. Each has a sacred place from which they, as a people, come. For example, for the Diné, or Navajo people, it is their four sacred mountains in the Four Corners region of the American Southwest. The connections that Indigenous Peoples have to these places and particular sites within their traditional homelands are culturally significant areas and sites. While others go to worship in "brick and mortar" structures, for Indigenous Peoples it is the places within their homelands.

The third factor differentiating IEJ from EJ for other people and communities is the continuing effects of colonization. These include changes in the ability to subsist—to live off the land—gathering, growing, and fishing or hunting for primary food sources. In the United States, most Native Americans were either removed to lands west of the Mississippi River in the 1830s under the Indian Removal Act or relocated to reservations under the Reservation-era system, as discussed earlier (Getches, Wilkinson, and Williams Jr. 1993). These actions disrupted traditional food systems; instead the government supplied Indians with rations early on, now known as "commodity foods," which do not provide the nutritional value of traditional food systems, and can in turn lead to health issues among Native Americans (see, for example, Joe and Young 1993). Some of these factors are also noted by Gilio-Whitaker (2019).

The rest of this chapter focuses on the connections Indigenous Peoples have to their traditional homelands and, in particular, culturally significant—sacred—sites. The loss of many traditional homelands resulted in the majority of those lands becoming public lands under the auspices of various federal agencies, including the National Park Service (NPS), the U.S. Department of Agriculture Forest Service (USDA Forest Service), and the Bureau of Land Management. As they are now public lands, protecting them and ensuring that American Indians retain access to those places to pray or to gather plants for traditional medicines has in many cases proved difficult or even impossible for Native Americans, in violation, many argue, of their First Amendment right to free exercise of religion.

LEGAL TOOLS FOR PROTECTION OF SACRED SITES

Legal tools specifically addressing protection of free exercise of religion include: The American Indian Religious Freedom Act of 1978 (AIRFA), the Religious Freedom Restoration Act (and the amended version of that law), Executive Order 13007–Indian Sacred Sites, the National Historic Preservation Act (NHPA), the Archeological Resources Protection Act (ARPA), the Native American Graves Protection and Repatriation Act (NAGPRA), Executive Order 13175, and the Tribal Forest Protection Act.

ARPA and NAGPRA relate to protecting artifacts and/or archeological structures, labeled as "ruins." Congress passed the American Antiquities Act of 1906 to protect "archaeological and cultural resources" and help stop illegal pot hunters—those searching for and taking Native-made pottery or shards on federal lands. This act was amended in 1979 to provide lengthier prison penalties and higher amounts for fines. These items in the amendment strengthened the previous legislation. NAGPRA (1990) requires federal agencies and museums receiving federal funds to inventory and then consult with tribal nations to repatriate cultural items, including human remains. Section 2 of this law pertains to burial grounds or cemeteries, archaeological sites with human remains and cultural items. The law also makes it illegal to traffic in human remains and makes grants available to both tribes and museums to facilitate compliance with other NAGPRA requirements (NAGPRA 1990 §2). It is important to note that all of the provisions of NAGPRA apply to Native Hawaiians as well as American Indians.

The passage of the NHPA followed closely after the national wave of urban renewal of the early 1960s, where old buildings had been destroyed to make way for new development. The intention was to save historic buildings and Traditional Cultural Properties, or TCPs, that were important to the history of particular places. Under the NHPA federal projects or any project using federal funds must comply with Section 106 of the law. The NHPA led to the creation of the National Register of Historic Places; however, the eligibility criteria and process to have a site listed on the National Register of Historic Places are long and complicated, and the process for having a site receive a TCP designation is the same as having a structure listed on the register (National Park Service 2012). While it remains one of the legal tools Native Americans use to protect culturally significant sites, it has not been widely successful as a strategy for protecting sacred sites. The NHPA has been far more successful with the repatriation aspects of the law.

AIRFA, a joint resolution of Congress, was the first law to specifically address the First Amendment rights of American Indians, Native Hawaiians, and Alaska Natives to free exercise of religion. This act directed federal agencies to consult with Native American traditional religious leaders and then to review their policies and procedures to ascertain "appropriate changes necessary to protect and preserve Native American religious cultural rights and practices" (AIRFA 1978). The act also announced that the policy of the United States was

> to protect and preserve for American Indians their inherent right of freedom to believe, express and exercise the traditional religions of the

American Indian, Eskimo, Aleut, and Native Hawaiians, including, but not limited to access to sites, use and possession of sacred objects and the freedom to worship through ceremonials and traditional rites. (AIRFA 1978)

While AIRFA seemed to offer promising protection for Native American religious freedom, as a law, it had no provisions for penalties for those who did not follow the law, and it provided no plan for ensuring implementation, beyond requiring the president to report back to Congress within one year with recommendations. AIRFA, in short, had no teeth and is often referred to as a largely symbolic piece of legislation. It was amended in 1994 to permit and acknowledge ceremonial use of peyote for those American Indians that use it as a sacrament (PL 193–344).

One recommendation that came from an AIRFA-directed review by federal agencies of their policies and procedures would not be acted on for nearly two decades. In 1996 President Clinton signed Executive Order 13007 (Executive Order 13007) on "Indian Sacred Sites." This order directed federal agencies with either statutory authority or administrative authority over federal lands "to the extent practicable or permissible by law, and not clearly inconsistent with essential agency functions, (1) accommodate access to and ceremonial use of Indian sacred sites by Indian religious practitioners and (2) avoid adversely affecting the physical integrity of such sacred sites" (1996). The order also required that agencies maintain confidentiality about the sites, and required each agency to deliver a report to the White House within one year. While Executive Order 13007 required more specific actions on the part of federal agencies especially regarding consultation with Native religious practitioners and tribes, it still has not resolved the issue of ensuring religious freedom for Native peoples accessing and utilizing sacred sites on public lands.

In 1993 Congress passed into the law the Religious Freedom Restoration Act (RFRA), another law focusing on Native American religious freedom. The RFRA was a response to the decision by the U.S. Supreme Court in *Employment Division Department of Human Resources of Oregon v. Smith*, in 1990. In *Smith*, an American Indian, Alfred Smith, was fired and denied unemployment benefits for using peyote. Smith argued that his use of peyote as a religious sacrament was protected under his right to free exercise of religion. In deciding the case, the U.S. Supreme Court declined to exercise the *Sherbert* standard often used in unemployment benefits cases. *Sherbert* requires the government to demonstrate it has a "compelling interest" in denying such benefits and has used "the least restrictive means" on religion in the pursuit of its compelling interest. The individual has to have demonstrated a "sincere religious belief" and that the governmental action in the case has resulted in a "substantial burden" on the individual's ability to exercise that belief (U.S. Legal n.d.). Instead, the Court used the "general applicability" test, a much less rigorous test of infringement on religious freedom. Under the general applicability test, a person who violates a law that is otherwise generally applicable to individuals, even it is for religious purposes, is not protected by the free exercise clause.

The RFRA sought a remedy for the outcome in *Smith* by requiring the government to demonstrate a compelling interest for its action and use the least restrictive means to achieve that interest. In 1997 part of the RFRA was ruled unconstitutional, as the U.S. Supreme Court determined that the RFRA did not apply to state governments.

One reason that the legal tools described above have failed to protect Native Americans' First Amendment right to religious freedom in cases where lands—particularly public lands—are involved, is the confluence of issues noted earlier: the no establishment clause and the continuing issues of how some non-Indians view Native Americans and, in turn, their religious practices and sacred places. In some cases where Native Americans attempt to pursue their free exercise of religion rights—particularly when it comes to protecting a sacred site on what is now public land— those who oppose them claim that federal agencies who try to close an area, stop a ski-area development, prevent rock climbing, or whatever the opposition's issue is, would be violating the no establishment of religion clause by privileging the religious practices of the Native Americans involved (McLeod 2001).

Such was the case of the Devil's Tower in Wyoming, where in 1995 the National Park Service (NPS) asked rock climbers to cease rock climbing in the month of June each year so that American Indian religious ceremonies held there for generations could proceed undisturbed. Some of the rock climbers and others in the area protested that the Park Service's accommodation of the American Indians constituted an establishment of religion by privileging their religion over others in violation of the no establishment clause of the First Amendment. This claim is particularly ironic, given the clear establishment of religion Native Americans were subjected to by the federal government under Grant's peace policy. The courts upheld the NPS's accommodation, stating that the NPS was simply removing barriers to create a more peaceful atmosphere for the ceremonies, not promoting the religion itself (McLeod 2001; Indian Law Resource Center n.d.). While in this case American Indians won a victory for their religious rights involving access to a sacred place on federal land, the victory was incomplete. To those practitioners of the tribes who hold the mountain sacred, rock climbers pounding metal pieces into the mountain wound it (McLeod 2001). Additionally, the accommodation does not require rock climbers to cease climbing in June—not climbing is voluntary, and some rock climbers respect it, while others refuse to and still climb during June (McLeod 2001). These are just a few examples of laws and legal tools involved in religious freedom cases where Native Americans have used religious freedom tools and arguments rather than using an EJ approach to secure access to and protection of their sacred places. The following section discusses examples of current conflicts for Native Americans seeking relief for their rights to freely exercise religion, which are also IEJ issues.

CURRENT AND RECENT INDIGENOUS ENVIRONMENTAL JUSTICE ISSUES

Protecting Indian and Native Hawaiian sacred sites and access to them often proves difficult, as evidenced in the two cases below, the *Lyng* case and the ongoing Oak Flat tragedy. One case of note decided during the current policy era of American Indian Self-Determination deserves discussion to understand some of the difficulties in achieving EJ for American Indians where sacred sites and issues of religious freedom are involved. *Lyng v. Northwest Indian Cemetery Protective Association* 1988 involved a sacred area—the Chimney Rock area—within the Six Rivers National Forest. The area was used for religious purposes by three Indian tribes, the Yurok, Karok, and Talowa peoples. The Forest Service wanted to build a logging road in the area. Due to comments opposing the road received on the draft environmental impact statement, the Forest Service authorized a study on the cultural and religious practices of American

Indians in the Chimney Rock area (*Lyng v. Northwest Indian Cemetery Protective Association* 1988). As cited in *Lyng*, the study determined that "constructing the road along any of the available routes would cause serious and irreparable damage to the sacred areas which are an integral and necessary part of the belief systems and lifeway of Northwest Indian Peoples" (*Lyng v. Northwest Indian Cemetery Protective Association* 1988).

After considering the finding in the report, the Forest Service elected to build the road anyway. The Northwest Indian Cemetery Protective Organization sued and won a victory at the district court level. The case eventually wound its way through the appellate process, and the U.S. Supreme Court granted certiorari—meaning it chose to hear the case. In the Court's analysis, they did not apply the compelling interest test. Rather, Justice O'Connor, writing for the majority, indicated that the government's action would not "coerce the Indians into violating their religious beliefs" but rather that the infringement on religious beliefs and practices was an incidental effect of the government's action (*Lyng vs. Northwest Indian Cemetery Protective Association* 1988). The lack of coercion meant the government's choice to build the road did not violate the free exercise of religion clause in this case. While the majority decision failed to uphold the First Amendment right to free exercise of religion, it is worth noting that, in the dissent, Justice Brennan wrote, "Where dogma lies at the heart of Western religions, Native American faith is inextricably bound to the use of the land. The site-specific nature of Indian religious practice derives from the Native American perception that the land is itself a living sacred being" (*Lyng vs. Northwest Indian Cemetery Protective Association* 1988). What is particularly noteworthy is that, unlike the majority, those justices dissenting recognized clearly that the vital difference between traditional religious practices of American Indians and Western religions is that Native American religions are land-based. This difference remains the core of the difficulty in protecting Indigenous sacred lands. The following is a current case that clearly illustrates that point.

OAK FLAT (CHI'CHIL BILDAGOTEEL)

In a high desert area, amid a majestic landscape, approximately sixty-five miles east of Phoenix and nestled between two Arizona towns, Globe and

Superior, sits the Oak Flat campground area. Oak Flat is part of the San Carlos Apache's traditional homelands. At some point it became part of the Tonto Apache Forest and under management by the USDA Forest Service. The Oak Flat area includes a site known as Apache Leap, sacred to the San Carlos Apache people. Now it belongs to a mining company, Resolution Copper, as the result of the outcome of a public–private land exchange.

Starting in 2005 bills were unsuccessfully introduced in several different sessions of Congress to complete a land exchange in which the USDA Forest Service would transfer the Oak Flat area into the hands of Resolution Copper. In exchange, Resolution Copper would transfer parcels of land it owned to the Forest Service. Many members of the San Carlos Apache Tribe, including a now former chairman of the tribe, made the federal government aware—from the Tonto National Forest where the land was located, to the White House—that they opposed this land exchange because it was the Apache's sacred area (anonymous pers. comm. 2010, 2011, 2015; Apache Stronghold n.d.). While the bill had failed many times before, this time lawmakers in favor of the land exchange, including Senators John McCain and Jeff Flake from Arizona's delegation of lawmakers, attached it as a rider to a bill sure to pass, the National Defense Authorization Act of 2015. While the USDA Forest Service is still required to prepare an Environmental Impact Statement under the terms of the bill, the land will be transferred to the mining company within sixty days of the final Record of Decision.

Those trying to protect Oak Flat successfully pursued a Traditional Cultural Property designation, and on March 4, 2016, Chí' chil Bildgateel (Oak Flat) was added to the National Register of Historical Places. However, in August 2019 the Tonto National Forest issued the Draft Environmental Impact Statement (USDA, Tonto National Forest 2019). In this statement the USDA Forest Service acknowledges, in part, the harm to Native nations and peoples that the land exchange and mining activity will have, saying:

> Native American communities would be disproportionately affected by the land exchange because Oak Flat would be conveyed to private property and would no longer be subject to the NHPA (see section 3.12). Loss of the culturally important area of Oak Flat would be a substantial threat to

the perpetuation of cultural traditions of the Apache and Yavapai tribes. The land exchange would have a disproportionally adverse effect on Native American communities as a result of the effects on tribal values and concerns and cultural resources (USDA, Toñto National Forest 2019, 678).

STRATEGY AND SUCCESS

Two cases in particular demonstrate the variety of tools necessary for achieving IEJ: A power line project in western New Mexico involving Forest Service and private lands, and a case of retaining access to a sacred site by crossing private land.

ZUNI HEAVEN (KOLHU/WALA:WA)

Generation after generation, the Zuni people, whose lands today encompass part of eastern Arizona and western New Mexico, undertake a journey every four years to a site on their land in eastern Arizona to pray. Today, those outside the tribe refer to it as "Zuni Heaven," while to Zunis it is known as Kolhu/wala:wa (Seibert 2005; Hart 1995). The Zuni participate in numerous traditional cultural practices that require caring for particular springs and numerous shrines, and includes their pilgrimage to Zuni Heaven. For many years, Zuni Heaven, like many of the sites the Zunis care for and maintain, was no longer part of their reservation, established in 1877. Hart writes, "According to the Zuni religion, Kolhu/wala:wa is the place where Zunis go after death, and where the supernatural Kokko reside under a sacred lake fed by the waters of a precious spring" (Hart 1995, 199). Every four years, up to sixty Zuni religious leaders chosen to the make the journey make the pilgrimage to Zuni Heaven, covering 110 miles roundtrip over four days. Zunis have been making the pilgrimage for more than one hundred years (Seibert 2005, 111; Hart 1995, 208). Like many Native American tribes, over time parts of their traditional homeland were lost. The Zunis acquired title to Zuni Heaven itself in 1984; however, in 1946, part of the pilgrimage trail from the reservation in New Mexico to Zuni Heaven in eastern Arizona became private land. The landowner, a rancher named Earl Platt, objected to the Zunis crossing parts of his land in Apache County on their pilgrimage (Seibert 2005; Hart 1995; Rubin 1989). Still, the Zunis would make their trek every fourth year. As the 1985 pilgrimage loomed, Platt indicated he would take action to stop the trek (Rubin 1989; Hart 1995, 208). Platt spoke openly about his feelings about the trek and the Zunis, saying "I don't like Indians," and "I'm going to stop them somehow" (Rubin 1989; Hart 1995, 210). The Zunis secured a temporary restraining order from a federal judge and the 1985 pilgrimage proceeded (Rubin 1985), but the Zunis wanted a permanent solution. The Zunis were concerned about bringing a legal challenge for multiple reasons, including that the *Lyng* case was winding its way through the courts at that time (Hart 1995, 209). If the Court denied religious freedom rights in favor of government interest in *Lyng*, the Zunis thought a court case regarding their pilgrimage could go badly for them (209–10). What they did have in their favor was documented continuous use for well over one hundred years, and adverse possession (continuously making their pilgrimage with the knowledge that someone else owned the land they were crossing) (Seibert 2005; Hart 1995, 210–12). As trustee for the Zuni tribe, the federal government brought suit in 1985 against the rancher (Hart 1995, 212). The suit purposefully did not make a First Amendment free exercise of religion claim (210–11). While the purpose of the pilgrimage was religious in nature, as stated earlier, the claim was not for protection of First Amendment rights. Instead, in a legally astute move, the claim was for a prescriptive easement (211). Both Zuni Heaven and Platt's ranch are located in Arizona. The State of Arizona law requires two elements in order to grant a prescriptive easement, which are (1) "peaceable and adverse possession," and (2) for a continuous period of ten years or more (212). As the Zunis were able to document quadrennial use for far longer than a ten-year period, they easily met that requirement. Elders testified about the pilgrimage, as well as non-Indians in the area who had observed the Zunis on their trek several times (212–14). Also well-documented was the participants' knowledge that the land they were crossing was owned by someone else, yet they continued to do so (a simplified, nonlegal explanation of adverse possession).

On February 8, 1990, the district court in Phoenix, Arizona, rendered its decision, granting a prescriptive easement to the Zuni tribe (*U.S. on Behalf of Zuni Tribe of New Mexico v. Platt* 1990). The court held that the Zuni tribe had met all of the elements of adverse possession under the

Arizona statute. The easement was limited to use on a quadrennial basis and the right to cross the land, with no camping or fires permitted (*U.S. on Behalf of Zuni Tribe of New Mexico v. Platt* 1990). The Zuni tribe found victory and justice because of the legal claim they chose and because of the one they did not choose; by using land-use law rather than making a free exercise of religion claim, they achieved victory for their religious pilgrimage.

POWER LINE PROJECT

About twenty-five miles south and slightly east of Taos, New Mexico, sits the town of Peñasco. Taos is a popular place known for skiing, art, and museums. Taos Pueblo, a Native American community, is adjacent to the town. Approximately six miles away is Talpa, and approximately nineteen miles south of Talpa is the small, quiet town of Peñasco. The decades-old power line running between Talpa and Peñasco needed upgrading for some time. By 2002, electrical service became spotty between the two places, and a new power line became necessary. The line would cross state, federal, and private land at times, including land within the Carson National Forest (CNF) (USDA, Carson National Forest 2002). Some of the area involved was within the traditional homeland of one American Indian tribal nation. The Camino Real district of the CNF, the district responsible for producing the needed Environmental Impact Statement (EIS), is located next door to an American Indian tribe, Picuris Pueblo (Jarratt-Ziemski 2006).

The National Environmental Policy Act (1969) requires an EIS describing various alternatives and the potential environmental impacts of each one whenever a federal agency is considering an action with possible environmental impacts. For the EIS a scoping process takes place where potential impacts are identified, alternative actions are generated, and the draft EIS is produced. The general public has a certain number of days to comment on the draft EIS, and those comments must be addressed in the final EIS; however, where a tribal nation is potentially affected by the action(s), federal agencies are required to "consult and coordinate" with them (Executive Order 13175). In implementing the order, federal agencies engage in formal consultation that typically includes letters notifying the tribe of the proposed action and formal meetings. In this author's experience, however, the coordination piece of the executive order some-times consists of little to no activities. Executive Order 12898 requires agencies, as discussed previously, to make achieving EJ part of their mis-sion; however, Executive Order 12898 is sometimes considered "just" a procedural order—meaning that as long as the agency follows the process, they are not required to "do anything" (anonymous pers. comm. 2006). In the case of the Forest Service, as an agency of the U.S. Department of Agriculture (USDA), they are required to follow the regulation promul-gated by USDA Regulation 5600–2 on Environmental Justice. Heading Number 9 of Regulation 5600–2 details outreach activities that agencies must include in their efforts to communicate about proposed activities to those populations included in Executive Order 12898. Examples of those activities listed in the regulation include Outreach efforts in the Power-line Case by the staff person responsible for outreach on the Camino Real District of the CNF. Her efforts were both simple and extraordinary, and are an example of successful consultation. The effort included the for-mal consultation required under Executive Order 13175, but also included efforts consistent with Executive Order 12898, and USDA Regulation 5600–2 on Environmental Justice. In additions to letters and phone calls, the district archaeologist asked members of the affected tribes to join her in the field at various points along the power line, where she explained in lay language what would occur under each possible alternative (anon-ymous pers. comm. 2006). Although no one from the tribal delegation (elected officials as well as traditional practitioners) spoke during her pre-sentation of each alternative, at the end of the presentation of alternatives, they offered vitally important feedback. The tribal delegation indicated that they did not like any of the alternatives, but pointed out the one that was least problematic for them. After listening, waiting, and a few questions, the Camino Real staff person learned what lay at the heart of their objects to the project. Various, unspecified things were buried at certain points along the project route, and could have been disturbed and/or damaged during the project; however, the exact nature and loca-tion of the times were confidential, not to be shared with those outside of the tribe. After consideration of how to address their concerns, the Camino Real staff person contacted the power company, who agreed to hire a tribal monitor. The monitor would accompany those digging for the project, and ask them to stop digging temporarily when/if they neared a spot where there was something of cultural significance, whether it was a burial site or cultural items. The tribe would then "take care of" the items, presumably reburying them in another location or removing them, and then contact the power company to resume operations (Jarratt-Ziemski 2006). Confidentiality about the items was maintained, the tribal nation's concerns were addressed, and the project proceeded.

In this case, EJ and the solution to a religious freedom issue were achieved for Native people with a relatively simple solution, with no mention of religion. The actions of the Camino Real archaeologist, though, are clearly what ensured a just outcome for the American Indian tribe involved. While not mentioning either Executive Order 12898 or Regulation 5600–2, the Camino Real staff person did talk about the importance of consultation *and* coordination in her communication with the tribe. Over time, the district archaeologist built a relationship of trust with the tribe and learned how best to communicate. While only a few of the many legal tools available in the EJ and, in turn, religious freedom, "tool box" were applied, they were effective due to the Forest Service's staff person's understanding of the spirit of these orders and regulations. In short, the district archaeologist chose activities that offered opportunities for *meaningful* participation for the affected EJ population—the tribal nation. Meaningful participation, not just activities that one can check off on the list to fulfill the absolute minimum in consultation, or the absolute minimum in community outreach to fulfill Executive Order 12898 requirements, made the difference in this case. Because one Carson National Forest staff member ensured the process in this case was one of fulfilling the spirit as well as the "letter of the law" of these two executive orders, it led to a just outcome for the tribe. Environmental justice—not injustice—was achieved.

CONCLUSION

Using EJ processes for protection of and access to culturally significant, or sacred, sites may offer a better chance of success than religious freedom First Amendment claims, an argument that Gilio-Whitaker (2019), also makes. Jocks (2020) also argues that, given the failure of religious freedom claims to protect sacred sites, other avenues such as the NHPA, discussed here as a legal tool for achieving IEJ, may offer more hope for protecting Indigenous sacred sites than First Amendment claims. Other examples beyond Zuni Heaven and the Power line project show similar results and point to opportunities for protecting sacred sites (see, for example, Jarratt-Ziemski 2006; McLeod 2001). Differences in values between land-based Indigenous lifeways and the religions that accompanied settler colonialism still find their way into court decisions affecting American Indian peoples, as is evident in *Lyng* and, more recently, the San Francisco Peaks cases (*Oliphant v. Suquamish Indian Tribe* 1978; *Navajo Nation v. U.S. Forest Service* 2008; *Save the Peaks Coalition v. US Forest Service* 2012). The issue, Justice Brennan wrote in the dissent in *Lyng*, is that Native Americans' religions are land-based and site specific. As long as the U.S. Supreme Court uses the standards applied in *Lyng* (1988) and *Smith* (1990), or the general applicability test, Native Americans will continue to see their free exercise of religion rights denied in public-lands cases.

Alternative strategies, however, offer a chance for better success. EJ does offer tribes an opportunity to protect and access their sacred lands, but relying on a single legal tool, such as Executive Order 12898 on Environmental Justice (1994) will likely be insufficient. Success requires an examination in each case of all the legal tools available in the "tool box" and selecting the right ones for the issue at hand.

The executive order on EJ itself does not create a right to pursue legal action. The policies and regulations an agency create in order to implement the order, however, do offer an opportunity to hold agencies accountable for effective outreach and, in turn, a more just solution for Native nations. Additionally, Executive Order 13175 on Consultation and Coordination with Indian Tribes (2000) used in concert with other legal IEJ tools may offer better opportunities for *meaningful* participation early and continuously in the process. Other legal tools, such as pursuing TCP designation, are also underutilized means in protecting sacred lands.

Tribal nations have opportunities to become more strategic in attempts to protect their sacred lands. Getting involved in the process early on and remaining involved is critical to pursuing an EJ approach. To that point, federal agencies should better train staff on effective outreach tools for tribal nations and utilize them early and continuously throughout the process (Jarratt-Ziemski 2006). While the onus is on federal agencies to reach out to tribal nations, low-income and minority populations, such federal agencies don't always do so, as demonstrated by the San Francisco Peaks snowmaking case in the Coconino National Forest. Tribal nations objecting to the ski area making snow with reclaimed wastewater lost administrative appeals and legal cases asserting that their free exercise of religion rights had been violated (Jarratt-Ziemski 2006). Tribal nations sometimes have only one or two staff members in environmental departments, while federal agencies have multiple staff—an entire Interdisciplinary Team—to work on environmental reviews. To be successful in protecting sacred lands, tribal nations may need to use all of the legal tools and strategies available.

At the heart of the matter lay the same attitudes about Indians and religion evident from the Doctrine of Discovery until the present day. Understanding of and appreciation of the religious practices of Indigenous Peoples and their connections to sacred homelands is not widely understood or accepted by the American public, including those within federal agencies and the courts. In short, if there is not a brick-and-mortar church on it, it is not sacred enough to protect from mining, road building and logging, rock climbing, or any governmental activity with an "incidental" and simultaneously devastating effect on the religious freedom of Native Americans. Some will continue to claim that the government cannot allow protection of sacred sites without violating the no establishment clause. Until that day when American society as a whole recognizes the inherent right of Native peoples to protect parts of their original homelands—sacred places—EJ may offer a better avenue for protecting those places without entering a religious fight, and thus may produce a more effective strategy for protecting culturally significant sites for Native Americans.

NOTE

1.   Interviewees wished to remain anonymous. All identifying information has been omitted.

REFERENCES

Apache Stronghold. n.d. http://www.apache-stronghold.com/.

Davidson, Osha Gray. 2016. "How a Huge Arizona Mining Deal Passed—and Could Be Revoked." *High Country News*. February 2, 2016.

Deloria, Vine, Jr., and David E. Wilkins. 1999. *Tribes, Treaties, and Constitutional Tribulations*. Austin: University of Texas Press.

EPA (Environmental Protection Agency). n.d.-a. "Environmental Justice." https://www.epa.gov/environmentaljustice.

EPA. n.d.-b. "Environmental Justice for Tribes and Indigenous Peoples." https://www.epa.gov/environmentaljustice/environmental-justice-tribes-and-indigenous-peoples.

Getches, David H., Charles F. Wilkinson, and Robert A. Williams, Jr. 1993. *Cases and Materials on Federal Indian Law*. 3rd ed. St. Paul, Minn.: West.

Gilio-Whitaker, Dina. 2019. *As Long as Grass Grows: The Indigenous Fight for Environmental Justice, From Colonization to Standing Rock*. Boston, Mass.: Beacon Press.

Gordon, Susan Barranger. 1985. "Indian Religious Freedom and Governmental Development of Public Lands." Faculty Scholarship. Philadelphia: Penn Law—Legal Scholarship Repository.

Gubi, Jason. 2008. "The Religious Freedom Restoration Act and Protection of Native American Religious Practices." *Modern America* 4 (2): 71–79.

Hart, E. Richard. 1995. *Zuni and the Courts*. Lawrence: University of Kansas Press.

Heise, Tammy. 2017. "Religion and Native American Assimilation, Resistance, and Survival." Religion in *Oxford Research Encyclopedias*. http://religion.oxfordre.com/view/10.1093/acrefore/9780199340378.001.0001/acrefore-9780199340378-e-394.

Imoda, J. C., and Francis J. Weber. 1969. "Grant's Peace Policy: A Catholic Dissenter." *Montana: The Magazine of Western History* 19 (1): 56–63.

Indian Law Resource Center. n.d. "Indian Religious Freedom at Devil's Tower National Monument." http://indianlaw.org/projects/past_projects/cheyenne_river.

Jarratt-Ziemski, Karen. 2006. "Meaningful Participation in Environmental Justice: Policy Designs and Implications for Re-envisioning, Reinstating, and Reinforcing Tribal Sovereignty." PhD diss., Northern Arizona University.

Jocks, Chris. 2020. "Restoring Congruity: Indigenous Lives and Religious Freedom in the US and Canada." In *Traditional, National and International Law and Indigenous Communities*, edited by Marianne O. Nielsen and Karen Jarratt-Snider. Tucson: University of Arizona Press.

Joe, Jennie Rose, and Robert S. Young. 1993. *Diabetes as a Disease of Civilization: The Impact of Culture Change on Indigenous Peoples*. New York: Mouton De Gruyter.

Keller, Robert. 1967. *The Protestant Churches and Grant's Peace Policy: A Study in Church-State Relations, 1869–1882*. PhD diss., University of Chicago. ProQuest Dissertations and Theses.

Levine, Richard E. 1985. "Indian Fighters and Indian Reformers: Grant's Peace Policy and the Conservative Consensus." *Civil War History* 31 (4): 329–52.

McLeod, C., dir. 2001. *In the Light of Reverence*. Oley, Pa.: Bullfrog Films.

National Park Service. 2012. "National Register of Historic Places-Traditional Cultural Properties (TCPs): A Quick Guide for Preserving Native American Cultural Resources" (Draft). https://www.nps.gov/history/tribes/Documents/TCP.pdf.

The Pluralism Project. n.d. "Religious Freedom for Native Americans." Harvard University. http://pluralism.org/religions/native-american-traditions/issues-for-native-peoples/religious-freedom-for-native-americans/.

Rubin, Paul. 1989. "Platt's Last Stand." *Phoenix New Times*. March 8, 1989. http://www.phoenixnewtimes.com/news/platts-last-stand-6412912.

Siebert, David, ed. 2005. "Sacred Lands and Gathering Grounds: A Toolkit for Access and Protection." (Binder toolkit.) Flagstaff, AZ: Northern Arizona University.

U.S. Legal. n.d. "Sherbert Test Law and Legal Definition." https://definitions.uslegal.com/s/sherbert-test/.

LEGAL RESOURCES

American Antiquities Act. 16 U.S.C. 431–433 (1906)

American Indian Religious Freedom Act. PL 95–341 (1978)

———. Amendment. PL 193–344 (1994)

Archaeological Resources Protection Act. PL 96–95 (1979)

Employment Division Department of Human Resources of Oregon v. Smith. 404 U.S. 872, 110 S Ct. 1595, 108 L. Ed. 2d 876 (1990)

Executive Order 12898. "Federal Actions to Address Environmental Justice in Minority and Low-Income Populations" (1994)

Executive Order 13007. "Indian Sacred Sites" (1996)

Executive Order 13175. "Consultation and Coordination with Indian Tribes" (2000)

Johnson v. M'Intosh. 21 U.S. 543, 5 L. Ed. 681 (1823)

Lyng v. Northwest Indian Cemetery Protective Association. 485 U.S.439, 208 S. Ct. 1319, 99 L.Ed.2d. 534 (1988)

National Defense Authorization Act for 2015. PL 113–291

National Environmental Policy Act. 42 U.S.C. §4321 et. Seq. (1969)

National Historic Preservation Act. PL 89–665, 54 U.S.C. 300101 et. Seq. (1966)

Native American Graves Protection and Repatriation Act. PL 101–601 (1990)

Navajo Nation v. U.S. Forest Service. 535 F3d 1058 9th Cir. (2008)

Oliphant v. Suquamish Indian Tribe. 435 U.S. 191, 98 S.C.t. 1011, 55 L.Ed. 2d 209 (1978)

Public Law 98–408 (1984)

Religious Freedom Restoration Act. PL 103–141 (1993)

Save the Peaks Coalition v. US Forest Service. 669 F.3d 102 9th Cir. (2012)

Tribal Forest Protection Act 25 U.S.C. §3115a (2005)

United States Constitution, Bill of Rights. Amendments 1–10 (1791)

U.S. on Behalf of Zuni Tribe of New Mexico v. Platt. 730 F. Supp. 318 D. Ariz. (1990)

U.S. v. Wong Van Ark. 169 U.S. 649 (1898)

USDA (U.S. Department of Agriculture). "Regulation 5600–2: Environmental Justice." Washington, D.C. (1997)

USDA, Carson National Forest. "Record of Decision and Final Environmental Impact Statement for a 69kV Transmission Line from Talpa to Peñasco, NM" (2002)

USDA, Tonto National Forest. DRAFT Environmental Impact Statement: Resolution Copper Project and Land Exchange (August 2019)

3

ENVIRONMENTAL INJUSTICES AND STATE-CORPORATE CRIME ON NAVAJO AND HOPI LANDS

LINDA M. ROBYN

UNPARALLELED BEAUTY is found on the Navajo Nation and the Hopi Nation, which exists inside the borders of the Navajo Nation.[1] Those who live on these reservations have experienced exceptional environmental injustices through corporate and government efforts to dispossess them of valuable resources for political and monetary gain. The Navajo and Hopi people have been subjected to uranium mining and coal mining, as well as gas and oil drilling, because the rest of the world wants these materials at the lowest possible cost. As will be discussed in this chapter, coal mining and uranium mining on the Navajo and Hopi Nations are two instances of environmental injustices that can be defined as state-corporate crimes.

STATE-CORPORATE CRIME AND INDIGENOUS NATIONS

State-corporate crime is a form of social harm that refers to "illegal or socially injurious [i.e., social harms] actions that occur when one or more institutions of political governance pursue a goal in direct cooperation with one or more institutions of economic production and distribution" (Kramer and Michalowski 1990, 3). Therefore, "within a capitalist economy, state-corporate crimes are the harmful consequences of deviant inter-organizational relationships between business and governments. This definition can be applied to illegal or socially injurious practices in societies organized around private-production systems and in those based on centrally planned economies" (Kramer and Michalowski 2006, 20–21). Kramer and Michalowski (2006, 21) write:

> The deviant interorganizational relationships that serve as the basis for state-corporate crime can take two forms. One is state-initiated corporate crime, and the other is state-facilitated corporate crime. State-initiated corporate crime occurs when corporations employed by a government engage in organizational deviance at the direction of, or with the tacit approval of, that government. State-facilitated corporate crime occurs when government institutions of social control are guilty of clear failure to create regulatory institutions capable of restraining deviant business activities, either because of direct collusion between business and government or because they adhere to shared goals whose attainment would be hampered by aggressive regulation.

State-corporate crimes are different from "street crimes" (murder, rape, robbery, aggravated assault, burglary, larceny, etc.) in that corporate crimes are not usually committed for personal gain, even though certain individuals directly benefit from them. Corporate crimes on the Navajo and Hopi Nations were committed to further the goals of the corporations, as well as to meet the government's need for uranium and coal. There are many links between corporate "power elites" and the government on all levels (see Friedrichs 2007, 27).

State-corporate crime concepts can be applied to the United States' interest in energy and mineral resources found on and underneath American Indian reservations. These reservations are of strategic importance to corporations and the government because they constitute one of the largest and previously least-known mineral repositories on the continent: nearly 5 percent of U.S. oil and gas, one-third of its strippable low-sulfur coal, and one-half of its privately owned uranium (Gedicks 1993, 40). Today, Indigenous Peoples "struggle to control some of the greatest acreage of energy mineral-rich lands in North America, even as their populations remain relatively small (at less than 1 percent of the total U.S. population) and economically marginalized" (Powell 2018, 9). Social and economic inequalities can be measured by quality of life indicators. On American Indian reservations, the Navajo reservation included, approximately "14 percent of households have no access to electricity, ten times the U.S. average. On both the Pine Ridge (Lakota) reservation and in the Navajo Nation, 40 percent of tribal citizens lack electricity" (U.S. Department of Energy, quoted in Powell 2018, 9).

Natural resource extraction on or in close proximity to Native communities has numerous "environmental, social, and economic justice implications[,] . . . because the lands granted to Native Americans under reservation treaties were later discovered to store significant resources desired by corporations and the federal government" (Lynch and Stretesky 2011, 109). The result of resource extraction is that both Navajos and Hopis live "in dangerously close proximity to major coal mines and power plants, with their noxious effects realized locally, as well as on a regional scale" (Powell 2018, 10). This, however, leads to another significant problem faced especially by Navajo populations that experience a "high incidence of cancer and lack of access to cancer treatment, screening, and prevention services" (Guadagnolo et al., quoted in Lynch and Stretesky 2011, 107).

It is important to recognize that the environmental harms on the Navajo and Hopi reservations are a product of elite power games in business and politics, thereby making corporate capitalism central to environmental injustice issues on Indigenous lands. The federal government used various means in the past to the disadvantage of Native Americans. These mechanisms included threats to rescind or modify treaties to retake control of Native lands, reorganizing Native American forms of governance, and "entering into coercive contract arrangements, a practice that has also been followed by the corporate mining sector" (LaDuke, quoted in Lynch and Stretesky 2011, 110; see also Forbes 1979). The American energy industry has been disproportionately reliant on Indigenous resources, and "the extraction of energy's raw materials (uranium, coal, oil, natural gas, water, and increasingly, wind and sunshine) has devastated Native lands, while Native people often benefit the least in terms of economic development and cheap energy—a phenomenon that can be shorthanded as energy injustice" (Voyles 2015, 9).

Environmental injustice is connected to a system of social inequality. In Indigenous communities subject to environmental injustice, "the origins of exposure to toxic hazards relate to the wealth of natural resources found beneath their lands" (Lynch and Stretesky 2011, 114); however, Native cultural values about the way lands and resources need to be cared for are vastly different from the exploitation of capitalistic enterprises. One group views their homelands "as sacred landscapes[,] . . . and the other sees these same areas as wastelands of little economic and productive value, suitable primarily for environmental experimentation and ultimately sacrifice" (Kuletz 1998, xiii). And when economic and political powers pursue common interests of resource extraction, the potential for harm is magnified. These types of harmful collaborations are state-corporate crime.

Before examining the actions or inactions taken by some multinational corporations on the Navajo and Hopi reservations, it is important to note that corporations have contributed much to our society; for example, they employ us, many are philanthropic, and they have enriched our lives. The majority of corporations do not conspire to commit illegal or harmful practices, but corporations exist in a capitalist society to make money. Making a profit is the bottom line, and in the case of the Navajo people, as well as many other populations living in low-income communities, the bottom line is making a profit regardless of environmental concerns or resulting harms to those living in these areas.

It may be difficult for many people to think of corporations as working in cooperation with government bureaucracies in ways that create harm. When working together, corporations and the government are not evil entities plotting to see whom they can take advantage of and harm; however, the history of the development of Indian policy and exploitative economic development on Indian lands suggest that this *has* been the case, as illustrated first by the history of coal mining on Navajo and Hopi lands.

COAL MINING ON NATIVE LANDS

The Navajo Nation encompasses the Hopi Nation, covers an area the size of West Virginia, and extends from Arizona into Utah and New Mexico. The nation covers approximately 27,425 square miles and is larger than ten of the fifty states in the United States (Navajo Nation n.d.)

The Hopi and Navajo living on Black Mesa (now split between the Hopi and Navajo reservations) were promised compensation in exchange for signing strip-mining leases for coal. This was the catalyst for the great injustices that resulted from the Navajo–Hopi land dispute and the Bennett Freeze. An analysis of these two events is helpful in understanding that harms from state-corporate crime encompass more than environmental destruction.

THE NAVAJO–HOPI LAND DISPUTE

Historically, the development of Indian policy and economic exploitation that includes illegal and unethical actions by the U.S. government started in the 1830s with Indian removal, and illegal and unethical conduct by the United States working with corporations began mainly after the Mexican–American War in 1848. At that time the Treaty of Guadalupe Hidalgo allowed the Mormon colonies of southwestern Utah and the settlers in New Mexico and Arizona to attack the Navajo through military expeditions to stop Navajo raids on the settlers. The military response led to the raiders' defeat by Colonel Christopher "Kit" Carson, and two-thirds of the Navajo population (eight thousand) being forced to endure the Long Walk before being incarcerated at Fort Sumner, New Mexico (Churchill 1997, 144). When the surviving Navajos were allowed to return from Fort Sumner, they found themselves on a reservation one-fourth the size of their original territory (Mudd and Florio 1985).

Non-Mormon expansion into Montezuma Creek and the Aneth area, Mormons settling in the Tuba City and Moenkopi areas, and the huge cattle industry of San Juan County in Utah made competition for scarce resources inevitable. Congress opened public domain lands for both Native and settler-colonist use, but the Navajos and Utes utilized the land in ways that whites did not believe to be prosperous, which accounts for the long historical struggle between Native peoples and whites from 1868 to 1991 (Mudd and Florio 1985).

The *Healing v. Jones* case (1959) set the stage for conflicts and disputes between the Navajo and Hopi regarding boundary lines. The case is named after Hopi and Navajo tribal chairmen Dewey Healing and Paul Jones, and was later referred to as "the greatest title problem of the West" (Benedek 1992, 37). This case brought to light the idea that government can give and take Indian land as it sees fit with no restraint whatsoever, with the state and corporations reaping the benefits from energy-resource development.

In 1955 Stewart Udall, congressman from Arizona, knew that Hopi and Navajo livestock grazing land overlapped somewhat, and that there were tensions between the two tribes about this, but thought that the issue could be easily resolved by building a fence so livestock wouldn't roam (32). Then in 1958 Udall was approached by lawyers from both tribes asking him to introduce a bill into Congress to allow the tribes to sue one another for their fair share. When he returned from Washington in 1980, he found that the small boundary dispute that grew from his bill "had become one of the largest relocations of civilians in the United States since the internment of Japanese-Americans during WW II" (32). Udall learned this was not just a simple livestock boundary line dispute, but involved 1.8 million acres shared by both tribes (32).

Understanding and untangling the dispute brought about by Udall's bill introduced in 1958 is not an easy task. Some events and dates described seem to be out of order but also serve to explain where the dispute came from, why certain events ended in specific ways, and just how complicated the land dispute is. To unravel the dispute and the land grabs that followed with the *Healing v Jones* (1959) case, the subsequent appeal decided in 1962, and the resulting disastrous environmental results, we have to go back to events that occurred in 1882 to see why a reservation (Joint Use Area, or JUA) was created in the first place by President Chester Alan Arthur's 1882 executive order.

The conflict that brought about the 1882 executive order did not begin as a dispute between the Navajo and Hopi, but was actually a disagreement among Indian Agent J. H. Fleming, E. H. Merritt, and Dr. J. Sullivan over Indian education (Benedek 1992, 33). The Indian agent wanted to send Hopi children to New Mexico to boarding school, and the Hopi were vehemently opposed. Sympathizers Merritt and Sullivan helped the Hopi oppose the government's program to send the children away. The Indian agent wanted to evict Merritt and Sullivan, but could not because Hopi lands were public lands (33). Fleming was so upset that he threatened to quit, so Commissioner Hiram Price sent a telegraph to Fleming asking him to outline boundaries "for a reservation that will include Moqui (Hopi) villages and agency large enough to meet all the needful purposes and no larger" (quoted in Benedek 1992, 34). Fleming drew an arbitrary square around an area he thought best, and it was sent to President Arthur (34).

On December 16, 1882, President Chester A. Arthur, by executive order, set aside a rectangular piece of land in Arizona, "seventy miles north to south and fifty-five miles east to west for the use and occupancy of the Moquis [Hopis] and such other Indians as the Secretary of the Interior may see fit to settle thereon, and became known as the 1882 Executive Order Area" (37). This order set aside 2.5 million acres around most of the Hopi villages (Lacerenza 1988). However, Arthur's executive order was not the end of land divisions on the Hopi and Navajo reservations. Between 1868 and 1905 there were eight further boundary changes that increased the area of the reservation to the north, east, and west as the territory changed hands many times at the behest of Congress.

The final extension occurred in 1934 as part of the Indian Reorganization Act (explained in more detail later in this chapter). A portion of this act centered around conservation methods to "protect Indian land from misuse and exploitation by whites" (Benedek 1992, 36). But to the Hopi and Navajo, this meant soil conservation and livestock control, and this was accomplished by creating grazing districts to keep Navajo livestock from intruding on Hopi lands. At this time, a Hopi-exclusive livestock district called District 6 was set aside for Hopi use and "followed the Parker-Keam line. The rest of the 1882 land was divided into Navajo grazing areas" (36–37). The Hopi were not happy with this because it limited them to only part of their 1882 reservation. District 6 was the first partition of the land between the Hopis and Navajos. And "although the Commissioner for Indian Affairs told the Hopis it would not compromise their rights to the rest of the 1882 reservation, District 6 was enlarged and the final boundary set in 1943" (36).

With Udall's 1958 statute (PL 85–457) mentioned earlier, the tribes could sue one another. After the partition was finalized, the Hopi chairman filed a friendly lawsuit against the chairman of the Navajo tribe in the famous 1959 case known as *Healing v. Jones* mentioned above (37). In 1960 a special panel of judges convened in Prescott, Arizona, to hear the case. Arguments between the two tribes over the 1882 executive order area ended two years later in 1962. At that time the court "determined that the Hopi tribe, subject to trust title of the United States, 'has the exclusive right and interest, both as to the surface and subsurface, including all resources,' to District 6. The court further found that the Hopi and Navajo tribes, subject to trust and title of the United States, 'have joint, undivided and equal rights and interests both as to the surface and subsurface, including all resources' of the land of the 1882 area outside of District 6" (quoted in Benedek 1992, 37). Upon appeal, the U.S. Supreme Court affirmed the lower court's decision on June 3, 1963. With all in agreement, the justices concluded "that District 6 belonged to the Hopis and that both tribes had equal interests in the 1.8 million acres that comprised the rest of the 1882 area" (37).

In effect the government, with Arthur's 1882 executive order–created reservation and Udall's apparently naïve ideas about Hopi and Navajo cultures, created a situation that resulted in boundary-line disagreements between the Navajo and Hopi that seemed to have no end. It seems as though these conflicts between neighbors with different values ended up with both sides feeling intruded upon and not protected by the U.S. government, leading to layers of frustration that have continued since 1882.

THE CREATION OF THE TRIBAL COUNCILS

Tribal councils were formed by the federal government in 1923, first on the Navajo Nation, and later with the Hopi. The creation of a tribal council on the Navajo Nation was foreign to the Navajo, who originally had someone chosen by the clan to deal with tribal matters. In contrast, tribal councils "were political entities set up by the U.S. government" (Lacerenza 1988, n.p.). According to a report filed by the U.S. Commission on Civil Rights, the tribal council was "created in part so that oil companies would have some legitimate representatives of the Navajos through whom they could lease reservation lands on which oil had been discovered" (quoted in Lacerenza 1988, n.p.). Basically, the Navajo Tribal Council "was created in order to legitimize resource extraction in the 1882 Executive Order Reservation," and to this day, binding decisions cannot be made without the signature of the secretary of the Interior (n.p.).

THE INDIAN REORGANIZATION ACT OF 1934

The basic idea behind the Indian Reorganization Act (IRA) was that Indians were not being successfully assimilated in the way the government had hoped. Boarding schools and other efforts to assimilate the Navajo and Hopi did not work well. Instead, they tried replacing traditional tribal structures of governance with a political system designed in Washington. This act subsidized schools, roads, and health services, but the IRA "concentrated its support chiefly on the development of natural resources" (Spicer 1997, 352–53). By usurping what was left of traditional Indigenous governments, the federal government "designed and maintained tribal councils whose function was/is mainly to sign off on federal development programs on the reservations, thus fostering the false impression of native consent to massive resource expropriation" (Churchill 1997, 292).

The American government is based on colonialism, and with the creation of tribal councils and the IRA, the Navajo and Hopi were set up to be exploited by the state and corporations. Corporations wanted the energy resources under those lands, and if necessary, if one tribe or the other got in the way, the people could easily be relocated and their ways of life sacrificed. "Under this system of colonial domination, the federal government determines which resources will be exploited on which reservations, at what pace, for what purpose, by which vendors, at what royalty rates, under what safety standards, and with what, if any, post-extraction cleanup requirements" (Churchill 1997, 292–93).

After World War II, Navajo lives were changed. Some had gone to work in munitions factories during the war or mined uranium used to make the atomic bomb. No one warned them about the dangers of radiation (Mudd and Florio 1985). When the war ended, the government continued to subsidize the defense energy industry in the West. Cities in the West like Phoenix, Los Angeles, Salt Lake, and Las Vegas were growing and had excessive energy needs. Utility companies needed new sources of electric power and began developing coal-fired power plants in the Four Corners region of the Southwest to turn coal into energy. Approximately one-third of the nation's strippable coal and one-half of its uranium is on Indian lands, and incredible wealth lies beneath and on the surface of Hopi and Navajo lands (Mudd et al. 1985).

Enter John Sterling Boyden. Now that the boundary lines had been redrawn, and eager to take advantage of the wealth to be had on the Hopi reservation after the war, John Boyden solicited the Hopi tribe to be their claims attorney in 1947. Boyden told the Hopi that they needed an attorney to protect their interests. The Hopi heard rumors that Boyden wanted to strip-mine their lands, so when the five traditional Hopi tribes would not consider his application, Boyden resorted to trickery to convince them to hire him. Boyden lied to the Hopi by suggesting that, with his help, they would be able to recover more land through the claims process, even though he knew full well that only the Indian Claims Commission could authorize this (Benedek 1992, 135).

Boyden realized the Hopi had their own method of governance, and in order to get around his rejection by the traditional people, he held a fraudulent election and received enough "yes" votes from the more progressive Hopis to be elected as the Hopi claims attorney. In order to be considered as Hopi tribal claims attorney, Boyden had to convince the Bureau of Indian Affairs (BIA) that the few "yes" votes of the more progressive villages should carry more weight than the "no" votes from the traditional villages. Based on Boyden's fraudulent strategy, the BIA cobbled together a very shaky argument in favor of Boyden, so that he was approved as the Hopi claims attorney. Writing about Boyden years later, the Indian Law Resource Center (cited in Benedek 1992, 135) concluded:

> In this play on numbers, a few poorly attended village meetings were characterized as a full-scale referendum of resident Hopis. Despite the fact that . . . traditional Hopi government was again ignored or avoided, and despite the fact that a false hope of possible return of land was being offered, Boyden's contract to represent the Hopis as their claims attorney was approved in Washington on July 27, 1951.

It became clear very quickly that Boyden's reasons for taking the position of tribal claims attorney would serve his own interests, just as the traditional members of the Hopi government believed. "A memorandum of a meeting between the BIA and Boyden not long after his claims contract was approved shows that Boyden had mineral development on his mind" (Benedek 1992, 135). Boyden pointed out that getting paid for his services would depend "largely on working out solutions to many of the Hopi problems to such a point that oil leases will provide funds" (135). To make matters worse, the Hopis' deep beliefs about being caretakers of the land and their close ties to and love for the land was considered merely an obstacle that could easily be pushed aside. So it was their lawyer/advisor, John Boyden, who sold the Hopi out to the federal government for his own gain.

Boyden's treachery knew no bounds. He was a corrupt attorney who also worked for Peabody Western Coal. In a blatant conflict of interest, Boyden was also representing the Hopi in negotiations with Peabody for Black Mesa coal (Dougherty 1997, n.p.). Douglas Brugge writes that, during the *Healing v. Jones* appeal in 1960 (decided in 1962) regarding the land dispute, Boyden made the Hopis appear to be "impoverished saints and the Navajos as nomadic aggressors" (1994, 69). The motivation underneath all the rhetoric was the mineral wealth that might exist on the reservation. A story in the *Arizona Republic* claimed, for example, "The land was recently evaluated rich in oil and uranium deposits," and the *Republic* quoted the Hopis as saying that "the Navajos have illegally settled on the potentially rich oil and uranium ground" (quoted in Brugge 1994, 90). Allegations made by Boyden helped set the stage for the creation of the dispute and the need for boundary lines to be redrawn; he claimed that the Navajo were criminal miscreants in their conflicts with the Hopi.

With Navajo families being displaced as lines were redrawn and some families refusing to leave their homelands, the government could easily make a case for a dispute between the two tribes that would eventually call for government action. Despite the protests of the Hopi and Navajo people against forced removal, the Navajo were forced out by the federal government from homelands they had occupied from time immemorial. No one in State or tribal political leadership stepped in to do anything to stop it (Mudd and Florio 1985). For the Navajo, to be relocated (for which there is no Navajo word) is to disappear and never be seen again (Mudd and Florio 1985).

This controversy opened lands for the exploitation of oil, natural gas, and minerals such as copper, coal, and, later, uranium by large corporations and the U. S. government at the expense of the Navajo and Hopi people. Environmental destruction soon followed.

Because of the extreme harms caused by John Boyden, tribes no longer use a single attorney for all legal matters, and resentment between the Navajo and Hopi still runs high. "Such is the legacy of the man, who remains revered in Utah by many, that left a continuing scar on the long tainted history of our relations with Native Americans while pursuing the goals of Manifest Destiny and our relentless push for development in the West" (New Mexico Wild News 2012, n. p.).

THE BENNETT FREEZE

After the *Healing v. Jones* decision that determined the tribes' respective rights to the 1882 area, there still remained the problem that the jointly owned land was almost completely inhabited by Navajos (Benedek 1992, 143). In 1966 BIA commissioner Robert L. Bennett enacted the socially and environmentally harmful Bennett Freeze. Because of the intense pressure to open reservation lands for energy development, it was not difficult to convince political leaders in Arizona at the time that a dispute existed between the tribes, and something needed to be done to avoid possible adverse actions between the Hopi and Navajo. The Bennett Freeze was an attempt to force relocation of its Navajo residents and thereby a supposed resolution of this alleged dispute between the tribes. He placed restrictions on Navajo families who refused to leave their homelands, and for forty years any kinds of infrastructure or home improvements were all but impossible (Minard 2012, n.p.). Life virtually stood still for those living in the Bennett Freeze area, while many other areas of the reservation received improvements such as electricity and running water.

At a Box Springs Chapter House meeting I attended on the Navajo Nation in December 2010, I learned firsthand about the social harms inflicted on the people living in this area of the Bennett Freeze. At that meeting people spoke about living in homes barely held together with baling wire, cardboard, tarps, and whatever they could salvage. People in the general population of the United States would likely have been amazed that there are people in this country asking for just basic necessities that all human beings have a right to, like adequate shelter and clean and running water; they are not asking for luxury items. Kathy Helmes (2010, A1, A2) interviewed Robert Begay, a veteran of the Korean Conflict and a victim of the Bennett Freeze. Robert said, "It's a lot of suffering—mentally, spiritually. What it does to you as a human being, it messes with your mind and you give up hope."

On another visit to the reservation in 2010, a Navajo resident living in the Bennett Freeze area told me that, to build a corral for their animals, fence posts had to be put up one at a time over a long period so that when helicopters flew over to check, improvements would not be detected. If people were detected making improvements (building corrals, etc.), they could be arrested and their house could be bulldozed to the ground. Robert Begay cited in Helmes (2010) gives another example,

> When I came back [from the Korean Conflict], the Bennett freeze took place. I built a hogan in Coppermine. When my hogan was halfway completed, I had a visit from Hopi, and they said, 'You're in the Bennett Freeze, you can't do that.' So we left there and we went to Bodaway and we build a stone house there." Just as that house was completed and they were digging a waterline, they had another visitor who told them the same thing, "You're in the Bennett Freeze. (A2)

Robert and his family moved to a rented trailer south of Tuba City where they now live near a former uranium mill site. Robert continued,

> My children do not have a piece of land. They do not have a home of their own. When I went to the Korean War I was told that I was fighting for my country and my right[s] and religious right and all that. But that was denied because of the Bennett Freeze. (A2)

Similarly, Myrtle Yellowhorse, eighty-four-years-old and suffering from cancer, said:

> I can't express enough how this land dispute has devastated people and how many lives it has taken on the Navajo people. . . . My ancestors have always said this is Diné Bikeyah. Those stories have been passed on by my forefathers, so it is very difficult for me to swallow the fact that there is a land dispute and the Hopis are taking claim to these lands they call Hopiland. (A2)

Richard Anderson Jr. of Whitecone on the Navajo Nation also experienced the social harms that came from one of the largest forced relocation efforts by the U.S. government. When the boundary lines were repartitioned, his family became one of many who found themselves squatters on their own land. He and his family were forced to move, and he was deprived of a place to call home. Richard said:

The relocation devastated my family. It killed my grandma, my grandpa. It killed a few of my uncles and aunties. They took our land. All of my civil rights under the Constitution were violated . . . my religious rights, my pursuit to happiness. My umbilical cord was buried in the hogan which ·was bulldozed by the government. My relatives' graves were bulldozed, too. Relocation is just a government word for genocide. That's all they are doing is killing us. They've been doing it for 500 years and they're doing it to this day and it's not right. (A2)

Some residents outside the Bennett Freeze who are on the reservation do have access to running water and electricity if they live where these hook-ups are available. Finding information about the number of people living without running water and electricity on the Navajo Nation is difficult (see also Hammersley, this volume), but for those still living in the Bennett Freeze area, only 3 percent of families have electricity and only 10 percent have running water, even though the Freeze is ended. The reason is that when cities and towns were developed across the country, water, plumbing, and similar utilities were included, but the people on this reservation (and others) lost out because they did not have the right to vote until 1948 in Arizona state elections, with New Mexico following suit in 1962 (the last state to enfranchise Native Americans). Access to waterlines was never planned for these communities (Weber 2015, n.p.).

Because of the former ban on infrastructure improvements within the Bennett Freeze area, along with no plans for water in these communities as far back as the 1940s, there is no indoor plumbing for food preparation or sanitation, no gas lines for heat or cooking, and no electricity for lights or refrigeration. There are no paved roads, and the dirt roads are in grave disrepair. People living in this area have to either haul water fit for human consumption or drink from the same contaminated wells as their livestock.

On a third visit to the Navajo reservation, I photographed a sign posted on a well in Black Falls that reads, "This water has been tested and found to exceed NAVAJO EPA and U.S. EPA human drinking water standards for uranium or other contaminants. Navajo Nation policy is that livestock-use-only wells are not to be used for human drinking water." Along with that sign, I have a photo of Navajo people taking water from that very well. People in this area have to travel long distances to find water fit to drink; there are no places close by to purchase drinking water, and the nearest well may be up to fifty miles away. If a family does not have a truck, they have to either depend on someone to haul large quantities of water for them or use their car and several fifty-five-gallon drums to collect enough water for a few weeks.

On May 9, 2009, President Barack Obama lifted the Bennett Freeze (Donovan 2009); however, it will take decades and billions of dollars to rebuild the damage from forty years of disrepair caused by state-corporate crime.

URANIUM MINING ON NATIVE LANDS

Eager to take advantage of the mineral wealth for political and monetary gain, companies began to mine uranium on the Navajo nation in 1944, ending in 1986. The U.S. government was the sole customer for uranium mined on the reservation during the Cold War era, and private companies operated the mines without safety regulations to protect the miners (Brugge, Benally, and Yazzie-Lewis 2006, 27). During this period, nearly thirty million tons of uranium were extracted from Navajo Lands under leases with the Navajo Nation (EPA 2017, n.p.). During this boom, American Indians in the Colorado Plateau area, "including the Navajo, Hopi, Southern Ute, Zuni, Laguna, and several other Pueblo nations, with their intimate knowledge of the land, often led miners to uranium resources during this exploration boom" (Moore-Nall 2015, 15). In some cases Navajos did so after being told they would be helping their country, meaning the United States (Pasternak 2010).

During the Cold War years that started about 1947 and lasted until the collapse of the former Soviet Union in 1991, mining companies flourished on the vast Navajo Nation. In the 1960s and 1970s, intense pressure grew again in mining in order to meet the energy demands of the Southwest's population growth. Gedicks (1993, xiii) writes that during this time, "two-thirds of all uranium resources within the borders of the United States lie under Native reservations, with Indians producing one-hundred percent of all federally-controlled uranium in 1975." This uranium mining contributed to the already-existing radioactive pollution in the Southwest caused by the World War II race to build an atomic bomb. Wilshire, Nielson, and Hazlett (2008, 181) write that every step of the uranium mining process, from mining the uranium for bomb fuel and purifying and enriching uranium to make plutonium, to detonating bombs to test them and disposing of the wastes[,] . . . currently contaminate[s] buildings, soil, sediment, rock, and underground or surface water within more than two million acres administered by the U.S. Department of Justice in eleven western states.

More importantly, Wilshire, Nielson, and Hazlett (2008, 182) note that "more alarming is the U.S. government's historic carelessness with atomic energy which has destroyed hundreds of thousands of our own citizen's lives."

During that time, mining companies extracted approximately four million tons of uranium ore on the Navajo Nation. Once the demand and prices for uranium made it no longer profitable to mine the ore, the mining companies left approximately 520 Cold War–era sites, with numerous abandoned mines on each one, along with massive radioactive waste piles (Diep 2010, n.p.; Landry 2017). Since that time, the Navajo people have been inhaling radioactive dust and drinking water contaminated with uranium and arsenic. Uranium ore's deadly properties are released upon extraction from the ground. Additionally, sheep play an important role in Navajo life. Uranium has been found in sheep, which are in turn ingested in the form of mutton by Diné people (see chapter 4 of this volume; Ingram n.d.). These deadly properties then decay into radon that further decays into a series of radioactive isotopes giving off alpha particles lodging in the body and creating conditions conducive to cancerous growth.

If we look back to the first half of the twentieth century, Navajos did not have access to the same kind of contemporary education found in the rest of our society. They were sheepherders who did not live close to industrial areas and were not exposed to industrial jobs until uranium mining came to the reservation. Having the chance to work for a living wage in the uranium mines was an opportunity not to be missed; however, only after an epidemic of lung cancer and other respiratory illness appeared years later were the miners finally told the truth kept from them by the government (Udall 2006, xi).

By 1949 the association between working in uranium mines and lung cancer was well known. "Radon builds up in the mines and its decay products (called 'radon daughters') lodge in the lung, delivering large amounts of radiation to the surrounding tissue" (Brugge, Benally, and Yazzie-Lewis 2001, 18). The U.S. government knew about the dangers of uranium mining, were warned of such by public health officials, and still allowed mining to occur with no safety measures in place. "Navajo miners knew nothing of all this and they and other miners were prevented from gaining too much knowledge by the complicity of the government and mining companies in choosing not to tell the miners" (18).

Eichstadt (1994) describes what the government knew and how uranium affects those who come into contact with this lethal mineral. He writes:

As uranium breaks down into other elements, the energy release has three different forms: alpha and beta particles, and gamma rays. Alpha particles are potent but can be stopped easily by such things as a sheet of paper or even human skin. However, this does not mean these little particles are harmless. Once alpha particles are taken into the human body, they lodge in tissues, bones, or organs, and steadily radiate and pelt surrounding cells. Beta particles are very similar, but thicker, denser materials are needed to stop them, and they can burn skin. Once inhaled they wreak havoc in the body. Gamma rays are highly penetrating . . . and require about an inch of lead or a foot of concrete to be stopped. These rays pass right through the human body. . . . Intense doses from such earthbound elements as radium can be fatal. (48–49)

Eichstadt also states:

In the uranium mines [on the Navajo Nation], sensitive lung tissues were constantly subjected to small but steady doses of radiation. These small, steady doses have recently been found to be more likely to cause cancer than a single heavy dose of radiation. . . . The earliest lung cancers found among the miners were what is known as the oat cell type, producing death within six months. Later work showed that other types of lung cancer were also related to mining. (49)

Because of nonexistent safety measures in the mines, miners had no place to shower or change clothes. They unknowingly brought contaminated clothing home to be put in the family wash. Very few of the

underground mines had any ventilation. The smaller companies' excuse
was that they could not afford ventilation because it would reduce their
profits. "Others, eager to remove as much uranium as possible per hour,
regularly sent workers back into the mines within minutes after blasting"
(50). Ventilation did come to the mines in the 1960s, but ventilation shafts
were oftentimes placed in the middle of residential areas and released the
same potent mixtures of radon, thoron, and other toxic substances suffered by the miners working in the mills. The pumped-out groundwater
seeping into deeper shafts was heavily contaminated as well (Churchill
1997, 308).

To stress the negative impacts upon the physical well-being of those
working underground in the mine shafts as well as their families and
communities, Clemmer (cited in Churchill 1997, 308) writes:

> The vents of one mine run by the Gulf Oil Company at San Mateo, New
> Mexico, were located so close to the town's school that the state's Depart-
> ment of Education ordered closure of the institution—but not the mine—
> because of the obvious health risk to the children attending it. Meanwhile,
> the local groundwater was found to be so contaminated by the corporation's
> activities that the National Guard was forced to truck in drinking water at
> tax-payer expense. (Clemmer, quoted in Churchill 1997, 308)

When miners began to fall ill, the U.S. Public Health Service became
concerned about the working conditions in the mines as well as their
health effects on miners. Henry Doyle, an engineer working for the Public Health Service, inspected several Navajo Nation mines and reported
radon samples "as much as 750 times the generally accepted limits, even
by 1950 standards" (Eichstadt 1994, 52). Clean, uncontaminated drinking
water was not provided. In the mines that had damp walls, the miners
drank water that dripped or beaded down the walls (53). Miners never
stood a chance, and neither did the families drinking contaminated water
resulting from tailings piles (radioactive sand-like materials left over from
uranium mining), carelessly and negligently left behind by mining companies (see NIH n.d.).

Toxic houses built with radioactive debris from the 1960s through the
1980s are also part of the lethal legacy left behind by uranium mining. In
every corner of the reservation, sandy mill tailings and chunks of ore were

released during blasting. People picked up these chunks of radioactive material left at old mines and mills and made them into bread ovens, cisterns, foundations for houses, fireplaces, floors, and walls. Federal and tribal officials fixed or replaced about twenty houses, then due to the cost of removal, walked away from the problem while Navajos continued to use mine waste as construction materials (Pasternak 2006, A1, A9). These homes are being passed from one generation to the next. Getting help to rectify this housing situation is difficult because of a lack of funds. The EPA estimates it will cost $250,000 to demolish each structure, haul away debris, and rebuild. So far, the EPA has assessed 117 structures and demolished 27 of them. Thirteen have been or will be rebuilt, and the owners of the others have received financial settlements (Fonseca 2009).

Pasternak (2010) writes that, before uranium mining on the Navajo Nation, people living there were believed to have a special immunity to cancer, but something happened in the 1950s and 1960s to cause severe changes in the health of many residents. In 1982 physician Richard Auld came to the reservation after completing his residency in internal medicine at the University of California, San Diego. Auld began working at Indian Health Services in Shiprock, New Mexico. Within two years he treated six cases of stomach cancer. Two of the patients were women eighteen and twenty years of age. Because these women were so young, this became cause for concern for the doctor. Auld worked with another specialist and found the incidence of stomach cancer for people living in some areas near uranium deposits to be fifteen times the national average. These cancers were not limited to former miners. In two western parts of the reservation filled with old pit mines, stomach cancer was two hundred times the U.S. average for women aged twenty to forty (Pasternak 2010, 142–43).

New evidence shows gastric cancer rates rose 50 percent during the 1990s among Navajo in two New Mexico counties with uranium sites. Uranium has been linked a sharp increase in breast, ovarian, and other cancers among young women still in their teens. Rates for these types of cancers are reported to be seventeen times the national average (Wenz 2001, 66). These lethal health impacts on the Navajo people contribute to the controversy about renewed uranium mining.

With this exposure to lethal levels of radiation, the correlation between uranium mining on the Navajo Nation and cancer rates among the

Navajo people living there is difficult to refute. There is a connection between uranium mining and the Bennett Freeze lands; as time went on and modern methods of extracting tons of uranium by large corporations were implemented, this area became the dumping grounds for tons of lethal mill tailings. There are uranium tailings in areas other than the Bennett Freeze, but it is especially important to people living in the Bennett Freeze because they were (and still are) forced to gather water from wells contaminated with uranium and arsenic. During the Freeze, more than one hundred million tons of mill tailings with a half-life of 4.46 billion years accumulated in the Four Corners area of the Southwest (Institute for Energy and Environmental Research 1997, 2001).

This is clearly a state-facilitated crime because the government failed to create and regulate safety standards due to shared goals with multinational corporations. With full knowledge, the Atomic Energy Commission left safety measures up to the mining companies that knew little about the hazards of uranium mining (Udall 2006, xi). In the 1940s it was not illegal for corporations to ignore safety hazards, but the resulting social harms committed by the government and multinational corporations left innocent people exposed to lethal levels of radiation and certain death. And the danger is not over, with the renewed interest in uranium mining since about 2016.

RENEWED INTEREST IN URANIUM MINING

President Ulysses S. Grant signed the General Mining Law in 1872 to promote the development and settlement of publicly owned lands in the western United States (Earthworks n.d.). This archaic U. S. federal law authorizes and governs prospective mining for economic minerals on federal public lands. During the late nineteenth century, mining had limited impact on the environment: miners staked their claims on the Colorado Plateau, they used picks and shovels to gather ore, and burros or donkeys hauled out the ore. Miners were not concerned with environmental protection, and the law does not contain environmental protection provisions (Earthworks n.d.). All one had to do was "find a bit of federal land that appears to contain gold, silver or other 'hard-rock' minerals, pound stakes at its corners to warn off others, dig, and . . . cash in" (McClure and Schneider 2001, n.p.).

The General Mining Law of 1872 is still in force today and is a source of frustration in trying to create regulations for hard-rock mining. Mining companies say they are regulated enough and realize that more recent federal laws such as the Clean Water Act (1972) and the National Environmental Policy Act (1970) must be adhered to. Still, the law is in need of drastic reform. In 1976 legal provisions were updated somewhat with the implementation of the Federal Land Policy and Management Act. Many of the provisions of the Federal Land Policy and Management Act revised the surface uses allowed on mining claims under the 1872 law by halting or restricting unnecessary or undue degradation of public lands. New rules effectively replace many of the 1872 provisions and require reclamation, financial guarantees for reclamation to the federal government, mining-claim occupation permits, and detailed mining plans of operations to be submitted to the governing agencies before disturbing the surface. Mining companies have been able to head off many other attempts at reform by arguing that overhauling the 1872 General Mining Law would risk national security (McClure and Schneider 2001, n.p.).

Even with new provisions, we need to be better prepared for new uranium mining. Mining uranium is not going to end, especially with the current administration in the White House. Industry and environmental groups are concerned that the Trump administration will turn attention to reopening part of the Grand Canyon watershed to uranium mining. In Arizona there is already a grandfathered uranium mine south of the Grand Canyon set to open, and lifting the ban on uranium mining could result in many mines opening in the future. The uranium mining industry continues to exert pressure on Arizona senators to open more areas near the Grand Canyon for mining. Denison Mines opened its Arizona 1 uranium mine in 2009 (Mining technology n.d.). The first inspection did not take place until September 2010. During the inspection the Arizona Department of Environmental Quality (ADEQ) found four major violations: (1) there were no pumps in the mine to eliminate water, (2) a test measuring the permeability of the rock in the mine had not been done, (3) a pipe was sticking out through a lined pond that is intended to prevent groundwater contamination from ore or water pumped out of the mine, and (4) plans for the mine did not match what inspectors found during their visit (IAEA 2011). ADEQ also found federal violations for worker safety, citing Denison and contractors with air-quality violations, failure to properly label power switches, equipment safety violations, and a lack of firefighting equipment. Most of the thirty-eight possible mine safety violations found by ADEQ are being contested by Denison (IAEA 2011).

Given the circumstances surrounding uranium mining, considering the safety (or lack thereof) and looking back at the definition of state-corporate and state-facilitated crime, it is clear that where the interests of the mining industry and key government officials intersect, the propensity for harmful actions is increased. As can be seen from the Denison example above, standards still are not adhered to, and safety measures are not always followed.

Much of the damage done by mining in the West happened decades ago, but the environmental problems still exist. Cleanup efforts are underway in some places, but we can still drive past huge uranium tailings piles near Cameron, Arizona, and see other mounds beside the Colorado River near Moab, Utah. In fact, with all the abandoned mining sites and four former uranium mills, the U.S. nuclear program has left a legacy of "scars on the land and people to this day" (Brugge, Benally, and Yazzie-Lewis 2006, xv). Nevertheless, mining companies once again are setting their sights on exploring for uranium in this region of the Southwest, but not without much opposition.

At a meeting held by three mining companies in Flagstaff, Arizona, in March 2008 to propose exploration for uranium in the Kaibab National Forest south of the Grand Canyon, the companies claimed that the unfortunate incidents that occurred more than fifty years ago would not happen again. Tribal leaders and citizens were present whose goal was to gain support for a House bill to put about one million acres in House Rock Valley, the Arizona strip west of the Kaibab National Forest, and the Tusayan section of that forest (right next to the Grand Canyon), off limits to new uranium claims. There are approximately 2,800 claims in Tusayan alone where miners could still work existing claims, even though it would be years before they would be allowed to do so. VANE Minerals received approval in January of 2008 for exploratory drilling on 39 sites, some only two miles from the Grand Canyon (Cole 2008).

Mining for uranium is safer than it was during the mid-twentieth century, but promises of safer mining were made before, and the legacy of uranium mining left no one, other than the mining companies, in a better place. In the 1940s and 1950s, mining companies exploited Navajo workers by paying them substandard wages while exposing them to radioactive dust. Even though safety standards have improved for miners with better ventilation and protection from radiation exposure, even though there are strict controls for processing mills that have to cap and seal tailings piles immediately, that is not good enough. The United States government and multinational corporations have exploited and turned the area where the Navajo live into a sacrifice area. It may be naïve to believe or expect the federal government to oversee and regulate this industry.

People living on the Navajo Nation are not willing to risk such a potentially hazardous chance. On April 19, 2005, the Navajo Nation Council voted 63–19 to pass the Diné Natural Resources Protection Act, signed into law by Navajo Nation President Joe Shirley at the Crownpoint Chapter House. This new tribal statute bans uranium mining and processing anywhere on the Navajo Nation ("Choike" 2006). In addition, several members of the U.S. Congress said they would support Shirley and the prohibition of mining (Brugge, Benally, and Yazzie-Lewis 2006, 172). Shirley met with New Mexico governor Bill Richardson to inform him of Strathmore Minerals Corporation of Canada's desire to reopen its Church Rock and Roca Honda uranium mines located in McKinley County, which it purchased from Kerr McGee Nuclear and Rio Algom. Shirley said, "The Navajo Nation as a government and a people has said we're not going to have uranium mining on Navajoland or in Navajo County . . . we'd like to see that law stick. Because of exposure to uranium, many of my medicine people have died, many of my elderly have died. I'd sure hate to go back there. Too many people have died . . . the powers that be committed genocide on Navajoland by allowing uranium mining" (Hardeen 2005, n.p.).

CLEANUP AND COMPENSATION

Bills need to be introduced with tougher penalties for existing and new mines based on past violations. The open-pit and tunnel mining used fifty years ago are long gone. Breccia pipe mining involves sinking a shaft down alongside a vertical pipe of uranium, thereby eliminating injection of water and exposure to air. This, however, does not ensure that safety standards are adhered to, and safety measures are not always followed, creating potential hazards as with the Dennison mines.

The legacy of uranium mining and the environmental and physical devastation that it caused to the Navajo people stretches back decades. Radiation exposure to those working in the mines and their families is believed to have caused serious diseases and various cancers. Yet it has taken the government and mining companies nearly fifty years to resolve the longstanding health and environmental issues caused by uranium. Brugge, Benally, and Yazzie-Lewis (2006) write:

> In the early 1960s widows started talking about their husbands' deaths and how they died. . . . The meetings had a snowball effect and more people came together, formed a committee, and the committee talked more and more about the death of the uranium miners. The committees eventually hired an attorney. . . . And after many years of struggle they got the Radiation Exposure Compensation Act (RECA) in 1990 which was supposed to provide 'compassionate compensation' to miners and their survivors since they continued to have their claims denied. In 2000, RECA was amended to attempt to correct some of its shortcomings. (xvii–xviii)

The Radiation Exposure Compensation Act (RECA) provides one-time cash benefits to some people exposed to radiation, including those present at a test site during an atmospheric weapons test, down-winders who were present in certain areas during testing, and certain uranium miners, millers, and ore transporters. All benefits are a one-time lump sum and are not adjusted to reflect changes in wages or the cost of living, and no medical or other benefits are provided (Szymendera 2017, 3). In this document there are requirements involving exposure geography, participation, occupations, and certain diseases that must be met in order to receive the benefits. For example, uranium miners must meet specific exposure and disease requirements and have worked in an above-ground or underground uranium mine for at least one year between January 1, 1942, and December 31, 1972.

The red tape involved is incredible; for example, exposure data does not exist for all the uranium mines that miners worked. Exposure data on individual miners were rarely collected, making it very difficult to meet RECA requirements. Actually receiving compensation from RECA is difficult, and it can take years for a claim to be processed. Important amendments to RECA in 2000 lowered the level of exposure required for compensation due to the fact that many former miners were ill from substantial exposure to radon in the mines but did not qualify under the old legislation (Brugge, Benally, and Yazzie-Lewis 2001). Even with new amendments, concerns still remain. Many people hire an attorney to help them through the maze of rules, which results in an extra expense for the victims. The path to compensation is long, and money that is received does not replace a loved one, but the funds do help care for those left behind.

Even though there are still variables that need to be worked out, the federal government has reached a settlement with the Navajo Nation that will clear the way for cleanup work to continue at abandoned uranium mines across the reservation, along with some sort of compensation (*Arizona Daily Sun* 2016, A7). The Navajo Nation, the United States government, and two subsidiaries of the Freeport-McMoRan mining company have reached a $600 million settlement to address the legacy of uranium mining. The settlement, announced by the U.S. Department of Justice, calls for Cyprus Amax Minerals Company and Western Nuclear Inc. to clean up ninety-four abandoned uranium mines on the Navajo Nation, with the U.S. government covering half the cost (Landry 2017).

Of the approximately 520 abandoned uranium mining sites on the reservation, this settlement will be used to clean up about 200 of them (Landry 2017, n. p.). Significant cleanup and environmental restoration are long overdue on Navajo lands, but a healthier future for the Navajo people will result in the coming years. Navajo Nation President Russell Begaye said, "We appreciate the efforts of mining companies like Freeport that are coming forth to clean up the uranium contamination that they have caused on the Navajo Nation . . . and the Navajo Nation will work very closely with Freeport to make sure that the cleanup is done properly" (n. p.).

According to Landry (2017, n.p.), "The settlement addresses mining operations that started with the high demand of atomic weapons at the end of World War II. At that time, state-facilitated crimes and social harms were visited upon the Navajo people when private companies exploited the reservations with the Atomic Energy Commission being the sole purchaser of the uranium until 1970." It is right and fitting that the Justice Department address the legacy of mining to fairly and honorably resolve the historic grievances of the Navajo Nation and take responsibility for helping build a better future for Indigenous Peoples.

THE HOPI NATION, THE NAVAJO NATION, AND STATE-CORPORATE CRIME

Resistance by the Navajo and Hopi to keep their land base and protect their resources threatened the privilege and control of the powerful corporations and the state (Potter 2002, 101). So portraying those who resisted mining projects as people against progress, and as deviant and "un-American," made it easy to mobilize public opinion in favor of mining corporations. In fact, the federal government did all it could to aid and abet the coal and uranium mining industries to take as many minerals as they could for the billions of dollars this revenue would produce. A case in point is *United States v Navajo Nation* (2009), in which the Navajo Nation initiated proceedings in the Court of Federal Claims, alleging that when they sought the assistance of the United States secretary of the Interior to renegotiate their original lease agreement with Peabody Coal in 1984, the secretary of the Interior had been influenced by the coal company, breaching the government's fiduciary duty to the Navajo Nation when he approved the 1987 lease agreements. While the case was upheld in the court of appeals, it was reversed and remanded by the U.S. Supreme Court (see Cornell University Law School, n.d.). Basically, there was a manipulation of the money Navajo people could expect for coal extraction, which was less than what other landowners would receive.

Exploitation of Indigenous Peoples is often the unfortunate result of state-corporate crime because one common threat that exists for many of the 573 federally recognized American Indian nations is that they are economically disadvantaged, and therefore easy to exploit (or powerful entities may at least be tempted to exploit them). Unemployment rates on reservations can range anywhere from 30 percent to as high as 50 percent (Smith 2000, 72). Limited socioeconomic opportunity leads to substandard health care and education, substance abuse, high rates of violence, and lack of the basic necessities for subsistence. Under such circumstances, it is easy to see how this population of people, who are on the frontline of contemporary struggles, become prime targets for exploitation.

Today, Navajo families are still recovering from relocation, and the Hopi and Navajo reservations have been strip-mined for uranium and coal, with massive machinery tearing into Mother Earth. "The mining of Black Mesa has desecrated sacred sites, forcibly removed 12,000 Navajo people from the land, pumped 325 million tons of carbon dioxide into the air, drained an invaluable desert aquifer, and decimated native plant species, permanently altering the local ecosystem" (Nies, cited in Clifford and Edwards 1998, 338). Sufficient water is necessary for both the Navajo and Hopi people, and in the arid desert Southwest, adequate, clean drinking water is precious for both tribes. But the devastation of the environment by multinational corporations has meant that "tailings from uranium mines have contaminated wells in the western part of the sprawling Navajo Reservation, and many water sources on Hopi lands have four times the accepted safe levels of arsenic" (Krol 2017, n.p.).

Politics, economics, and cultural dislocation led to Native people quickly learning about the complexities and power of the federal government. They have also been disappointed in the elected representatives who were supposed to be upholding treaty rights (Brugge and Goble 2002). With the sanctioning of these types of power arrangements by the federal Bureau of Indian Affairs, corporations and federal agencies have pressured, bribed, cajoled, and enticed their way onto Indian lands to mine for strategic minerals, which would environmentally devastate the reservations.

Where the interests of the U.S. government and huge corporations intersect, state-corporate crime flourishes. One might rightfully ask why this is a crime. After all, the purpose of a corporation is to make money for its stockholders. But at what point does a corporation take responsibility for its actions? In the course of doing business there are times when corporations create harms to humans and the environment. Corporate efforts to make a profit may be legal, but when basic human rights are violated in doing so, making a profit at the expense of others certainly is not right. "Many corporate activities are 'crimes' in the broadest sense of the term, without being illegal" (Friedrichs 2007, 58). There is no overriding theory that explains crime in all its different shapes and guises, but from a social harms perspective, what happened to the Navajo and Hopi people is a series of crimes because the results of uncontrolled, unsafe mining devastated the environment and took the lives of many people. No one person, corporation, or government entity was taken to task for these harms because legally mining, no matter how dangerously done, is not a crime; yet the actual incidence and degree of harm to the environment and people cannot be measured.

CONCLUSION

Today, after strip-mining Hopi lands for coal and mining uranium on Navajo lands, the energy needs of the Southwest have been met but at a very steep cost to the Hopi and Navajo People. The Hopi and Navajo people of Black Mesa and in the Bennett Freeze area have suffered destruction of their environment, degradation of their health, dwindling water supplies, destruction of archeological sites, and removal from ancestral homelands. The Navajo–Hopi land dispute has been presented for decades as a conflict between the Hopi and Navajo people, when in reality corporate greed and state facilitation of corporate exploitation of Indigenous lands, regardless of social harms to the Navajo and Hopi people, have been the forces used to divide and conquer these nations in order to open lands for mineral exploitation.

It is difficult to tell a story of legal theft by state-corporate entities that have the ability to pass laws and use their power to exploit people and natural resources to extend their personal wealth and political power. And even though cleanup efforts and addressing contaminated water on the Navajo and Hopi Nations are underway, the history and continued suffering of Indigenous Peoples continues to be an ongoing story that many American Indians live each day.

NOTE

1.   Portions of this chapter originally appeared in Robyn (2011).

REFERENCES

Arizona Daily Sun. 2016. "Feds Reach Uranium Settlement with Navajos." July 20, 2016.

Benedek, Emily. 1992. *The Wind Won't Know Me: A History of the Navajo-Hopi Land Dispute.* Norman: University of Oklahoma Press.

Brugge, Douglas M. 1994. *The Navajo-Hopi Land Dispute: An American Tragedy.* Albuquerque: University of New Mexico Press.

Brugge, Doug, Timothy Benally, and Esther Yazzie-Lewis. 2001. "Uranium Mining on Navajo Indian Land." *Cultural Survival Quarterly* 25 (1): 18–21.

Brugge, Doug, Timothy Benally, and Esther Yazzie-Lewis, eds. 2006. *The Navajo People and Uranium Mining*. Albuquerque: University of New Mexico Press.

Brugge, Doug, and Rob Goble. 2002. "The History of Uranium Mining and the Navajo People." *American Journal of Public Health* 92 (9): 1410–19.

"Choike: Native Community Wins Battle Against Uranium Mining in Arizona, USA." 2006. *Third World Network Features* (reprinted from WISE/NIRS Nuclear Monitor 627, May 13).

Churchill, Ward. 1997. *A Little Matter of Genocide: Holocaust and Denial in the Americas, 1492 to the Present*. San Francisco: City Lights Books.

Clifford, Mary, and Terry D. Edwards. 1998. *Environmental Crime*. Burlington, Mass.: Jones and Bartlett.

Cole, Cindy. 2008. "Uranium's Toxic Legacy Looms Large." *Arizona Daily Sun*. March 28, 2008.

Cornell University Law School. n.d. "US v. Navajo Nation." https://www.law.cornell.edu/supct/html/07-1410.ZS/html.

Diep, Francie. 2010. "Abandoned Uranium Mines: An 'Overwhelming Problem' in the Navajo Nation." *Scientific American*. December 30, 2010. https://www.scientificamerican.com/article/abandoned-uranium-mines-a/?print=true.

Donovan, Bill. 2009. "Obama Signs Bennett Freeze Repeal." *Navajo Times*. May 14, 2009. http://www.navajotimes.com/news/2009/0509/051409freeze.php.

Dougherty, John. 1997. "A People Betrayed." *Phoenix New Times*. May 1, 1997. https://www.phoenixnewtimes.com/news/a-people-betrayed-6423155.

Earthworks. n.d. "General Mining Law of 1872." Accessed June 18, 2019. https://earthworks.org/issues/general_mining_law_of_1872/.

Eichstadt, Peter. 1994. *If You Poison Us: Uranium and Native Americans*. Santa Fe, N.M.: Red Crane Books.

EPA (Environmental Protection Agency). 2017. "Navajo Nation: Cleaning Up Abandoned Uranium Mines." https://www.epa.gov/navajo-nation-uranium-cleanup.

Fonseca, Felicia. 2009. "Navajo Homes Razed—Uranium Contamination." *San Francisco Gate*. June 21, 2009. https://www.sfgate.com/green/article/Navajo-homes-razed-uranium-contamination-3294703.php.

Forbes, Jack D. 1979. *The Papago-Apache Tribe of 1853: Property Rights and Religious Liberties of the O'Odham, Maricopa, and Other Native Peoples*. Davis: University of California, Davis.

Friedrichs, David O. 2007. *Trusted Criminals: White Collar Crime in Contemporary Society*. 3rd ed. Belmont, Calif.: Thompson, Wadsworth.

Gedicks, Alan. 1993. *The New Resource Wars: Native and Environmental Struggles Against Multinational Corporations*. Cambridge, Mass.: South End Press.

Hardeen, George. 2005. "Navajo Nation President Joe Shirley, Jr., Seeks Support of New Mexico Gov. Bill Richardson To Keep Navajo Uranium-Free." Press release, Office of the President and Vice President, The Navajo Nation. August 25, 2005. http://www.navajo-nsn.gov/Archived_Webpages_News_Releases/2005/augustnews.htm.

Helmes, Kathy. 2010. "Relocation Victims Tired of Status Quo." *Gallup Independent*. August 7–8, 2010.

IAEA (International Atomic Energy Agency). 2011. *National Reports for Joint Convention on the Safety of Spent Fuel Management and on the Safety of Spent Radioactive Waste Management*. https://www.iaea.org/topics/nuclear-safety-conventions/joint-convention-safety-spent-fuel-management-and-safety-radioactive-waste.

Ingram, Jani, C. n.d. "Cancer Risk from Exposure to Uranium Among the Navajo." National Institute of Health Presentation. Accessed June 17, 2019. https://www.niehs.nih.gov/news/events/pastmtg/assets/docs_c_e/cancer_risk_from_exposure_to_uranium_among_the_navajo_508.pdf.

Institute for Energy and Environmental Research, International Atomic Energy Agency. 1997. *Annual Report*. iaea.org/publications/reports/annual-report-1997.

Institute for Energy and Environmental Research, International Atomic Energy Agency. 2001. *Annual Report*. iaea.org/sites/default/files/anrep2001_full.pdf.

Kramer, Ronald C., and Raymond J. Michalowski. 1990. "Toward an Integrated Theory of State-Corporate Crime." Paper presented at the American Society of Criminology, Baltimore, Md.

Kramer, Ronald C., and Raymond J. Michalowski. 2006. "The Original Formulation." In *State-Corporate Crime: Wrongdoing at the Intersection of Business and Government*, edited by Raymond J. Michalowski and Ronald C. Cramer, 1–17. New Brunswick, N.J.: Rutgers University Press.

Krol, Debra Utacia. 2017. "Water Settlement for Navajo and Hopi Tribes Inches Forward." *NewsDeeply*. June 15, 2017. https://www.newsdeeply.com/water/articles/2017/06/15/water-settlement-for-navajo-and-hopi-tribes-inches-forward.

Kuletz, Valerie L. 1998. *The Tainted Desert: Environmental and Social Ruin in the American West*. New York: Routledge.

Lacerenza, Deborah. 1988. "An Historical Overview of the Navajo Relocation." *Cultural Survival Quarterly Magazine*. September. https://www.culturalsurvival

.org/publications/cultural-survival-quarterly/historical-overview-navajo
-relocation.

Landry, Alysa. 2017. "Navajo Nation Abandoned Uranium Mines Cleanup Gets
$600 Million." *Indian Country Today*. February 14, 2017. https://newsmaven
.io/indiancountrytoday/archive/navajo-nation-abandoned-uranium-mines
-cleanup-gets-600-million-moboWFJcbUy6mZFjVEKmrQ/.

Lynch, Michael J., and Paul B. Stretesky. 2011. "Native Americans and Social
and Environmental Justice: Implications for Criminology." *Social Justice* 38
(3): 104–24.

McClure, Robert, and Andrew Schneider. 2001. "The General Mining Act of
1872 Has Left a Legacy of Riches and Ruin." *Seattle Post-Intelligencer*. June
10, 2001. https://www.seattlepi.com/news/article/The-General-Mining-Act
-of-1872-has-left-a-legacy-1056919.php.

Minard, Anne. 2012. "The Bennett Freeze's Surreal Nightmare Should Be Ending—
but It's Not." *Indian Country Today*. December 18, 2012.https://newsmaven.io/
indiancountrytoday/archive/the-bennett-freeze-s-surreal-nightmare-should
-be-ending-but-it-s-not-nT7hzZ9P7oCObmVPN1c2Gw/.

Mining Technology. n.d. "Arizona 1 Uranium Project." mining-technology.com/
projects/arizona-1-uranium/.

Moore-Nall, Anita. 2015. "The Legacy of Uranium Development on or Near
Indian Reservations and Health Implications Rekindling Public Awareness."
Geosciences 5: 15–29.

Mudd, Victoria and Maria Florio, dirs. 1985. *Broken Rainbow*. New York: Earthworks Films.

NIH (National Institute of Health, U.S. National Library of Medicine). N.d.
"Uranium Tailings." ToxTown. https://toxtown.nlm.nih.gov/sources-of
-exposure/uranium-tailings.

Navajo Nation. n.d. "Official Site of the Navajo Nation." www.navajo-nsn.gov.

New Mexico Wild News. 2012. "John Sterling Boyden: A History of Coal Mining
and One of the Greatest Conmen of Modern Times." http://www.nmwild
.org/news-2/john-sterling-boyden-a-history-of-coal-mining-and-one-of-the
-greatest-conmen-of-modern-times?tmpl=component&print=1.

Pasternak, Judy. 2006. "Mining Firms Again Eyeing Navajo Lands." *Los Angeles
Times*. November 22, 2006.

Pasternak, Judy. 2010. *Yellow Dirt: An American Story of a Poisoned Land and a
People Betrayed*. New York: Free Press.

Potter, Gary. 2002. *Controversies in White-Collar Crime*. Cincinnati, Ohio:
Anderson.

Powell, Dana E. 2018. *Landscapes of Power: Politics of Energy in the Navajo Nation.* Durham, N.C.: Duke University Press.

Robyn, Linda. 2011. "State-Corporate Crime on the Navajo Nation: A Legacy of Uranium Mining." *Indigenous Policy Journal* 22 (2): 1–16.

Smith, Dean Howard. 2000. *Modern Paths to Self-Sufficiency and Tribal Cultural Integrity in Indian Country Development.* Walnut Creek, Calif.: AltaMira Press.

Spicer, Edward H. 1997. *Cycles of Conquest: The Impact of Spain, Mexico, and the United States on the Indians of the Southwest, 1533–1960.* Tucson: The University of Arizona Press.

Szymendera, Scott D. 2017. *The Radiation Exposure Compensation Act (RECA): Compensation Related to Exposure to Radiation from Atomic Weapons Testing and Uranium Mining.* Congressional Research Service 7–5700, R43956. https://www.hsdl.org/?search&exact=CRS+Report+for+Congress%2C+R43956&searchfield=series&collection=documents&submitted=Search&advanced=1&release=0&so=date.

Udall, Stewart L. 2006. "The Navajo People and Uranium Mining." In *The Navajo People and Uranium Mining,* edited by Doug Brugge, Timothy Benally, and Esther Yazzie-Lewis, xi–xii. Albuquerque: University of New Mexico Press.

Voyles, Traci Brynne. 2015. *Wastelanding: Legacies of Uranium Mining in Navajo Country.* Minneapolis: Minneapolis: University of Minnesota Press.

Weber, Brandon. 2015. "Some Native Americans Reservations Have No Access to Basics like Water. Why? Look to 1948." *Upworthy News.* August 27, 2015. https://www.upworthy.com/some-native-american-reservations-have-no-access-to-basics-like-water-why-look-to-1948.

Wenz, Peter S. 2001. "Just Garbage." In *Faces of Environmental Racism: Confronting Issues of Global Justice,* edited by Laura Westra and Bill E. Lawson, 57–71. Lanham, Md.: Rowman and Littlefield.

Wilshire, Howard G., Jane E. Nielson, and Richard W. Hazlett. 2008. *The American West as Risk: Science, Myths, and Politics of Land Abuse and Recovery.* New York: Oxford University Press.

LEGAL RESOURCES

Clean Water Act. 33 U.S.C. 1251 et seq. (1972)

Diné Natural Resources Protection Act (2005)

Executive Order (1882)

Federal Land Policy and Management Act. 43 U.S.C. § 1744 (1976)

General Mining Law Sess. 2, ch. 152, 17 Stat. 91 (1872)

Healing v. Jones. 174 F. Supp. 211 (D. Arizona) (1959)
Healing v. Jones. 210 F. Supp. 125 (D. Arizona) (1962)
Indian Reorganization Act. 25 U.S.C. (1934)
National Environmental Policy Act. 42 U.S.C § 4321 (1970)
Public Law. 85–547 (1958)
Radiation Exposure Compensation Act. 42 U.S.C. (1990)
Treaty of Guadalupe Hidalgo (1848)
United States v Navajo Nation. 501 F. 3d 1327 (2009)

4

ENVIRONMENTAL RACISM

Contaminated Water in Indigenous and Minority Communities

LINDA M. ROBYN

WATER IS the source of life. Nations and communities the world over revolve around water, and for many Indigenous Peoples, water is sacred. We rely on water that is diverted from rivers, lakes, streams, canals, and hydrogenerating stations, and water that comes from aquifers deep underground. Water is an element that humans cannot live without, but for people of color, both on and off reservations, who live in low-income communities that are exposed to environmentally harmful levels of pollution, this precious life source has become gravely compromised. Social and economic inequality helps explain the degree and extent of environmental injustice experienced by people of color, including Native Americans living on reservations (Lynch and Stretesky 2012, 104).

Environmental-related harms, regardless of legality per se, that are facilitated by the state as well as corporations, have the capacity to shape official definitions of environmental crime in ways that allow or condone environmentally harmful practices. The state and corporate environmental harms leading to water contamination on the Navajo Nation and other parts of Indian Country, and near the Standing Rock Sioux Reservation, are examined in this chapter as examples of the many environmental harms that have plagued Native Americans for generations. These are compared and contrasted with the water issues in Flint Michigan in terms of the degree of public awareness each has garnered and the criminal charges that resulted. These examples are then used to discuss the relationship between colonialism and environmental justice.

THE NAVAJO NATION, INDIAN COUNTRY, AND ANCESTRAL LANDS

A large portion of the Navajo Nation water supply has been under attack since the 1950s. Uranium mining on the northern and western part of the Navajo Nation began in 1948, peaked in 1955 and 1956, then declined to zero by 1967 (Brugge, Benally, Yazzie-Lewis 2006, 28). Because of mining tailings (radioactive sand-like materials left over from uranium mining) that were left behind by the corporations that mined uranium, much of the water supply is contaminated with uranium and arsenic, and today more than one thousand abandoned mines are estimated to lie on Navajo land (P. Charly, cited in Brugge, Benally, Yazzie-Lewis 2006, 28). Until recently, multinational corporations that mined uranium were not required to clean up abandoned mines. Cleanup efforts are currently underway, but people and their livestock have no choice but to drink water contaminated with uranium and arsenic. On the Navajo Nation, and for other Nations within Indian Country, the health impacts on those living in environmentally devastated areas are well known to doctors and scientists alike (see Brugge, Benally and Yazzie-Lewis 2006; Eichstaedt 1994; Pasternak 2010; as well as chapter 3 in this volume).

Because multinational corporations could mine on Native lands without cleaning up after mining operations ended, as of June 2014, there were 532 Superfund sites in Indian Country, nearly 25 percent of the 1322 active Superfund sites in the USA (Hansen 2014, n.p.). Superfunds are lands in the United States that have been contaminated with toxic waste and are slated for cleanup because they pose a threat to humans, animals, and the environment. "The name, Superfund, is used to describe the law called the Comprehensive Environmental Response, Compensation and Liability Act of 1980, or CERCLA. Superfund is also the trust fund used by Congress to handle emergency and hazardous waste sites needing long-term cleanup" (Schons 2011, n.p.). It is important to note that "Indian Country" as used here is not limited to the statutory definition but includes ancestral lands; therefore, all superfund sites across the country have effects on

Indian communities and nations. From Alaska to New York, Superfund sites exist on tribal lands in Indian Country where environmental degradation of water has occurred unbeknown to those living there. Waters in Indian Country have been contaminated with lead, cadmium, arsenic, uranium mining tailings, and other contaminants. Examples of water contamination within Indian Country were investigated and described by Terri Hansen (2014), a few of which follow.

For twenty-five years (1916–41), Native peoples living in the federally recognized Village of Kasaan located on Kasaan Bay of Prince of Wales Island in southeastern Alaska, regularly consumed fish and seafood from waters surrounding their home. They were totally unaware for decades of the dangers of tailings from the copper-palladium-gold-silver Salt Chuck Mine.

In Cour d'Alene, Idaho, the Bunker Hill Mining and Metallurgical Complex is the site of one of the largest environmental and human health cleanups in the country. Bunker Hill Mining has contaminated the river basin for decades from mining, milling, and smelting operations, leaving behind a legacy of suffering and toxic pollution. With toxins left behind from mining operations in over 150 miles of river, lake, and tributary, approximately three-quarters of children living in the area since the 1970s have been found to have unhealthy levels of lead in their bloodstream.

Located on the St. Lawrence River in the northernmost part of New York, the General Motors Massena Superfund site contains PCBs (Polychlorinated biphenyls) and other industrial wastes that contaminate groundwater, the Raquette River, Turtle Cove, and Turtle Creek. The Akwesasne and St. Regis Mohawk tribes have been exposed to these carcinogens from the General Motors plants. These toxins can affect immune, reproductive, nervous, and endocrine systems, as well as cause many other health effects. The Centers for Disease Control and Prevention established that young Akwesasne Mohawk adults exposed to these toxins have twice the levels of PCBs as the national average.

Lastly, part of the land of the Quapaw tribe from Picher, Oklahoma, was home to zinc and lead mining until 1967. When mining ended, the Quapaw were left with abandoned mine shafts and a million tons of lead-laced tailings; and acid mine water leaking from bore holes contaminated the water. At one point 34 percent of the children tested had extremely high levels of toxins in their blood that raised the chances for brain or nervous system damage. Because the environmental damage was so great, the federal government paid people to leave. Cleanup by the tribe is underway with the goal of making their land productive once again. (See also chapter 3 in this volume).

Environmental injustice stems from mining uranium, coal, oil, natural gas, and other minerals by extraction industries that have caused some of the most environmentally devastated areas on Indian lands nationwide. Cleanup efforts by the United States and the companies responsible have created agreements that will help protect people's health now and in the future, but the environmental harms and contaminated waters continue to exist. Since about the late 1990s, mining corporations have reinvented themselves to be more socially and environmentally responsible; however, the 2015 waste water spill into a river in Colorado that flowed downstream to the Navajo Nation from the Gold King mine in Silverton, Colorado, is just one example of the failure of the state and the Environmental Protection Agency (EPA) to deal with environmental devastation that continues to occur.

THE STANDING ROCK SIOUX (LAKOTA) RESERVATION

The Standing Rock Sioux Nation is a current example of an American Indian Nation trying to prevent water contamination on their lands. For over 150 years, many demonstrably harmful activities have occurred in the Dakotas. As far as the Lakota are concerned, under the provisions of the Fort Laramie Treaty of 1868, the land on which they live is Lakota land. The Standing Rock Sioux tribe "retained sovereignty over the sacred Black Hills and parts of the Missouri River and certain off reservation hunting rights. . . . But in 1877, U.S. Congress, without tribal consent, passed an act removing the Black Hills from Standing Rock's jurisdiction, curtailing tribal members' capacity to honor the sacred places of the Black Hills" (Powys Whyte 2016, n.p.). Since the early 1970s, however, the federal government has argued that, under the Homestead Act of 1868, this land is non-Indigenous land, and it has told both peoples Indigenous and non-Indigenous that the other is trying to take their land (Churchill 1997). Both Indian and non-Indigenous people have pointed accusing fingers at each other over who owns land and who is trying to steal land. The legacy and history of U.S. colonialism that is a significant part of the political relationship with Native Americans continues today with the possible contamination of the Standing Rock Sioux water by the Dakota Access Pipeline (DAPL) that connects production fields in North Dakota to refineries in Illinois.

There were two broad concerns that surrounded the construction of the pipeline: The first was that the pipeline passes under the Missouri River, at Lake Oahe, which is just one-half mile upstream of the tribe's reservation boundary, and a pipeline rupture that close to tribal lands has the potential to be culturally and economically catastrophic (NARF 2017). Second, the pipeline passes through areas of culturally significant sacred sites as well as burial grounds that federal laws protect (NARF 2017).

According to federal government policy, tribes must be consulted before any project is undertaken that may affect tribal well-being. The Standing Rock Sioux argued that the Army Corps of Engineers (the state), and Energy Transfer Partners (the corporation) should have consulted extensively with the tribe, but did not (Plumer 2016). Instead, the Army Corps of Engineers and Energy Transfer Partners consulted with the Standing Rock Sioux Tribe about the pipeline venture in a way that would legitimize federal infringement. In July of 2016, therefore, "the Standing Rock Sioux and the nonprofit Earthjustice sued the Army Corps of Engineers in federal court, arguing that the agency had wrongly approved the pipeline without adequate consultation" (Plumer 2016, n.p.).

The Native American Rights Fund worked with the tribe's attorneys, and Earthjustice, and took the lead "to develop and coordinate an effective amicus brief strategy in support of the Standing Rock Sioux tribe in their lawsuit against the U.S. Army Corps of Engineers" (NARF 2017). In June 2016 U.S. district court judge James Boasberg ruled that the approval of the Dakota Access Pipeline by the Trump administration violated the law, but fell short of ordering a halt to the oil that now flowed through the pipeline (Zacarias 2017). Then, on October 11, 2017, a federal court judge ruled that the Dakota Access Pipeline could continue operating, pending another environmental review by the Army Corps of Engineers to be completed by April 2018 (Earthjustice 2017).

On November 1, 2018, the Standing Rock Sioux Tribe filed a supplemental complaint against the U.S. Army Corps of Engineers challenging federal permits for the Dakota Access Pipeline. The complaint was in response to the newly released report by the corps that continued to dismiss the Nation's concerns about the risks of an oil spill on the Missouri River, one-half mile upstream from the tribe's reservation. Chairman of the tribe, Mike Faith Jr., stated that the corps has conducted a "sham process" with the same conclusions for a second time. Faith stated that the pipeline "represents a clear and present danger to the Standing Rock Sioux Tribe and its people, and we will continue to fight until the Corps complies with the law" (Earthjustice 2018, n.p.).

On the surface the DAPL protests seemed to be an isolated grievance between the Standing Rock Sioux Tribe and Dakota Access, LLC (a subsidiary of Energy Transfer Partners) that gained fleeting national attention, but the fact is that the Standing Rock Sioux tribe has not been alone in its resistance. Beginning in 2016 hundreds of Indigenous people and their allies used nonviolent means to try to stop the pipeline from going through the ancestral territories of the Standing Rock Sioux tribe.

The primary fear about the pipeline expressed by Indigenous protesters was the result of a major oil spill that happened on December 5, 2016, 150 miles from the Dakota Access Pipeline protests in North Dakota (Dichristopher 2016). Tara Houska, National Campaigns Director for Honor the Earth, a nonprofit organization focused on raising awareness and financial support for Indigenous environmental justice, stated, "Oil companies' interest is on their profit margins, not public safety" (quoted in Medina 2016, n.p.). The spill contaminated a tributary of the Little Missouri River. The Belle Fourche Pipeline Company reported that about 12,615 barrels, or 529,830 gallons, of oil spilled as a result of a pipeline leak the company believes started on December 1 and was discovered by a landowner on December 5, 2016 (Dalrymple 2017).

Belle Fourche is part of a larger corporation, True Companies of Wyoming, which is also responsible for another 30,000-gallon pipeline oil spill, contaminating the drinking water supply for the city of Glendive, Montana. While the population did not suffer ill effects from the oil spill, one landowner reported losses of cattle he attributed to the spill. Bill Suess, investigation program manager for the state Department of Health, reported that traces of benzene were detected in the creek, but that the spill did not reach the river (Dalrymple 2017). Consequences to the Bell Fourche Pipeline Company and True Companies of Wyoming included a notice of violation by the health department but no proposed fine, and the federal Pipeline and Hazardous Materials Safety Administration issued a corrective order late in December 2016 (Dalrymple 2017).

After news of the Belle Fourche pipeline spill reached thousands of DAPL protesters who were such a short distance from the catastrophe, the Standing Rock Sioux felt vindicated. The central argument of the DAPL protesters was that "despite assurances from Energy Transfer Partners (the Dallas-based company funding the $3.7 billion project) an oil spill would be inevitable" (Medina 2016, n.p.). If another pipeline oil spill were to occur, the possibility exists that the Missouri River would be devastated and the drinking water would be at risk not only for the Standing Rock Sioux tribe but for millions of other people.

The concerns of the tribe are well-founded because, since President Trump's decision to allow the pipeline to become fully operational in June 2017, there have been three leaks on three separate occasions (Earthjustice 2017). Even though the pipeline is currently operational, the Tribal Supreme Court Project and Native American Rights Fund will continue to support the tribe to provide a strong, unified voice in the federal courts (NARF 2017). The decision to allow the pipeline to operate is another example of the historic pattern of corporate greed on the part of the U.S. government and corporations while Indigenous Peoples continue to experience risk and harm.

COLONIALISM AND INDIGENOUS WATER RESOURCES

The Dakota Access Pipeline is just one of many instances where the actions of the U.S. government and corporations have resulted in grave social harms to the people living on reservations. As with most other American Indian tribes on reservations, colonialism has set the stage for massive exploitation of Native lands to mine uranium, coal, natural gas, and oil that has not only devastated the environment but dealt harms to Indigenous Peoples who are simply in the way. (See also chapter 3 of this volume). Harms rising from colonialism can be immediate or take time to manifest in the water (and air), as with uranium and coal mining. Breaches in oil pipelines will damage soil and drinking water as well as endanger animals and their habitats. Rather than explore and invest in renewable technologies, our reliance on fossil fuels will likely continue. The risks associated with the pipeline are unacceptable to the tribe because of the irreversible harm that results when pipelines rupture.

The movement behind the Water Protectors' attempt to stop DAPL, therefore, is about stopping colonial methods of extracting resources that result in environmental devastation and other social harms to Indigenous Peoples. The Water Protectors were not only against the pipeline, "they stood for something greater: the continuation of life on a planet ravaged by capitalism" (Estes 2019, 15). As Tuck and Yang (2012, 1) state, "Decolonization . . . is not a metaphor." Historically, Indigenous Peoples and their waters have been threatened by outside interests, as with Standing Rock, the Navajo Nation, and other parts of Indian Country. Their waters in many areas are irreversibly contaminated with uranium and arsenic, causing untold cancers, birth defects, and economic hardships. For them, the internationally recognized right to clean water takes on new meaning.

Because many of the Superfund sites in Indian Country are not cleaned up, and some, as on the Navajo Nation, are still active, this environmental injustice on Native lands will continue for generations to come. Even with Superfund cleanup, it will take decades for the land and people to heal. When people are socioeconomically and politically disadvantaged, live with fewer civil liberties and rights, and are excluded from environmental decision-making, as are so many American Indian people, they become easy targets for environmental exploitation. This is the same for minority and low-income people living in Flint (Stretesky and Hogan 1998, 268–87). The link between exclusion from environmental decision-making, "vested private interests, state interests and environmental harm" substantially contributes to environmental exploitation as well (White and Heckenberg 2014, 31).

FLINT, MICHIGAN

As is the case in Indian Country, problems in Flint, Michigan, disproportionately affect low-income communities. In 2011 Flint, Michigan, faced bankruptcy and financial ruin. Once a politically significant and important industrial city, Flint has become an economically depressed area. Approximately seventy miles north of Detroit, 41.6 percent of residents live below the poverty line, the median household income is $24,679 (according to the U. S. Census Bureau), and the population is mostly Black (Smith and Moorhead 2016; Martinez 2016). Because of the financial emergency in Flint, Michigan, Governor Rick Snyder decided to appoint an emergency manager to run the city, thereby taking away any real power from the mayor (Hanna-Attisha 2018, 28). Snyder also appointed emergency managers in Detroit and Pontiac, which meant that by 2013 "over half of the African-American population in Michigan did not have elected representatives running their cities—the cities had been effectively colonized by the state" (28).

The emergency managers did not answer to the people but to the governor, and came up with the idea of changing Flint's tap water source to save money. A team of elected officials and members of the governor's office decided that one way to save money would be to stop buying clean, safe water from the Detroit Water and Sewerage Department, and instead build a new pipeline to Lake Huron. In the meantime, and to save more money, a decision was made to change the water source to the Flint River—a monumental mistake (Hanna-Attisha 2018). The people living in Flint were not consulted, and had no say in the decision to switch the water supply.

The environmental disaster and harms incurred by the people of Flint that were a direct result of changing the water source to the Flint River were more than simply a result of government mismanagement. It was common knowledge to residents living in the area that "the Flint River had been a toxic industrial dumping site for decades, even if in recent years the river water didn't look quite as brown or *as thick and flammable* (it was said to have twice caught fire) as it had before the 1972 Clean Water Act" (Hanna-Attisha 2018, 29; emphasis in original). Not unique to Flint is the history of environmental harms caused by structural problems inherent in a legacy of multiple industries from the production of automobiles and chemicals to coal and agriculture (Carmody 2016, n.p.).

The decision to switch Flint's tap water source to the Flint River led to a manmade public health disaster that embroiled Michigan governor Rick Snyder's administration in scrutiny and led to criminal charges against a number of public officials (Associated Press 2017). Community advocates charged that Flint residents were victims of environmental racism because race and poverty were a factor in why Flint was not adequately protected, its water contaminated to the point of being undrinkable (Martinez 2016).

The decision to switch Flint's water supply from Detroit to the Flint River to save money demonstrates that people living in Flint are a structurally disadvantaged community, and the association between income and environmental injustice is clear. The people who live in Flint now have to cope with the idea that none of this probably would have happened if they had been residents of Grosse Point, an affluent Michigan suburb just an hour away. Had they lived in a place with economic and political clout, maybe there would have been a greater sense of urgency in addressing their concerns (Hill 2016, 163). As in other cases of state and corporate crime, water contamination in Flint was not intentional; however, if affluent neighborhoods existed in Flint, more would probably have been done more quickly. NAACP president and CEO Cornell Brooks drew a direct connection between Flint's socioeconomic factors and the toxic drinking water by stating "Environmental Racism + Indifference = Lead in the Water & Blood" (Martinez 2016, n.p.).

Water contamination has existed in Indian Country for decades, but what happened in Flint brought to the attention of the rest of the country the environmental racism that people of color living in poor communities face.

THE MEDIA

Flint was important to the media because, before the financial emergency, the city was politically significant as a major population center as well as for its importance to the automotive industry. The media therefore were eager to report on the economic crisis and the environmental devastation that followed. The protests surrounding DAPL, named #NoDAPL, along with their many famous, mainly non-Native celebrity supporters, also caught media attention. On the other hand, what the media have not reported on is the many decades of water contamination on the Navajo Nation and other parts of Indian Country.

National media and television stories reported to the world that the water quality in Flint, Michigan, had become poisoned with lead. The media were slow to begin reporting about the crisis, but since 2016 there have been many editorials and nationwide news reports about the public health crisis and state of emergency that ensued. It took almost two years before the public found out that, due to residents having little choice but to drink water from the Flint River contaminated with extremely high levels of lead, hundreds of children were diagnosed with lead poisoning (Strup 2016, n.p.).

News reports focus on politics, technology, and middle- and upper-class life but fail to report on issues important to poor communities, and even less on Indigenous reservations that are of little economic, productive value and that are primarily used as an environmental sacrifice. Unlike the water contamination in Flint, news media gave very little attention, if any, to illnesses Native people have suffered from consuming unsafe drinking water. Native people and their lands continue to be made invisible, and their perspectives on land-use issues are mostly silenced; hence, the media fail to tell the stories of Indigenous Peoples.

Major environmental crises, as with Flint, the Navajo Nation, and Standing Rock disproportionately affect people of color, but fail to get media attention until the crises begin to escalate beyond people of color. The stories of people of color about environmental injustice are often disproportionately ignored, and their exploiters often go unpunished because contamination resulting from mining uranium, coal, and natural gas, and from oil spills are not violations of criminal law, but of regulatory law. "From a juridical standpoint violations of regulatory law are not crimes" (Michalowski and Kramer 2006, 4). The EPA bears responsibility for enforcing regulations, and on the Navajo Nation, the EPA continues to research and identify Potentially Responsible Parties under Superfund laws to contribute to cleanup costs (Hansen 2014, n.p.).

CRIMINAL CHARGES

One of the most significant justice issues today is environmental and climate degradation. Even though much of the environmental devastation on lands in Indian Country cannot be viewed as legal crimes, environmental injustice occurs when groups of people suffer from the social harms caused by major companies mining for uranium, coal, and natural gas, and from oil spills from pipeline leaks. One very big difference between the water contamination in Flint, Michigan, compared to water contamination in Indian Country, is that Flint officials, including the head of the state health department, are being formally charged with involuntary manslaughter for widespread lead poisoning in children and the deaths of twelve people from Legionnaires' disease caused by bacteria that can be harbored in mismanaged water systems (Sheppard, Delaney, and D'Angelo 2017). Based on my extensive research and consultation with other scholars and Navajo court officials regarding Superfund sites in Indian Country, no one who played a part in contamination of water on Navajo and Hopi tribal lands has ever faced criminal charges, and probably no one will.

When the economic interests of some large corporations and the interests of the state are in line with one another, state-corporate crimes may be the result. Even though some of the environmental devastation, including contaminated water, that has occurred as a result of corporation mining are not actual crimes according to law, social harms and physical destruction to people and the environment still occur. The same is true for the economically oppressed people in Flint, Michigan, when their clean drinking water was replaced by a contaminated water source for purely economic reasons (see Kennedy 2016). The antecedents in Indian Country, however, are rooted in colonialism, making issues of "Indigenous environmental justice" different from "environmental justice."

The Environmental Protection Agency defines environmental justice as the fair treatment and meaningful involvement of all people, regardless of race, color, national origin, or income, with respect to the development, implementation, and enforcement of environmental laws, regulations, and policies (EPA 2018, n.p.). However, Kuehn (2000) cites three reviews of empirical evidence indicating "that the distribution of pollution is inequitable by race and income, with race the most strongly correlated indicator," and adds that "an unpublished 1995 Colorado State University review of 30 studies on the distribution of 46 different environmental risks showed race and class disparities" (10685). Environmental justice, then, has a broad definition of the environment, and "many people of color and lower income communities believe that they have not been treated fairly regarding the distribution of the environmental benefits and burdens" (10681). So "whether by conscious design or institutional neglect, communities of color in urban ghettos, in rural 'poverty pockets,' or on economically impoverished Native American reservations face some of the worst environmental devastation in the nation" (Robert Bullard, quoted in EPA 2018, n.p.).

Environmental assaults on American Indian lands, resources, and self-determination have occurred "since the beginning of American settler colonialism" (Gilio-Whitaker 2019, 12). Indigenous environmental justice looks at the negative impacts of injustices against both individuals and communities; "Communities are as much the victims of inequity as are individuals" (Schlosberg and Carruthers 2010, 18). The most important part of Indigenous environmental justice is empowerment. Indigenous activists see threats to their lands as assaults against people but also as an assault against cultural practices, beliefs, and "the ability of their communities to reproduce those traditions" (18). The overall emphasis is on "health of the environment, the protection of local economies, and the preservation of local and traditional cultures and practices, and also the political freedoms and self-determination and a political voice necessary for their communities to function fully" (18).

Another aspect of environmental justice is "corrective justice" that involves not only inclusiveness—treating all members of a community fairly in decision-making processes—but also "fairness in the way punishments for lawbreaking are assigned and damages inflicted on individuals and communities are addressed" (Kuehn 2000, 10693). Corrective justice would place the burden of proof "on those who seek to pollute and in redressing existing inequalities by targeting enforcement and cleanup actions." Corrective justice means violators should be caught and punished, not reap benefits for disregarding legal standards, and that injuries caused by acts of another, whether in violation of the law or not, are remedied (10693).

A recent example of the importance of corrective justice occurred on June 13, 2019, when all pending charges in the Flint Water Case were dropped for now in order to conduct a more thorough investigation. Solicitor General Fadwa Hammoud and Wayne County prosecutor Kym L. Worth wanted to remind Flint residents that "justice delayed is not always justice denied, and a fearless and dedicated team of career prosecutors, and investigators are hard at work to ensure those who harmed you are held accountable" (Egan 2019, n.p.). Eight people in this case pleaded no contest to misdemeanors, "with expectation they would cooperate with other pending prosecutions and their records would eventually be wiped clean" (n.p.). Those charged "feel fantastic and vindicated" while resident and grassroots organizer Nayyirah Shariff feels that this is a "slap in the face of Flint residents" (n.p.). A community conversation was set for June 28, 2019, in Flint with Solicitor General Hammoud, who is handling the criminal charges (n.p.). It remains to be seen what will happen with this test of corrective justice.

EXPLANATIONS OF STATE-CORPORATE CRIME IN THE CONTAMINATION OF INDIAN COUNTRY WATER

To understand the arguments about state-corporate crime and water contamination on Indigenous lands, we need to look back historically. Europeans came to these shores with colonial and linear ways of thinking, meaning that "thought is rationalizing how something originates at point A, is affected by some force or influence and transforms into point B, to point C, and so forth" (Fixico 2003, 15). Colonialism and this type of thinking were foreign to Native peoples. Europeans found Native logic and thinking to be vastly different from the Western way of thinking. Natives at that time, and traditional Native people today, use a more abstract paradigm in their philosophies and methods of living that form a circle, rather than a single line of thought. Fixico explains:

> The circular method is a circular philosophy focusing on a single point and using familiar examples to illustrate or explain the point of discussion. The circular approach assures that everyone understands, and that all is considered, thereby increasing the change for harmony and balance in the community and with everything else. As each person or being relates to the focal point, and if lines were drawn to indicate this relatedness, then the results would be the spokes of a wheel, and all the participants are encircled by the unity of this experience. (16–17)

Native ways of thinking did not fit U.S. settler colonialism that undermined "the political, military, social, psychocultural, value system, and law and order knowledge bases of the colonized while imposing the values and culture of the colonizer" (Robyn and Alcoze 2006, 71–72). An examination of the protests against the Dakota Access Pipeline (#NoDAPL) is more than "what corporation or government entity met with what tribe to come to an agreement, how many times, and when." There is a larger story, one that includes how DAPL is an environmental injustice not only to the Lakota Nation but to everyone. As LaDonna Brave Bull Allard of the Standing Rock Sioux tribe reminds us,

> We must remember we are part of a larger story. We are still here. We are still fighting for our lives, 153 years after my great-great-grandmother Mary watched as our people were senselessly murdered. We should not have to fight so hard to survive in our own lands. (quoted in Powys Whyte 2017, 154)

Indigenous Peoples have been fighting to survive on their own lands for centuries. Estes (2019, 10) writes, "Over the last 200 years, the US military has waged relentless war on the Oceti Sakowin as much as it has on their kinship relations, such as Pte Oyate (the buffalo nation) and Mni Sose (the Missouri River). What happened at Standing Rock was the most recent iteration of an Indian War that never ends." These seemingly never ending wars "include centuries of genocidal policies, treaty violations, illegal land seizures, and environmental catastrophes perpetrated by the US settler government. . . . And the Dakota Access Pipeline was only the most recent intrusion into the Standing Rock Sioux's lands and sovereignty sending the message that they would not tolerate the further desecration of their treaty lands and the potential contamination of the water—especially for the sake of profits of a fossil fuel conglomerate and for which the tribe would see no benefits whatsoever" (Gilio-Whitaker 2019, 5).

Another part of the larger story includes differences in thinking about the earth. For many American Indians, their lands are thought about in a circular fashion with the Creator at the center of everything. All things used for survival come from the earth and are gifts from the Creator. If sacred lands are not cared for, then the earth cannot care for the people upon it. "And so it is possible to love land and water so fiercely you will live in a tent in a North Dakota winter to protect them" (Kimmer and Moore, quoted in Powys Whyte 2017, 156). The linear thinking of the U.S. government and corporations is, and always has been, in sharp contrast to the deep beliefs of Native peoples about being caretakers of the land. Navajo, Kasan, Quapaw, and Standing Rock Sioux tribal members' close ties to and love for the land were obstacles that could easily be dismissed by corporations and the state. Excluding Indigenous groups, or any minority group, from environmental decision-making that disproportionately exposes them to environmental hazards constitutes state-corporate crime.

State-corporate crime is a hybrid of white-collar crime. It is important to introduce the definitions of state-corporate crime in this chapter to form a clear picture between the linkage that exists among power elites and public and private entities and the crimes that are often the result. Ron Kramer, Raymond Michalowski, and David Kauzlarich, noted scholars in the area of state-corporate crimes, call for recognition of state-corporate crime, which refers to

> illegal or socially injurious actions that result from mutually reinforcing interaction between (1) policies and/or practices in pursuit of the goals of one or more institutions of political governance, and (2) policies and/or practices in pursuit of the goals of one or more institutions of economic production and distribution. (2002, 271)

They continue,

> This theoretical framework is based on the proposition that criminal or deviant behavior at the organizational level results from a coincidence of pressure for goal attainment, availability and perceived attractiveness of illegitimate means, and an absence of effective social control (273).

These can be either state-initiated or state-facilitated (Kramer, Michalowski, and Kauzlarich 2002), the latter being primarily the case in Indian Country. Tied into the previous comparison of media coverage of Indian Country and Flint, one hallmark of state-corporate crime when it comes to environmental crimes in Indian Country, as Gedicks (1993, 14) writes, is "the extraordinary reluctance of mainstream media to assign responsibility to the practices of specific corporations, banks, and government agencies." In the case of water contamination in Flint, Michigan, media coverage reached the public nation-wide because twelve people died and children were exposed to water contaminated with lead, but such is not the case for those living—and dying—in Indian Country.

Ecologically destructive ventures conducted by multinational corporations that threaten Native peoples' lives in Indian Country are rarely mentioned, until it is too late. The partnership between multinational corporations and development-oriented governments to procure as much cheap energy as possible, no matter the costs to people and the environment, continues today with efforts by the current administration to reduce the size of two national monuments in Utah by two million acres to open the land for fossil fuel development and to permit drilling in protected waters in areas of the Arctic and the Atlantic (Nordhaus 2018).

The argument is that opening lands for resource exploitation will create jobs. True, maybe for a while, but at what cost? Flint, Michigan, enjoyed years of a healthy economy, but the boom and bust economic cycle left people without jobs and with an environmentally devastated river that continues to cause harm to residents. Mining is a short-sighted solution to creating jobs. It is extremely capital-intensive and, for every dollar invested, actually produces few jobs (Gedicks 1993, 195), but it seems inevitable, no matter what the costs may be. Looking forward to the seventh generation is not in the cost–benefit analysis for most multinational corporations.

Gedicks (1993) writes that part of "the resource colonization process is, as John Bodley has emphasized in his classic work, *Victims of Progress*, 'that the prior ownership rights and interests of the aboriginal inhabitants are totally ignored as irrelevant by both the state and the invading individuals'" (13). In Flint, Michigan, the General Motors Company polluted the Flint River for decades in the process of manufacturing automobiles with no regard for social harms and no oversight by the state. The economy of Flint and General Motors was the bottom line. The difference is that the injustice faced by Native peoples is "not a result of something their Native life ways produced, but because the most technologically advanced societies on the planet have built their modern lifestyles on a carbon energy foundation" (Wildcat 2009, 4).

The corporate executives of large corporations like General Motors seem to believe that their economic enterprises can operate the same way in Indian country as they do off reservation lands, such as in Flint, Michigan. As a result, "manufacturing, mining and extractive industries are responsible for some of the most environmentally devastated places in Indian country, as specified under the Comprehensive Environmental

Response, Compensation and Liability Act (CERCLA), the official name of the Superfund law enacted by Congress on December 11, 1980" (Hansen 2014, n.p.).

As has been demonstrated, marginalized people of color are especially vulnerable to environmental harms that compromise not only health but psychological well-being (Bullard 1993, 15–39). The relationship between law and socially harmful events experienced by Indigenous groups is complex. Removal of Indigenous Peoples from their homelands for the purpose of land grabs and mineral extraction takes an emotional and psychological toll. When Native peoples, and any marginalized group, are excluded from decisions about what happens to them and their environment, the physical and mental health of the people suffer. Discriminatory practices have limited the ability of Native people to prevent potentially harmful practices from happening in their homelands. Even though the coal and mining industries provided employment to the Navajo Nation's depressed local economy, for example, the advantages were certainly diminished by hazardous working conditions and contamination of the soil and water. The intent of mineral extraction industries was not to harm Navajo people, but it happened anyway with full knowledge of the environmental harms that would occur (DOE 1995).

INDIGENOUS PEOPLES FIGHT BACK: PROTECTING SACRED WATER

Today tribes in Indian Country like the Lakota are utilizing traditional forms of protecting their cultures and the environment with "sophisticated forms of political protest, coalition-building, and international networking with environmental and human rights organizations . . . and have demonstrated that such ecologically-destructive megaprojects can be slowed down, modified, and even stopped" (Gedicks 1993, 14–15).

When political powers in the United States (and elsewhere) and those with economic power pursue common interests, the potential for harm is magnified, as with other state-corporate crimes (Michalowski and Kramer 2006). Historically, treaties were deceptively and unethically created in order to remove Indian people from land the government wanted to obtain and control (Robyn 2006), and since treaties were first written, they have been deceptively used to remove Indian tribes from lands desired by whites. As a crystalline example of state-corporate crime, American governments (state and federal) have violated treaties in order to advance the economic interests of large corporations. Past practices of corporations and the U.S. government running roughshod over Indigenous Peoples of North America may be coming to an end. The Standing Rock Sioux Tribe received overwhelming support from all across Indian Country and the United States in their fight to protect sacred sites—the irreplaceable water sources of the Missouri River.

CONCLUSION

This chapter demonstrates that we are a settler colonial society in which the state and multinational corporations are skilled at advancing their interests, which is at the heart of state-corporate crime. Environmental quality and inequality depend on one's place in the world. Environmental degradation in places where Indigenous populations and socioeconomically and politically disadvantaged people of all races live is "always linked to questions of social justice, equity, rights and people's quality of life in its widest sense" (Agyeman, Bullard, and Evans 2003, 1). Torras and Boyce (1998, 1) write that places with greater wealth distribution, civil liberties, political rights, and opportunities for quality education have higher environmental quality. In places where people live with less equal income, fewer rights and civil liberties, and lower education, there tend to be more environmentally degraded areas with less access to environmental stability. In fact, people of all races living at the bottom of the socioeconomic scale disproportionately bear the brunt of environmental devastation, as is the case with those living in Indian Country and those living in Flint.

The impact of settler colonialism has contributed greatly to environmental devastation and social harms to Indigenous Peoples, and there is no doubt that water contamination on the Navajo Nation and other superfund sites and the Dakota Access Pipeline present cold sober threats to the Navajo and the Lakota Nations with ramifications that will ripple through to other Indigenous nations on the North American continent. With tribal determination and the assistance of their allies, perhaps greater coordination and improved strategies for litigation that may affect the rights of all Indian nations will be accomplished. As the rights of all Indian nations are acknowledged and respected as they have been in the United Nations Declaration on the Rights of Indigenous Peoples, perhaps the right to clean water to all Indigenous nations and people of color will follow.

REFERENCES

Agyeman, Julian, Robert D. Bullard, and Bob Evans. 2003. *Just Sustainabilities: Development in an Unequal World.* London: Earthscan.

Associated Press. 2017. "A Timeline of the Water Crisis in Flint, Michigan." June 14, 2017. https://www.apnews.com/1176657a4b0d468c8f35ddbb07f12bec.

Brugge, Doug, Timothy Benally, and Esther Yazzie-Lewis. 2006. *The Navajo People and Uranium Mining.* Albuquerque: University of New Mexico Press.

Bullard, Robert D. 1993. "Anatomy of Environmental Racism and the Environmental Justice Movement." In *Confronting Environmental Racism: Voices from the Grassroots,* edited by Robert D. Bullard, 15–39. Boston: South End Press.

Carmody, Tin. 2016. "How the Flint River Got So Toxic." *The Verge.* https://www.theverge.com/2016/2/26/11117022/flint-michigan-water.

Churchill, Ward. 1997. *A Little Matter of Genocide: Holocaust and Denial in the Americas, 1492 to Present.* San Francisco: City of Lights Books.

Dalrymple, Amy. 2017. "Oil Spill in Creek Originally Underestimated, Making It One of the Largest in North Dakota History." *Bismarck Tribune.* March 23, 2017. https://bismarcktribune.com/news/state-and-regional/oil-spill-in-creek-originally-underestimated-making-it-one-of/article_93c58fa0-3d22-554c-a1ae-cfb08b248aee.html.

Dichristopher, Tom. 2016. "Pipeline Spills 176,000 Gallons of Oil into Creek 150 Miles from Dakota Access Pipeline Protests." *CNBC.* December 13, 2016. https://www.cnbc.com/2016/12/12/pipeline-spills-176000-gallons-of-crude-into-creek-about-150-miles-from-dakota-access-protest-camp.html.

DOE (U.S. Department of Energy). 1995. *Final Report of the Advisory Committee on Human Radiation Experiments.* Washington, D.C.: U.S. Government Printing Office.

Earthjustice. 2017. "Dakota Access Pipeline to Remain Operational, For Now." October 11, 2017. https://earthjustice.org/news/press/2017/dakota-access-pipeline-to-remain-operational-for-now.

Earthjustice. 2018. "The Standing Rock Sioux Tribe's Litigation on the Dakota Access Pipeline." November 1, 2018. https://earthjustice.org/features/faq -standing-rock-litigation.

Egan, Paul. 2019. "All Flint Water Crisis Criminal Charges Dismissed by Attorney General's Office—for Now." *Detroit Free Press*. June 13, 2019. https://www .freep.com/story/news/local/michigan/2019/06/13/flint-water-crisis-criminal -charges-dismissed/1445849001/.

Eichstaedt, Peter H. 1994. *If You Poison Us: Uranium and Native Americans*. Santa Fe, N.M.: Red Crane Books.

EPA (U. S. Environmental Protection Agency). 2018. "Learn About Environmental Justice." https://www.epa.gov/environmentaljustice/learn-about -environmental-justice.

Estes, Nick. 2019. *Our History Is the Future*. Brooklyn, N.Y.: Verso.

Fixico, Donald L. 2003. *"Indian Thinking" and a Linear World*. New York: Routledge.

Gedicks, Al. 1993. *The New Resource Wars: Native and Environmental Struggles Against Multinational Corporations*. Boston, Mass.: South End Press.

Gilio-Whitaker, Dina. 2019. *As Long as Grass Grows: The Indigenous Fight for Environmental Justice, from Colonization to Standing Rock*. Boston, Mass.: Beacon Press.

Hanna-Attisha, Mona. 2018. *What the Eyes Don't See: A Story of Crisis, Resistance and Hope in an American City*. New York: One World.

Hansen, Terri. 2014. "Kill the Land, Kill the People: There are 532 Superfund Sites in Indian Country." *Indian Country Media Network*. June 17, 2014. https:// newsmaven.io/indiancountrytoday/archive/kill-the-land-kill-the-people-there -are-532-superfund-sites-in-indian-country-LpCDfEqzlkGEnzyFxHYnJA/.

Hill, Marc Lamont. 2016. *Nobody: Casualties of America's War on the Vulnerable, from Ferguson to Flint*. New York: Simon and Schuster.

Kennedy, Merrit. 2016. "Lead-Laced Water in Flint: A Step-by-Step Look at the Making of a Crisis." *National Public Radio*. April 20, 2016. https://www.npr .org/sections/thetwo-way/2016/04/20/465545378/lead-laced-water-in-flint-a -step-by-step-look-at-the-makings-of-a-crisis.

Kramer, Ronald C., Raymond J. Michalowski, and David Kauzlarich. 2002. "The Origins and Development of the Concept and Theory of State-Corporate Crime." *Crime and Delinquency* 48 (2): 263–82.

Kuehn, Robert R. 2000. "A Taxonomy of Environmental Justice." *Environmental Law Reporter* 30:10681–703.

Lynch, Michael J., and Paul B. Stretesky. 2012. "Native Americans and Social and Environmental Justice: Implications for Criminology." *Social Justice* 38 (3): 104–24.

Martinez, Michael. 2016. "Flint Michigan: Did Race and Poverty Factor into Water Crisis?" *CNN*. January 27, 2016. http://www.cnn.com/2016/01/26/us/flint -michigan-water-crisis-race-poverty/?iid=ob_homepage_deskrecommended _pool&iref=obnetwork.

Medina, Daniel A. 2016. "Dakota Protesters Say Belle Fourche Oil Spill 'Validates Struggle.'" *NBC News*. December 13, 2016. https://www.nbcnews.com/ storyline/dakota-pipeline-protests/it-validates-our-struggle-dakota-access -protesters-nearby-oil-spill-n695191.

Michalowski, Raymond J., and Ronald C. Kramer. 2006. *State-Corporate Crime: Wrongdoing at the Intersection of Business and Government*. New Brunswick, N.J.: Rutgers University Press.

NARF (Native American Rights Fund). 2017. "Water Protector Legal Collective Defends Those Arrested at Dakota Access Pipeline Protests." October 1, 2017. https://www.narf.org/water-protector-legal-collective/.

Nordhaus, Hannah. 2018. "What Trump's Shrinking of National Monuments Actually Means." *National Geographic*. February 2, 2018. https://news .nationalgeographic.com/2017/12/trump-shrinks-bears-ears-grand-staircase -escalante-national-monuments/.

Pasternak, Judy. 2010. *Yellow Dirt: An American Story of a Poisoned Land and a People Betrayed*. New York: Free Press.

Plumer, Brad. 2016. "The Battle over the Dakota Access Pipeline, Explained." *Vox News*. November 29, 2016. https://www.vox.com/2016/9/9/12862958/dakota -access-pipeline-fight.

Powys Whyte, Kyle. 2016. "Why the Native American Pipeline Resistance in North Dakota Is About Climate Justice." *The Conversation*. September 16, 2016. https://theconversation.com/why-the-native-american-pipeline-resistance-in -north-dakota-is-about-climate-justice-64714.

Powys Whyte, Kyle. 2017. "The Dakota Access Pipeline, Environmental Injustice, and U.S. Colonialism." *Red Ink* 19 (1): 154–69.

Robyn, Linda. 2006. "Violations of Treaty Rights." In *State-Corporate Crime: Wrongdoing at the Intersection of Business and Government*, edited by Raymond J. Michalowski and Ronald C. Kramer, 186–98. New Brunswick, N.J.: Rutgers University Press.

Robyn, Linda, and Tom Alcoze. 2006. "The Link Between Environmental Policy and the Colonization Process and Its Effects on American Indian Involvement in Crime, Law and Society." In *Native Americans and the Criminal Justice System*, edited by Jeffrey I. Ross and Larry Gould, 67–84. Boulder, Colo.: Paradigm.

Schlosberg, David, and David Carruthers. 2010. "Indigenous Struggles, Environmental Justice, and Community Capabilities." *Global Environmental Politics* 10 (4) 12–35.

Schons, Mary. 2011. "Superfund." National Geographic Resource Library. www
.nationalgeographic.org/news/superfund/.

Sheppard, Kate, Arthur Delaney, and Chris D'Angelo. 2017. "Officials Charged
with Involuntary Manslaughter for Flint Water Crisis." *Huffington Post.*
June 15, 2017. https://www.huffpost.com/entry/nick-lyon-flint-involuntary
-manslaughter_n_5941314fe4b09ad4fbe4838b.

Smith, Jacque W., and Jeremy Moorhead. 2016. "Flint: It's Not Just About the
Water." *CNN.* March 6, 2016. https://www.cnn.com/2016/03/06/us/flint
-problems-unemployment-poverty-crime/index.html.

Stretesky, Paul B., and Michael J. Hogan. 1998. "Environmental Justice: An Analysis of Superfund Sites in Florida." *Social Problems* 45:268–87.

Strup, Joe. 2016. "How National Media Failed Flint." *Media Matters for America.* February 11, 2016. https://www.mediamatters.org/blog/2016/02/11/how
-national-media-failed-flint/208506.

Torras, Mariano, and James K. Boyce. 1998. "Income Inequality and Pollution:
A Reassessment of the Environmental Kuznets Curve." *Ecological Economics*
25:147–60.

Tuck, Eve, and K. Wayne Yang. 2012. Decolonization Is Not a Metaphor. *Decolonization: Indigeneity, Education and Society* 1 (1): 1–40.

White, Rob, and Diane Heckenberg. 2014. *Green Criminology: An Introduction to
the Study of Environmental Harm.* New York: Routledge.

Wildcat, Daniel R. 2009. *Red Alert! Saving the Planet with Indigenous Knowledge.*
Golden, Colo.: Fulcrum.

Zacarias, Michelle. 2017. "Federal Judge Rules Dakota Access Pipeline Permits
Were Illegally Issued." *People's World.* June 16, 2017. https://www.peoplesworld
.org/article/federal-judge-rules-dakota-access-pipeline-permits-were
-illegally-issued/.

LEGAL RESOURCES

Comprehensive Environmental Response, Compensation and Liability Act. 94
Stat. 2767 (1980)

Homestead Act (1868)

Treaty of Fort Laramie (1868)

United Nations Declaration on the Rights of Indigenous Peoples (2007)

PART II

INDIGENOUS COMMUNITY RESPONSES

INTRODUCTION BY MARIANNE O. NIELSEN AND KAREN JARRATT-SNIDER

P ART 2 of this book focuses mainly on the positive aspects of Indigenous community responses to Indigenous environmental injustices in two countries: the United States and Canada. It looks at success stories that reflect resilience and hope, two important Indigenous environmental justice characteristics not usually acknowledged as part of environmental justice. The four chapters also illustrate the main themes of this book, such as the continuing impacts of colonization and the lack of human rights that Indigenous Peoples have suffered for centuries. They give examples of the social harms caused by corporate and state greed through the legacy of leaving toxic wastes on land and in water (Jarratt-Snider), the contamination of water and air by a generating plant in the Southwest (Hammersley), and the impact of environmental injustice on urban Indigenous populations (Luna-Gordinier).

It is important to note that Luna-Gordinier's chapter on environmental justice leadership among Indigenous women focuses on Indigenous people living in urban areas, which is a particularly important contribution to the literature, since most academic interest still centers on Indigenous Peoples living on Indigenous lands. She makes it clear that Indigenous identity is still rooted to land, even when the Native people live in cities. As of 2010 "urban Indians" in the United States comprise about 71 percent of the American Indian / Alaska Native population (UIHI 2013) and, according to the Urban Indian Health Commission (UIHC 2015, 1), compared to the rest of the US population,

> racial and ethnic minorities, including American Indians and Alaska Natives, are at an even greater risk of receiving mediocre or even poor-quality care. Other than the few urban Indian health care programs sprinkled across the country, large-scale efforts to reduce these disparities in care often overlook the urban Indian population.

In addition, if Indigenous individuals are of mixed Indigenous ancestry and so are not qualified to become citizens of a particular tribal nation, or do not belong to a federal- or state-recognized group, they are not eligible for even these low-cost urban health services, which reflects the community health issues that can be associated with urban Indigenous environmental justice.

It is important to note that the lack of human rights is an underlying theme that frames the discussions and success stories in this part. Human rights were not a concern when environmental degradation began on Indigenous lands. First, there was the question of which human right protections Indigenous Americans could expect (see, for example, Echo-Hawk 2010); and second, the right to a safe and healthy environment for Indigenous Peoples did not appear comprehensively in international law until 2007 with Part 2 of Article 24 of the UN Declaration on the Rights of Indigenous Peoples, which states: "Indigenous individuals have an equal right to the enjoyment of the highest attainable standard of physical and mental health. States shall take the necessary steps with a view to achieving progressively the full realization of this right" (UN 2007).

The most important contributions of these chapters, however, are the positive themes that they illustrate, such as community resilience, as communities carry out environmental cleanup in Barrow and Tar Creek (Jarratt-Snider), and preserve access to traditional lands in the Arctic and British Columbia (Casey). They describe strategies for resisting natural resource development (Casey and Hammersley) and show how sovereignty issues are part and parcel of Indigenous environmental justice (all chapters). These chapters describe effective strategies and roles from which other Indigenous groups can learn. They are examples of Native peoples practicing de facto sovereignty as discussed in the introduction and conclusion to this book. Indigenous Peoples have been solving environmental injustice issues on their lands for decades. The chapters in this section show how it was and is being done.

REFERENCES

Echo-Hawk, Walter R. 2010. *In the Courts of the Conqueror: The 10 Worst Indian Law Cases Ever Decided.* Golden, Colo.: Fulcrum.

UIHC (Urban Indian Health Commission). 2015. *Invisible Tribes: Urban Indians and Their Health in a Changing World.* Urban Indian Health Commission and the Robert Wood Johnson Foundation. https://www2.census.gov/cac/nac/meetings/2015-10-13/invisible-tribes.pdf.

UIHI (Urban Indian Health Institute). 2013. *U.S. Census Marks Increase in Urban American Indians and Alaska Natives.* http://www.uihi.org/wp-content/uploads/2013/09/Broadcast_Census-Number_FINAL_v2.pdf.

UN (United Nations). 2008. *United Nations Declaration on the Rights of Indigenous Peoples.* http://www.un.org/esa/socdev/unpfii/documents/DRIPS_en.pdf.

5

TWO CASES OF NAVIGATING LEGAL COMPLEXITY

Environmental Justice in Barrow and Tar Creek

KAREN JARRATT-SNIDER

L EGAL INTRICACIES in environmental justice are the result of the unique legal and political status of American Indian tribal nations, combined with more than a century of shifting federal Indian policy.[1] The two cases discussed in this chapter are some of the most complex types of Indigenous environmental justice issues. The first, a case involving Alaska Natives, centers on a Formerly Used Defense Site (FUDS) in the Native Village of Barrow (NVB), Alaska. Adding the military to any environmental justice issue complicates it, as does the status and rights of Alaska Native tribes, who, unlike many tribal nations in the lower forty-eight states, have no treaties, making the legal landscape quite different from elsewhere in the United States. The laws that settled the rights of Native Alaskan villages are unique from those of tribes in other states. The case of the Tar Creek site is also representative of a particular category of Indigenous environmental justice issues. The Tar Creek site case involves the Quapaw tribe that has allotted lands, which has resulted in various land statuses that make solutions to this environmental injustice all the more complex. Tar Creek is also a case of environmental contamination caused from mining, and it is a Superfund site case. These three factors—multiple land statuses, Superfund, and mining—combine to create legal entanglements not found in every Indigenous environmental justice case. The stories of environmental injustice on Quapaw lands and for NVB are examined in this chapter. They represent two of the most legally complex and unique types of Indigenous environmental justice issues, as mentioned above, but they also offer examples of success stories. While there are many other cases that could be discussed, these cases may offer useful insights for Indigenous nations and their communities facing similar Indigenous environmental injustices.

THE NATIVE VILLAGE OF BARROW

The northernmost point in the United States is Point Barrow, Alaska. Two seas meet at Point Barrow, the Chuckchi from the west and the Beaufort from the east, with the North Pole a mere 1,200 or so miles away. Just about 3 miles south and west of Point Barrow is the former city of Barrow. The area is home to the Iñupiat people, who are attempting to revitalize their Native language. In October 2016 residents voted to change the city name from Barrow to Utqiagvik. Quiayaan Harcharek, one of the authors of the name-change ordinance, indicated that changing the name back to Iñupiat, the language of the local people, would, "promote pride in identity" and "would perpetuate healing and growth from the assimilation and oppression from the colonists" (quoted in Oliver 2016, n.p.).

The Iñupiat people of Utqiagvik are not, however, the only residents. Weather scientists and, in the last few years, climate scientists, also reside in the city, along with an occasional polar bear who wanders down from Point Barrow. Tourism is growing, as summer visitors want to see the northernmost point in the United States, known as the Top of the World. As the largest city in the North Slope Borough (a borough is similar to a county in other states), Utqiagvik has nearly five thousand residents and many of the essential services (a hospital, post office, and utilities, for example) that one would expect in any community, and a community college—Ilisaġvik College.

The Iñupiat chose to form a Native government in 1940 under the Indian Reorganization Act of 1934, established a constitution and bylaws, and became the federally recognized tribe known as the Native Village of Barrow (United States Department of Interior 1940). The Iñupiat people are largely a subsistence people, hunting caribou, Bowhead whales, seals, and other wildlife, and fishing. Subsistence hunting is not just a traditional lifeway; for Native people in Barrow, it is essential. There are no roads to or from Utqiagvik. The location of the town is within the Arctic Circle and experiences periods of twenty-four-hour darkness in the winter and twenty-four-hour sunlight in the summer. The extremely cold climate and permafrost make growing food impossible. Natives do gather a small wild plant, when it is available, but it is tiny. Food, like other things, is flown in via airfreight—the only way in and out of the town—except for a few weeks in the summer. For that short span of time when the sea ice breaks up, barges can reach the town by sea. The issue of having to transport food into the area by plane leads to exorbitant prices. When I visited in the second week of July 2011, I was struck by basic food item prices in the local grocery store: nearly $12.00 for a gallon of milk, and eggs at $1.05 each—not per dozen. With the cost of living so high, subsistence is not only a generations-old cultural tradition embedded in Iñupiat identity, it is a necessity.

MILITARY PRESENCE

The area had a widespread military presence from the early 1940s until the 1980s for several types of activities. In 1947 the Naval Arctic Research Laboratory (NARL), with seven scientists, began operations about a mile south of Point Barrow (Reed n.d.). At that time the area was part of the National Petroleum Reserve 4, and Barrow was the site of an oil exploration camp. During World War II, the Elson Lagoon area was the staging area for the Naval Petroleum Reserve Alaska initiative and brought a large personnel presence (DOD 2013). The Office of Naval Research was responsible for creating and opening the NARL to study the Arctic area. Over time, scientists from around the world came to the NARL to conduct research. During the Cold War era, a Long Range Radar Site was installed, and Barrow became a Defense Early Warning site, or DEW Line Site. The air force also had a presence for a time, as did the navy. An empty navy hangar building, the NARL buildings, the power plant, and the constructed metal mesh runway were still all present in 2011, no longer in use. In October 1963 a huge storm with a strong storm surge flooded the camp, drenching it in two to three and a half feet of water in various places (Reed n.d.; DOD 2013). The storm surge was so strong that numerous pieces of equipment and "tens of thousands" of metal drum containers were swept into Elson Lagoon (DOD 2013). They remained in the lagoon after the military left years later. Elson Lagoon, the place where the Iñupiat launched their boats, became a very dangerous place. With metal lurking under the surface of the water, the Iñupiat experienced torn fishing nets and damage to the bottoms of their boats—it had become a serious physical hazard.

Further south, approximately one and a half miles south of NVB, is a deep ravine just off the beach and along the shore of the Chukchi Sea. QIQU, as the Iñupiat call the ravine, was filled to the top with fifty-five-gallon drums of assorted waste by the time the military presence was gone. Iñupiat people began to refer to it as "the Valley of 10,000 Drums" (NVB 2010; anonymous pers. comm. 2011; DOD 2013). For years the NVB struggled, trying to get someone to clean up the enormous mess left behind. Finally, in 1996, they found an answer.

LEGAL STATUS OF ALASKA NATIVES

Alaska Native villages are, like some mainland U.S. tribal nations, federally recognized; however, many differences exist in their legal structure and rights. Until the mid-eighteenth century, colonial powers left Alaska undisturbed by colonization and settlement. Russia was the first colonizing power to claim Alaska, and established only two large settlements, in Kodiak and Sitka, comprising less than one thousand settler colonists (Getches, Wilkinson, and Williams Jr. 1993). When the United States purchased Alaska in 1867, the Treaty of Cession from Russia "said only that the uncivilized tribes were to be subject to such laws as the United States may, from time to time, adopt in regard to aboriginal tribes of that country" (912). The 1884 Territorial Organic Act of Congress stated:

> Indians or other persons in said district shall not be disturbed in the possession of any lands actually in their use or occupation or now claimed by them but the terms under which such persons may acquire title to such lands is reserved for future legislation by Congress. (912)

The Supreme Court, in a 1955 case, disagreed that the Organic Act acknowledged absolute ownership by Alaska Natives, instead saying that it acknowledged the continuing existence of Aboriginal rights (Getches, Wilkinson, and Williams Jr.1993). That case, *Tee Hit Ton Indians v. United*

States, denied the Alaska Native parties a property interest in a U.S. Department of Agriculture (USDA) Forest Service sale of timber within their Aboriginal homelands. The case set a negative precedent for the future of Alaska Native rights (See Echo-Hawk 2010; Williams 2005). In delivering the opinion of the Court, Justice Reed wrote, "Every American schoolboy knows that the savage tribes of this continent were deprived of their ancestral ranges by force and that, even when the Indians ceded millions of acres by treaty in return for blankets, food and trinkets, it was not a sale but the conquerors' will that deprived them of their land" (*Tee Hit Ton Indians v. United States* 1955).

Alaska, one of the last two U.S. territories to enjoy statehood, did not become a state until 1958. Shortly after that, oil was discovered in the state. Almost overnight, settling Native rights and claims in the state became an urgent matter. Unlike American Indians in the lower forty-eight states, Alaska Natives do not have treaties with the United States. Congress ended the practice of treatymaking in 1871, decades before Alaska became a state. Settler colonists were scattered and did not establish large settlements in Alaska; otherwise it would have made land cessions necessary to satisfy their land-hungry appetites—so no treaties were signed before Congress ended the practice. Likewise, oil discoveries would have necessitated treaties to settle Alaska Native mineral rights, but they came later. Still, once oil was discovered, Congress needed to settle Alaska Native rights quickly to facilitate oil development.

Congress, with input from Alaska Natives, developed and passed the Alaska Native Claims Settlement Act (ANCSA) in 1971 (Hensley 2010) and amended it in 1987. ANCSA, as it is referred to, extinguished all Native "reserves" (reservations and other land claims) in Alaska except for one, the Metlakatla Indian Community, and revoked all Native rights to fishing and hunting. The policy statements of ANCSA included the requirement that Alaska Natives have full consultation on their rights, and activist leaders worked on behalf of Alaska Native people (Case and Voluck 2012; Hensley 2010). Legal uncertainty, stemming in part from various legal decisions, left both Alaska Natives and other stakeholders in a position where negotiation was necessary (Case and Voluck 2012; Royster and Blumm 2002). Some subsistence rights were set aside nine years later (i.e., 1980) for both Alaska Natives and rural Alaskans under the Alaska National Interest Lands Conservation Act, or ANILCA

(Getches, Wilkinson, and Williams Jr.1993; Royster and Blumm 2002;
Case and Voluck 2012), and Congress indicated that "an ANILCA purpose was to preserve 'a way of life essential to Native physical, economic,
traditional, and social existence'" (Royster and Blumm 2002, 79). The primary components of ANCSA were the following:

(1) Native land claims were extinguished, except for the one reservation
    noted above.
(2) Twelve regional Native corporations to share in the oil revenues of
    Alaska oil development were established (every Alaska Native born
    by December 18, 1971, was entitled to one hundred shares of stock,
    while those born after that date could only inherit stock).
(3) The regional corporations would manage and make decisions about
    oil monies—including the original payment of more than $950
    million from the federal and state governments—and stocks in the
    corporation.
(4) The original payment was to be shared equally with the Native village
    corporations within each region.
(5) The Native village corporations would have the authority to purchase
    land for home sites and other limited purposes, such as needed for
    structures for the Native village government (the federally recognized
    Indian tribe).
(6) Lands purchased were fee simple title, not trust land, and had title
    restrictions, usually twenty years, prohibiting sale, and had limited
    taxation by the state (Getches et al. 1993).

The situation of Alaska Natives is arguably the most complex legal
situation in federal Indian policy and law (for an in-depth discussion of
ANCSA, ANILCA, and the legal complexity affecting Alaska Natives,
see Case and Voluck 2012).

THE NATIVE AMERICAN LANDS ENVIRONMENTAL
MITIGATION PROGRAM, THE NATIVE VILLAGE OF BARROW,
AND SELF-DETERMINATION

When one turns to untangling the entities involved in the cleanup of
a FUDS, the situation is further complicated, as will be shown shortly.

Two branches of the military, the navy and the air force, utilized the various Point Barrow facilities. Furthermore, there was no single program or entity the NVB could approach to clean up the environmental mess left behind until 1996, when the Department of Defense created the Native American Lands Environmental Mitigation Program (NALEMP) to address environmental contamination on or near lands of Alaska Natives and American Indians due to former DOD activities (DOD n. d.). In 1998 (likely through the government-to-government consultation that NALEMP utilizes), the DOD determined it was responsible for the cleanup of the site (DOD 2013).

The 2001 Cooperative Agreement through NALEMP funded the tribe to identify the exact location of pieces of debris to help ensure thorough and safe cleanup. The NVB then used an old barge, created and attached a grappling hook, and proceeded to pull out debris from Elson Lagoon between 2001 and 2005. Cleanup work was sometimes slowed by weather and could only be accomplished in the summer. Some summers, weather permitted work for three weeks, other summers for eight (anonymous pers. comm. 2011). Persistence by the workers (members of the NVB hired to do the work) augmented by donated staff time from the borough, eventually paid off. The NVB made the lagoon safe to once again launch boats, and returned the lagoon to its pristine condition. Before and after photos of Elson Lagoon are strikingly different. They were so different that, when I visited in July 2011, I stood at the edge of the lagoon, with the temperature at 37°F, and marveled at the crystal-clear water and peaceful environment.

The next site the NVB turned to for cleanup was the Drum Ravine site, or "The Valley of 10,000 Drums" (NVB 2010; DOD 2013). When the DOD continued NALEMP funding, the NVB began to focus cleanup efforts on the ravine. The drums posed a physical threat to Inupiat snowmobilers, who would encounter metal hiding under the snow. Additionally, the ravine is the site where Iñupiat people from the NVB collect a particular kind of clay for making pots. As with the Elson Lagoon cleanup, the drum ravine cleanup progress was dependent on weather. Additionally, the land had to be firm enough for heavy equipment to move without sinking. Drums were crushed, and after 2010, disposed of in a new local landfill (DOD 2013). Eventually, the ravine returned to being a ravine, rather than a dump site filled to the brim with drums of trash and other debris, but only after the NVB removed 1,385 tons of garbage and more than 10,000 drums (DOD 2013).

The Native Village of Barrow case is an example of a success story. Not only was the village able to achieve environmental justice, in their own words, "We did it ourselves" (anonymous pers. comm. 2011). That statement reflects simple, pure, de facto self-determination and sovereignty. The NVB persisted until the DOD accepted responsibility and paid them to clean up the mess left by the military, but it was NVB personnel themselves who brought their own ingenuity in designing the barge grappling tool, and their own hard work to actually carry out the cleanup. In doing so, they were able to utilize some of the DOD funds to pay their own people. They didn't create the mess left by the military, but they found a way to hold the DOD accountable, and did so in a way that no one could label dependency. Instead, they took charge. Taiaiake Alfred, noted Indigenous studies scholar, says that the Kanien'keha people have a word, *tewatotowie*, which means "we take care of ourselves" (Alfred 1999, 110). The people of the NVB did indeed "take care of themselves," or do it themselves, and in so doing, exercised their sovereignty by putting the "self" in self-determination.

TAR CREEK

In the northeastern corner of Oklahoma sit dozens of grey hills, devoid of any vegetation. As one draws closer to them, it suddenly becomes evident that they are not natural features of the landscape. The Quapaw Tribe of Oklahoma's lands are filled with these grey hills, the leftover environmental degradation resulting from mining. These are piles of lead chat (small pieces of gravelly lead waste), evidence of just one type of environmental contamination in Ottawa County, Oklahoma, and the lands of the Downstream People, as the Quapaw are known.

The Quapaw were removed to Oklahoma from Arkansas. Like most tribal nations in Oklahoma, the Quapaw became an allotment tribe during the Allotment and Assimilation Era in American Indian policy. The point of the policy was to solve "the Indian Problem" by breaking up Indian reservations into individual allotments and pressuring Indians to abandon their lifeways, languages, and manner of dress and appearance, and become "Americans" and good citizens (Getches, Wilkinson, and Williams Jr. 1993; Porter 2005). Even though American Indians would not become citizens until a 1924 Act of Congress, individual American Indians whom the Bureau of Indian Affairs (BIA) deemed "civilized" enough could become citizens under a special procedure of the BIA, informally known as the Shoot the Last Arrow Ceremony (Porter 2005). Each step of the ceremony emphasized leaving one's Indian identity behind and becoming someone else. At one point in the ceremony, the Indian person was handed a bow and arrow (irrespective of the fact that not all Indians used bows and arrows) and was instructed to "shoot your last arrow." The agent administering the ceremony would then proclaim, "(name), you have shot your last arrow. That means that you are no longer to live the life of an Indian. You are to live the life of a white man" (428), then the agent had the Indian touch a plow, and gave the individual a purse with coins and a pin of an American flag (Porter 2005). The idea of becoming a good citizen meant being a farmer, making money, and being a patriotic American (Porter 2005). Assimilation practices fostering these ideas were proselytized to school children as well as adults. Thomas J. Morgan, U.S. commissioner of Indian Affairs for six years, wrote to Indian agents, instructing them on "the Inculcation of Patriotism in Indian Schools," including that the agents should "carefully avoid any unnecessary reference to the fact that they are Indian" (quoted in Porter 2005, 426–27). Assimilation practices came to play a significant role in mining on Quapaw lands and the environmental disaster that followed.

Under the General Allotment Act, tribes were forced to have their reservations parceled out into 160-acre allotments for adults and 80 acres for every minor child (Getches, Wilkinson, and Williams Jr. 1993). Allotments were fee-simple title, but with a restriction that the land could not be sold for a certain number of years—usually twenty-five. In many cases the restriction was extended beyond the initial twenty-five years. In an astute move, the Quapaw tribe elected to self-allot, dividing their lands by the number of tribal members (Baird 1989). Indian lands where allotment took place often became a checkerboard over time, as non-Indians became landowners within the allotment area, or Indian jurisdiction area. That is the case with Quapaw lands as well, and has led to the legally complex situation regarding environmental cleanup that still remains.

MINING AND QUAPAW LANDS

Between 1902 and 1925 several discoveries of lead and zinc ore on and around Quapaw lands in Ottawa County turned a seventy-square-mile area, known as the Tri-State Mining District, into an important mining area (Johnson 2008; EPA n. d.-b). When World War I arose, the lead and zinc ore coming out of the district became important to the war effort. Johnson (2008, 111–12) writes that "after 1915, 80% of the district's ore came from the Picher-Cardin" area in Oklahoma. As of 1918 the Oklahoma part of the large Picher ore field that stretched from the Picher area of Oklahoma to the southern Kansas–Oklahoma border had over two hundred mines (EPA n. d.-b).

The need for additional ore meant prices were rising. Near the heart of it all were the Quapaw allotted lands (EPA n. d. b; Johnson 2008). As the time period coincided with the allotment and assimilation era (1887–1933) in federal Indian policy, Quapaw allottees were urged to sign mining leases for the ore on their lands. This would accomplish two goals. First, supporting the country's need for lead and zinc for the war effort was patriotic, and second, earning money was part of the formula for Indians being good American citizens as noted above (Baird 1989, 83–93; Porter 2005, 428). Some Quapaws signed mining leases. Others did not want to, and so the BIA took over and signed leases on their behalf, as they were declared incompetent to handle their own business affairs (Baird 1989, 83–93). Unethical business behavior also led to the "incompetent" classification, as some allottees were convinced to lease their allotment for mining for a pittance of the value of the lease (83–93). In 1892 the Quapaw tribe also gave forty acres to the Catholic Church, known as the "Catholic 40," to use for educational and religious purposes (Baird 1989; Kent 2018). The church and school established on that particular tract of land operated until 1927 (Kent 2018) when "the Quapaws' enthusiasm for Catholicism dramatically declined because of the rising influence of the Peyote religion" (Baird 1989, 93). In 1937 the Catholic Church signed a mining lease for that parcel, and then, in 1975, returned the deed for the land back to the Quapaw tribe (Kent 2018). The Catholic 40 is considered a culturally significant site by the tribe (Kent 2018).

CLOSURE OF THE MINES AND ENVIRONMENTAL CATASTROPHE

By the early 1970s, all mining activity in the area had ceased. In place of the booming mines, a great number of the grey hills, some of which were one hundred feet high or higher, were left standing on the land. After the mines became inactive, the naturally high water table began to fill the caverns left from the room and pillar mining activity.[2] The water in the abandoned mining rooms mixed with the minerals and, in some cases, abandoned equipment, and turned to acid mine water. The acid mine water, a rust-colored orange, began escaping from boreholes into Tar Creek. Once clear blue, the creek was turned an ugly rust orange by the acid mine water as it passed south of the Douthat Bridge, where borehole flows and water from mine shafts enter the creek (Personal Observation 2010). Downstream from the Douthat Bridge "most of the downstream biota were killed" (EPA n.d.-b). Tar Creek then continues downstream, merging with other bodies of water (EPA n.d.-b).

The lead chat piles, some literally right behind or adjacent to individual houses, left lead contamination in yards, exposing adults and children to unsafe levels of this metal. In 1994 the Indian Health Service found elevated levels of lead in the blood of more than one-third of the Indian children in Ottawa County. Finally, physical hazards from sinkholes where the rooms of abandoned mines caved in dotted the landscape in the area.

The sinkholes, orange creek, chat piles, and subsequent haze of grey lead dust over roads and riparian vegetation are part of the legacy of mining at Tar Creek. In 1980 Congress passed the Comprehensive Environmental Response, Compensation and Liability Act, otherwise known as "Superfund" (EPA n.d.-a). The law was designed to clean up hazardous spills, accidents, and emergency releases of pollutants and contaminants into the environment, and clean up abandoned or uncontrolled hazardous waste sites (EPA n.d.-a). The EPA is responsible for implementing Superfund and attempting to find responsible parties, and then "ensur[ing] their cooperation," using enforcement tools when necessary to "obtain private party cleanup" (EPA n.d.-a). If legally responsible parties cannot be identified or located, the EPA takes responsibility for cleanup (EPA n.d.-a). The EPA breaks large categories of tasks for remediation, or cleanup, into Operable Units (OUs). Starting in 1995, OU 2 consisted of the sampling of soil in yards for lead contamination, and where found, replacing the top twelve inches of soil with clean, uncontaminated soil. The goal was to reduce the immediate threat of exposure. By 2015 over 2,900 yards in the area had received clean soil (EPA n.d.-b). OU 1, in operation from 1983 to 1986, was devoted to reducing groundwater contamination, including capping dozens of old wells. Specifically, capping was done to try to prevent acid mine water from the Boone aquifer from leaking into the Roubidoux aquifer, used for drinking water (EPA n.d.-b.; EPA 2018). The EPA established a groundwater monitoring program, and noted that abandoned wells were still being discovered through the agency's Roubidoux groundwater monitoring program. Every five years, the EPA conducts and publishes five-year reviews of the site to assess whether the activities they've undertaken are still working to protect the environment, as well as public health (EPA Region 6 2018). The most current of those reviews indicated that the "remedy" selected, which includes the remediation activities at all of the operable units, is "protective of human health and the environment *in the short term*" and adds that the reviews will continue as long as remediation is ongoing and "in perpetuity" (EPA Region 6 2018, emphasis added). OU 4 remediation focuses on chat piles. OU 4 operations began in 2009 and continue today. Some chat piles have been sold for use in road paving (EPA n.d.-b.). Additionally, over forty-three thousand tons were injected into empty caverns below ground (EPA n.d.-b.). Contaminated wells in the area were capped, and residual tailings were also injected below ground (EPA n.d.-b.).

LEGAL COMPLEXITY

The Tar Creek Superfund Site involved two regions of the EPA, various agencies within the State of Oklahoma, the U.S. Fish and Wildlife Service, the BIA, and the Quapaw tribe of Oklahoma. With the checkerboard land area in the Tar Creek Superfund Site, legal jurisdictions vary due to various different land statuses, making a holistic solution for cleanup in the area difficult, as one would require land consolidation of the allotments. For example, non-Indian landowners have been able to sell the chat piles on their lands for use in road paving, while for many years trying to do the same, Indian allottees went through an unsuccessful process to receive permission from the BIA, the legally designated trustee as mentioned earlier.

Fewer chat piles now contaminate the area, and the water in Tar Creek still runs orange. The EPA has another Operable Unit, OU 5, looking at risk assessment and eventual remediation of sediment and water contamination from the downstream effects of Tar Creek contamination, including effects on the Quapaw (EPA n.d.-b). In 2012 the tribe signed a Cooperative Agreement with Region 6 of the EPA to carry out their own remediation activities; it is the first tribal nation to do so in connection with a Superfund site (EPA 2015). This cooperative agreement provided for the Quapaw tribe to carry out remediation activities on the culturally significant "Catholic 40" from which the tribe removed 107,000 tons of chat (EPA 2015; Kent 2018). On May 18, 2017, EPA Region 6 awarded $4.8 million to the Quapaw tribe of Oklahoma to carry out additional cleanup activities on tribal lands (EPA Region 6 2017). The tribe, through diversified economic development activities, was able to develop "construction contracting capabilities," and that, along with their environmental department's programs and expertise, as well as active political engagement by tribal chairman John Berrey, paid huge dividends. Having demonstrated success in their remediation activities, the Quapaws entered into further cooperative agreements with the EPA and interagency agreements with the State of Oklahoma to remediate other parts of the Tar Creek Superfund site.

CONCLUSION

Like the Native Village of Barrow, the Quapaw Tribe of Oklahoma exercised de facto sovereignty by taking initiative to help themselves. In the case of the NVB, the village's engagement with the DOD to secure an agreement to do the work themselves is a clear example of self-determination. Similarly, the cooperative agreements the Quapaw tribe of Oklahoma secured with the EPA to put their own people to work making their homelands clean and safe is a clear and strong statement of tribal sovereignty and self-determination. Both the NVB and the Quapaw tribe of Oklahoma faced numerous barriers and long odds, but their perseverance, political engagement, and consistent development of their own tribal environmental programs and department (Quapaw) served them well in finding environmental justice solutions. These particular cases can offer useful information to other Native nations facing similar situations with harmful environmental "leftovers" from large mining operations, especially for Native nations in that situation who also have multiple land statuses, including allotted lands. Particularly, the experiences of the tribe and Alaska Native village, and the choices they made to develop capacity in their environmental departments, as well as the consistent political engagement of their elected leadership, created conditions for them to succeed. For the Quapaw this meant developing arguably one of the most professional and technically capable tribal environmental departments in the country. In the case of the Native Village of Barrow, it stands as a model for cases of environmental injustice facing other Alaska Native villages, where jurisdiction is complex. It also can be instructive in other cases of Indigenous environmental injustice involving FUDS.

The work and actions of these two communities may serve as a model for other American Indian and Alaska Native nations facing similar monumental environmental disasters, including Superfund sites on other tribal lands.

Both the NVB and the Quapaw tribe of Oklahoma faced difficult circumstances, including jurisdictional and legal complexity, public health (Tar Creek) and environmental hazards, making finding Indigenous environmental justice solutions unlikely. These environmental injustices are examples of the continuing effects of settler colonialism on Native nations. In these cases, those effects led to what in current terms can be described as classic cases of Indigenous environmental injustice. They both also fit the category of procedural injustice described in Robert Kuehn's taxonomy (discussed in the introduction to this volume). In the case of the NVB, their story ended with a case of corrective justice as described by Kuehn. The polluters took responsibility and paid for the cleanup; however, it was the ingenuity, persistence, hard work and will of the Iñupiat people who took the opportunity to effect environmental justice through their own efforts.

In both cases, the situations might have been different if the NVB and the Quapaw Tribe had been involved in the environmental decision-making throughout the entire process, which is precisely what Kuehn refers to as procedural justice. The opportunity to be involved in the environmental cleanup efforts could have resulted in justice for both the NVB and the Quapaw much sooner. The Quapaw have made history in several ways. First, they were finally able to conduct remediation of their own lands. Second, they signed the first ever tribal cooperative agreement with the EPA to carry out remediation on and off of tribal lands. Third, the tribe signed an interagency agreement with the state of Oklahoma that was the first such nation-wide agreement to remediation of a "state-led" project beginning in June 2014 (Kent 2018). The importance of what the tribe has accomplished with the cooperative agreements, the interagency agreement with Oklahoma, and the quality of the work they have done in remediation cannot be overstated. They have accomplished what several government agencies failed to do, and like the Native Village of Barrow Iñupiat people, they are now able to proclaim, "We did it ourselves."

NOTES

1. Research study participants wished to remain anonymous. All identifying information has been omitted.
2. Room and pillar mining is a method of subsurface mining where great caverns, or rooms, are carved out for mining, sometimes nearing within a few feet of the surface. A column of earth is left standing in between to support the rooms. Some rooms were one hundred feet tall.

REFERENCES

Alfred, Taiaiake. 1999. *Peace, Power, and Righteousness: An Indigenous Manifesto.* Don Mills, Ont.: Oxford University Press Canada.

Baird, David W. 1989. *The Quapaws.* New York: Chelsea House.

Case, David S., and David A. Voluck. 2012. *Alaska Natives and American Laws.* 3rd ed. Fairbanks: University of Alaska Press.

DOD (U.S. Department of Defense). 2013. "Successful DOD-Tribal Partnership: Native Village of Barrow, Elson Lagoon and Valley of 10,000 Drums." May 2013. www.denix.osd/mil/na/nalemp.

Echo-Hawk, Walter. 2010. *In the Courts of the Conquerors: The 10 Worst Indian Law Cases Ever Decided.* Golden, Colo.: Fulcrum.

EPA (Environmental Protection Agency). 2015. *Tribal Leadership, Historic Preservation and Green Remediation: The Catholic 40 Cleanup Project in Northeast Oklahoma.* October 2015. https://semspub.epa.gov/work/06/500017890.pdf.

EPA. 2017. *Superfund Task Force Recommendations.* July 25, 2017. www.epa.gov/superfund/superfund-task-force-recommendations.

EPA. 2019. "Tar Creek (Ottawa County), Ottawa County, OK." https://cumulis.epa.gov/supercpad/SiteProfiles/index.cfm?fuseaction=second.cleanup&id=0601269.

EPA. n.d.-a. "Summary of the Comprehensive Environmental Response, Compensation, and Liability Act (Superfund)." Accessed June 18, 2019. www.epa.gov/laws/summary-comprehensive-environmental-response-compensation-and-liability-act.

EPA. n.d.-b. "Tar Creek (Ottawa County), Ottawa County, OK: Clean Up Activities." Accessed June 18, 2019. https://cumulis.epa.gov/supercpad/SiteProfiles/index.cfm?fuseaction=second.Cleanup&id=0601269#bkground.

EPA, Region 6. 2017. "EPA Partners with Quapaw Tribe of Oklahoma to Continue Cleanup at Tar Creek Superfund Site; EPA Awards over $4 Million to Tribe." May 18, 2017. https://www.epa.gov/newsreleases/epa-partners-quapaw-tribe-oklahoma-continue-cleanup-tar-creek-superfund-site-epa-awards.

EPA, Region 6. 2018. "EPA Officials Tour Tar Creek Superfund Site Celebrating the One-Year Anniversary of the Superfund Task Force." July 26, 2018. https://www.epa.gov/newsreleases/epa-officials-tour-tar-creek-superfund-site-celebrating-one-year-anniversary-superfund.

Getches, David H, Charles F. Wilkinson, and Robert A. Williams, Jr. 1993. *Federal Indian Law: Cases and Materials.* 3rd ed. St. Paul: West.

Hensley, William L. Iggiagruk. 2010. *Fifty Miles from Tomorrow: A Memoir of Alaska and the Real People.* New York: Sarah Crichton Books.

Johnson, Larry G. 2008. *Tar Creek: A History of the Quapaw Indians, the World's Largest Lead and Zinc Discovery, and the Tar Creek Superfund Site.* Owasso, Ok.: Anvil House.

Kent, Tim, and Quapaw Tribe of Oklahoma. 2018. "Quapaw Tribe Remedial Efforts at the Tar Creek Superfund Site." Presentation to Environmental Justice Forum, Dallas, Tex., June 12–13. https://www.epa.gov/sites/production/files/2018-06/documents/quapaw_tribe_remedial_efforts_at_the_tar_creek_superfund_site.pdf.

NVB (Native Village of Barrow). 2010. *Native Village of Barrow Newsletter.* March 2010. http://nvb-nsn.gov/doc/2010_newsletter_by_jaime_hopson.pdf.

Oliver, Shady Grove. 2016. "Barrow Voters Support Name Change to 'Utqiagvik.'"
    Anchorage Daily News. October 13, 2016. https://www.adn.com/alaska-news/
    rural-alaska/2016/10/13/barrow-voters-support-name-change-to-utqiagvik/.

Porter, Robert Odawi. 2005. *Sovereignty, Colonialism and the Indigenous Nations:
    A Reader*. Durham, N.C.: Carolina Academic Press.

Reed, John C. n.d. *The Story of the Naval Arctic Research Center*. Accessed June 18,
    2019. http://pubs.aina.ucalgary.ca/arctic/Arctic22-3-177.pdf.

Royster, Judith, and Michael C. Blumm. 2002. *Native American Natural Resources
    Law: Cases and Materials*. Durham, N.C.: Carolina Academic Press.

Williams, Robert A., Jr. 2005. *Like a Loaded Weapon: The Rehnquist Court, Indian
    Rights, and the Legal History of Racism in America*. Minneapolis: University of
    Minnesota Press.

LEGAL RESOURCES

Alaska Native Claims Settlement Act. PL 92–203, 43 U.S.C.1601–1624 (1971)
    ———. Amendment of 1987. PL 100–241 (1988)

Comprehensive Environmental Response, Compensation and Liability Act (1980)

Indian Reorganization Act. PL 73–383, 48 Stat 984 (1934)

General Allotment Act (Dawes Act). 25 U.S.C. ch. 9 § 331 et seq (1887)

Tee Hit Ton Indians v. United States. 348 U.S. 272 (1955)

Territorial Organic Act (1884)

Treaty of Cession from Russia (1867) 1940

United States Department of Interior, Office of Indian Affairs. Native Village of
    Barrow Constitution and By-Laws. https://www.loc.gov/law/help/american
    -indian-consts/PDF/41051357.pdf. (1940)

6

THE WATER–ENERGY NEXUS AND ENVIRONMENTAL JUSTICE

The Missing Link Between Water Rights and Energy
Production on Tribal Lands

MIA MONTOYA HAMMERSLEY

I N THE southwestern United States, urban areas have long relied on the
natural resources on tribal lands to support their growth and development. The Navajo Nation's lands are used to both extract and burn coal
to provide electricity, and consequently, water, to nontribal communities
across the West. This occurs at the expense of the health of their own
people and natural resources, particularly their water resources.

The environmental justice (EJ) movement began in response to
minority and low-income populations being exposed to environmental
health threats at a disproportionately high rate (Rechtschaffen, Gauna,
and O'Neill 2009). This disproportionate impact of environmental health
hazards came to be recognized as environmental racism, which, like other
forms of racism, is systemic and embedded within our political, social,
and legal structures (Cole and Foster 2001). The cultural and spiritual
connections that Indigenous Peoples have with the natural environment
make them particularly vulnerable to environmental racism and injustice (Grijalva 2008). Indigenous Peoples were perhaps the first victims
of environmental racism, as their fight for self-determination over their
natural resources began over five hundred years ago when first confronted
by foreign colonial powers (Cole and Foster 2001).

The political status of tribes as sovereign nations distinguishes them
from minority groups that are part of the EJ movement. The trust relationship between tribes and the federal government obligates the federal

government to manage tribal trust lands and resources in the best interests of the tribe (Warner 2017; Grijalva 2008). Despite this, due to legal, procedural, and regulatory failures, tribes may still be denied meaningful participation in environmental decision-making processes and the right of free, prior, and informed consent for development projects impacting their Aboriginal territories (Grijalva 2008; Article 28 of the United Nations Declaration on the Rights of Indigenous Peoples 2007).

A noteworthy example of this issue is the closing of the Navajo Generating Station; however, this also has the potential to be a solution. In February 2017 the Navajo Generating Station's four private utility owners voted to close the coal power plant by the end of 2019, about twenty-five years before the anticipated end of its productive life (Thompson 2017). The Navajo Generating Station was constructed in 1969 on the Navajo Nation in Page, Arizona. Using coal mined from Black Mesa, a region shared by the Hopi and Navajo Nations, the Navajo Generating Station has provided relatively cheap electricity to the cities of Phoenix, Tucson, Las Vegas, and Los Angeles for decades and generates approximately 90 percent of the electricity used to pump water uphill through the Central Arizona Project. The Navajo and Hopi tribes will lose nearly 54 million dollars in total annual royalties and income due to the closure (Thompson 2017). Despite this economic hardship, the closure may also represent an opportunity for these tribes to explore renewable energy development and recover from the cycle of corporate control of tribal natural resources at the expense of the health and welfare of tribal members.

Making the switch to renewable energy offers many potential benefits to tribes, from energy independence and development to economic growth and even carbon abatement. Yet cultural and economic barriers have largely deterred the Navajo Nation from developing its renewable energy resources (Pasqualetti et al. 2016). Overcoming these barriers and securing energy independence may serve as a tool to promote both tribal sovereignty and EJ. Because respecting a tribe's right as a sovereign nation to use its natural resources as it best sees fit is an important aspect of achieving EJ in Indian Country (Tsosie 2007), this chapter is not meant to condemn the actions of any tribal nation but rather to outline the potential benefits of tribal investment in renewable energy development.

The water–energy nexus describes the coupled relationship between water and energy production and infrastructure; particularly in the arid

Southwest, energy production is relied upon to satisfy demands for water, while the production of fossil fuel energy in turn consumes scarce water resources (Scott et al. 2011). The environmental injustices experienced by the people of the Navajo Nation as a product of the water–energy nexus are multifaceted and interconnected:

- Although, like many tribes, the Navajo Nation has senior federal reserved water rights, they stem from racist and restrictive water law doctrines.
- Federal and corporate incentives continue to threaten the ability of the Navajo Nation to effectively manage and develop its water resources, which are bound to electricity production.
- Nontribal companies mine coal on Black Mesa, which both uses and contaminates local water resources, desecrates sacred sites, and harms the health of those who live and work there.
- That coal is burned at the Navajo Generating Station, which draws cooling water from Lake Powell and emits toxins and greenhouse gases that pollute the air and contribute to climate change.
- This energy is exported off the reservation to supply electricity and water to non-Native populations, while residents of the Navajo Nation remain energy poor, with undeveloped water rights, and burdened by the impacts of decreased water quality and quantity.
- The exacerbation of climate change creates a feedback loop that perpetuates this cycle of disproportionate environmental harms being borne by tribal members as a result of this water–energy nexus, as tribal members are among the most vulnerable to the impacts of climate change (Tsosie 2007). On the Navajo Nation in particular, climate change is expected to further strain water resources.

The closure of the Navajo Generating Station provides an opportunity to break this cycle of environmental racism and environmental harm inflicted by extractive industries; it provides the Navajo Nation with a chance to develop its own renewable energy resources, as an exercise of tribal sovereignty, in a way that is consistent with tribal values and beneficial to the physical and economic well-being of tribal members.

Using the case of the Navajo Generating Station on the Navajo Nation, this chapter will provide: (1) an overview of the tribal water law framework and water rights of the Navajo Nation, (2) an argument for the renewable energy potential in Indian Country and the Navajo Nation in particular, addressing barriers to implementation of renewable energy projects, and (3) a discussion of Indigenous environmental justice (IEJ) at the nexus of water and energy on the Navajo Nation, looking toward a future impacted by climate change.

BACKGROUND

THE DEVELOPMENT OF THE SOUTHWEST

Urban development in the Southwest relied primarily on energy and water resources from the Navajo Nation (Powell 2018). Technological advances made it economically viable to construct power lines that could transport electricity hundreds of miles from the Navajo Nation to metropolitan areas (Needham 2014). Tribal leaders hoped that the arrangement would bring economic development and independence from the federal government, while federal agencies and private developers seized the opportunity to provide cheap energy to consumers. Post–World War II, the city of Phoenix began a campaign to rebrand itself as a place of luxury, pleasant weather, cheap housing, and modern amenities; this fueled growth in population and industry that resulted in a dramatic change of land use. By 1970 Phoenix consumed 2000 percent more electricity than it did in 1945, only twenty-five years earlier. This began a shift from reliance on hydropower to reliance on coal-fired power plants to meet growing demand (Needham 2014).

Population growth in the region also fueled an increased demand for water. Arizona in particular relied heavily on groundwater to feed this demand, and by the 1970s had significantly depleted its groundwater resources (Glennon 1995). The successful conclusion of several decades of litigation between Arizona and California over the apportionment of water rights in the Colorado Compact of 1922 paved the way for Arizona to construct the Central Arizona Project—a long-desired water infrastructure project that transports water from the Colorado River in Lake Havasu to central and southern Arizona. This, in addition to the passage of the Groundwater Management Act of 1980, enabled Arizona to shift from reliance on groundwater to surface water (Glennon 1995). This project, however, is energy intensive; it transports 1.6 million acre-feet of water, uphill, annually, requiring approximately 3,140 hours per acre foot (kWh/AF) to pump water to the end of the Central Arizona Project line in Tucson (Scott et al. 2011). The Navajo Generating Station provided much of this electricity (Thompson 2017).

THE NAVAJO NATION

The earth is at the center of the Navajo, or Diné, existence. The Diné have a matrilineal descent system, where women are both land managers and owners of livestock grazing permits (Powell 2018). Traditionally nomadic and resistant to external colonial forces, the Diné were never subdued by Spanish; the greatest impacts of foreign colonization came at the hands of the United States after the Mexican–American War, fueled by American desire for land and natural resources (Sherry 2002).

As the arrival of an increased number of settlers to Navajo ancestral lands led to escalating conflicts, the U.S. government established a military presence there. Beginning in the summer of 1863, American troops lead by Colonel Kit Carson began a systematic siege and destruction of Navajo natural resources (including burning plant foods and killing animals) and rounded up thousands of people in what would be known as "The Long Walk" to Fort Sumner in New Mexico (Sherry 2002; Hughes 1988). People were forced to march up to fifteen miles per day for over three hundred miles and endure atrocities at the hand of the U.S. military; some accounts report that captives who were not able to keep up, such as elders, pregnant women, and people who were ill, were shot and killed. Many others died of starvation and disease during the forced march and the years that followed at Fort Sumner (Sherry 2002; Hughes 1988).

In 1868 the few thousand survivors of captivity at Fort Sumner were allowed to return to their homeland pursuant to a treaty that established a reservation. Before this period of captivity, the Diné peoples did not consider themselves united as one nation, although they were traditionally linked through a clan system and shared cultural and linguistic commonalities (Sherry 2002). Today, the Navajo Nation is the largest Indian reservation in the country (Hughes 1988).

Soon, the newly established Navajo Nation faced external demands for Navajo natural resources. Pressure and encroachment from mining and oil and gas companies were extremely influential in the creation and organization of the official government of the Navajo Nation. The Navajo formed the first official tribal council in 1923 (Navajo Nation 2011, n.p.), after several attempts by the U.S. government to establish "business councils" to represent the tribe in natural resources dealings with outside corporations. Despite this history, the current tribal council serves as an important safeguard of tribal natural resources (Sherry 2002).

BLACK MESA AND PEABODY COAL

Today, about half of the Navajo Nation's annual budget is associated with the coal industry, creating a dependence that may not be easily remedied (Rowe 2013). Beginning in 1966, Peabody Coal acquired its mining lease-holds, which cover an area of about one hundred square miles, and strip mining commenced in 1970 (Kelley and Francis 1994). Peabody's operation also includes a lease to pump water from the Coconino aquifer, which is used to transport coal slurry (Gerke 2008). This area, known as Black Mesa, is a sacred landscape to the Navajo. Navajo oral tradition states that Black Mesa is a sacred site that cannot be disturbed; it also contains many historical sites with human remains and other cultural resources (Kelley and Francis 1994).

The coal mined at Black Mesa supplies the Navajo Generating Station, which in turn provides electricity and water, via the Central Arizona Project, for cities outside the reservation. Conversely, the water required to operate the strip mine has taken a heavy toll locally on both water quality and quantity, and the mine has harmed the health of tribal members who still live on the leasehold site (Kelley and Francis 1994). Although the coal industry brings economic revenue to the reservations, there are many negative social and environmental consequences to the surrounding community, including air and water pollution (Goffman 2016).

THE NAVAJO GENERATING STATION

The Navajo Generating Station is the largest coal-fired power plant in the western United States, consuming 15 tons of coal per minute (White

Hawk 2016). It is a main driver of the Navajo and Hopi economies, including by providing employment for 935 full-time employees, 90 percent of whom are tribal members (Thompson 2017); however, the environmental impacts from this power plant can be seen both on and off reservation. The Navajo Generating Station emits approximately 8.6 metric tons of carbon dioxide annually, in addition to 472 pounds of mercury, 4,370 of selenium, and 259 of arsenic, which are toxic air pollutants that permeate the ecosystems of neighboring national parks, such as Mesa Verde (Thompson 2017). The Navajo Generating Station is also a massive consumer of both groundwater and surface water; it draws approximately 1,200 acre feet of groundwater from the Navajo aquifer each year as well as 28,000 acre feet (or 9 billion gallons) of water from nearby Lake Powell to generate steam and cool the turbines (Scott et al. 2011; Thompson 2017).

ENVIRONMENTAL JUSTICE CONCERNS

The Navajo government permitted the Navajo Generating Station due to the promise of jobs and better economic opportunity (Goffman 2016); however, it eventually became clear that these economic benefits were not equally distributed, nor were the costs to human health and the environment. Despite the fact that the largest energy producer in the state is located on the reservation, 37 percent of Navajo households do not have electricity (White Hawk 2016). Nationally, approximately 14.2 percent of American Indian households do not have electricity, compared to only 1.4 percent of total households in the United States (White Hawk 2016). Out of that 14.2 percent, approximately 75 percent of those homes are located on the Navajo Nation (Jones and Necefer 2016).

This disparity in access to electricity permeates other aspects of the quality of life available on the Navajo reservation, including a lack of refrigeration for food storage, a lack of heating and cooling, and a lack of running water (Jones and Necefer 2016). Thousands of families on the reservation are still living without running water, and approximately 45 percent of tribal members on the Navajo reservation are unemployed (Rowe 2013; Sherry 2002). Furthermore, individuals who have been employed to work in the mines often face potentially life-threatening respiratory health problems from prolonged inhalation of coal dust, such as black lung disease (Rowe 2013).

THE WATER

OVERVIEW OF WATER LAW DOCTRINES

In the western region of the United States, the federal government owns 53.7 percent of all land, including Native American reservations (Thompson, Leshy, and Abrams 2013). Unlike the water rights doctrine of riparianism that governs the eastern United States, the prior appropriation doctrine does not inherently grant a landowner water rights with the land. Under prior appropriation, the first person to make a "beneficial use" of the water is granted the water rights for a fixed amount. In the early years of the prior appropriation doctrine, beneficial uses largely consisted of activities that contributed to the settlement of the West, such as mining and agriculture. The older a priority date of a water right is, the more senior the water right is; this is important because, in times of shortage, senior water rights holders are able to divert their full appropriation, while there may not be enough water for junior water rights holders to withdraw their full appropriated amount. Water rights can be lost by a period of non-use, abandonment, and forfeiture. The prior appropriation doctrine is largely governed on a state-by-state basis (Thompson, Leshy, and Abrams 2013).

Federal reserved water rights are unlike any other water rights; contrary to many aspects of the prior appropriation doctrine, they fulfill water rights to meet the needs of a given parcel of land without any demonstrated withdrawal of a previously fixed amount of water. Water rights reserved specifically for federally recognized Native American tribes are a large component of the federal reserved water rights system (Thompson, Leshy, and Abrams 2013). Under the Winters doctrine, these water rights are meant to satisfy the present and future needs of a reservation (Yale Law Review 1979). There is often, however, a lack of specification and certainty surrounding tribal reserved water rights regarding the quantity of the right, points of diversion, rules of transferability, and definitions of beneficial reservation uses. This lack of specificity can make it difficult for tribes to develop and implement water-management practices (Yale Law Review 1979).

The Winters doctrine emerged from the case *Winters v. United States* in 1908. This case established that water rights are inherently reserved for beneficial use of the land on Indian reservations; however, it did not provide a method of quantifying these rights (Yale Law Review 1979). The case stemmed from a conflict between the Fort Belknap reservation and upstream water users of the Milk River. In the late 1800s, white settlers had begun homesteading the land surrounding the reservation, using water from the Milk River for agriculture and watering their stock. The year of 1905 was unusually dry, and upstream water use left almost nothing for downstream users, including the reservation (Osborn 2013). The Court ruled in favor of the Fort Belknap reservation, referring back to the agreement of 1888 that outlined the provisions of a newly created 640,000-acre reservation. It stated:

> The reservation was a part of a very much larger tract which the Indian had the right to occupy and use, and which was adequate for the habits and wants of a nomadic and uncivilized people. It was the policy of the government, it was the desire of the Indians, to change those habits and to become a pastoral and civilized people. If they should become such, the original tract was too extensive; but a smaller tract would be inadequate without a change of conditions. The lands were arid, and, without irrigation, were practically valueless.

Thus reasoning that there is no value to land without water in situ because agriculture would then be rendered impossible and the tribes would not be able to live as "pastoral and civilized people," the Court upheld the tribe's federally reserved water rights.

Under the Winters doctrine, Indian reserved water rights are governed differently from other appropriated water rights (Thompson, Leshy, and Abrams 2013). Tribes are often the most senior water user, as their date of appropriation is usually set to the date the reservation was created or earlier, and their rights cannot be lost by non-use (Thompson, Leshy, and Abrams 2013). The establishment of federally backed reservations with senior water rights represented a large step in overcoming previously upheld court cases such as *Johnson v. M'Intosh* (1823). In *M'Intosh* the Court held that Indigenous Peoples' right to property ownership of their lands was extinguished by the doctrine of discovery and conquest by European powers, leaving them with only the right of occupancy. The Winters doctrine, however, still presents potential challenges and inequalities to tribal governments and communities, exemplified by the discourse of assimilation of tribal peoples through an imposition of an agricultural lifestyle that it furthers (Ross 2013; Burton 1991; McCool 1994).

In the following decades, there continued to be new legal developments regarding tribal reserved water rights (Burton 1991; McCool 2006). In 1952 Congress passed the McCarren Amendment, which waived sovereign immunity for federal reserved water rights and allowed them to be administered and adjudicated under state law (Stein 1988). This was problematic for tribes, who have historically turned to the federal government for protection against hostile states (Getches et al. 2011). Furthermore, the McCarren Amendment established that issues of transaction and transferability for tribal water rights would be administered by states— specifically, a change of purpose or place of use, change of the point of diversion, or leasing (Stein 1988).

Despite this ruling, tribal water rights were still protected, and the federal government still sought out new methods to open the reservations to settlement in order to allow water rights to be used by nontribal members (Osborn 2013). *Winters* was upheld by the Supreme Court of the United States in *State of Arizona v. California* in 1963. There, the appointed special master recommended a division of Colorado River water rights and, due to an intervention of the federal government, the water rights of the Colorado River Indian Tribe were successfully protected amid the dispute. This case also established a method to quantify tribal water rights by assessing the "practicably irrigable acreage," or PIA. Specifically for the western United States, this method calculates the amount of water needed to convert arid land to arable land. This quantification method helped to resolve some of the previous issues with determining the exact amount of water encompassed by a given tribal water right (Osborn 2013).

WATER RIGHTS OF THE NAVAJO NATION

Because the Navajo reservation spans across the borders of Arizona, Utah, and New Mexico, the tribe must reach water rights settlement agreements with each state. The Navajo Nation recently reached a settlement agreement with Utah over its rights to the San Juan River that entitles the Navajo Nation to 81,500 acre-feet per year (Minard 2016). The tribe reached a water settlement agreement with the state of New Mexico in 2013, which entitles the Navajo Nations to a total of 325,000 acre-feet per year (Fleck 2013). The Navajo Nation rejected a proposed water settlement with the state of Arizona in June, 2012, largely due to public opposition. Bill 2109, better known as the Navajo-Hopi Little Colorado River Water Rights Settlement Act was introduced to Congress in February of 2012, sponsored by Arizona senators John McCain and Jon Kyle (Navajo-Hopi Little Colorado River Water Rights Settlement Act 2012). The tagline of the bill stated that it was

> a bill to approve the settlement of water claims of the Navajo Nation, the Hopi Tribe, and the allottees of the Navajo Nation and Hopi Tribe in the State of Arizona, to authorize construction of municipal water projects relating to the water rights claims, to resolve litigation against the United States concerning Colorado River operations affecting the States of California, Arizona, and Nevada, and for other purposes.

The bill required the Hopi and Navajo Nations to give up their reserved water rights to the surface waters of the Little Colorado River and forfeit any ability to make claims on damages to or contamination of the Coconino aquifer. In exchange for the forfeiture of these water rights, the federal government offered to spend 315 million dollars on water infrastructure projects to deliver groundwater to communities located both on and off reservation (Navajo-Hopi Little Colorado River Water Rights Settlement Act 2012).

Although this could have provided tribal communities with a reliable source of drinking water, it also threatened to perpetuate a dependence on the federal government for water projects, which is less legally secure than ownership of senior federal reserved water rights. There was also federal pressure on the tribes to include the Navajo Generating Station in the Little Colorado River water lease, which could have exacerbated environmental concerns in the region (Roffman 2012). With the upcoming closure of the Navajo Generating Station, negotiations have included the possibility of turning over the water rights currently used for electricity generation back to Navajo and Hopi (Thompson 2017). Securing water rights for tribes located in the Southwest is likely going to become a more pressing issue as state and local lawmakers look to tribes' senior water rights as a source to bolster their own dwindling water resources in times of shortage; for example, a bill recently introduced, and quashed, in Arizona would have prevented the Gila River Indian Community from filing forfeiture claims to use the un-utilized water rights from upstream ranchers and farmers, contrary to decades of water law precedent (Arizona House Bill 2476; Fischer 2019).

THE ENERGY

THE RENEWABLE ENERGY MARKET

In spite of recent legislation enacted to sustain the coal industry, the renewable energy market is only expected to grow and expand (Obama 2017). Although the economic success of the renewable energy market may be partially attributed to the growing importance of curbing greenhouse gas (GHG) emissions, it is also due to a trend in market forces. The United States has experienced a period of concurrent reductions in GHG emissions and economic growth since 2008 (Obama 2017). This was also accompanied by a dramatic drop in the price of renewable electricity costs between 2008 and 2015, including a drop by 41 percent for wind power and by 54 percent for rooftop solar photovoltaic installations. These pricing mechanisms, in addition to the incentive of avoiding future costs incurred by the impacts of climate change on the global market, have influenced corporate decision-making toward further investment in renewables (Obama 2017).

In fact, over 360 companies signed an open letter to the then president-elect Donald Trump, President Obama, and members of Congress urging them to hold the United States to the Paris Climate Accord (Kennedy 2016). This letter asserts:

> Failure to build a low-carbon economy puts American prosperity at risk. But the right action now will create jobs and boost US competitiveness. . . . Implementing the Paris Agreement will enable and encourage businesses and investors to turn the billions of dollars in existing low-carbon investments into the trillions of dollars the world needs to bring clean energy and prosperity to all.

President Obama echoed that the United States' commitment is crucial to the success of the Paris Climate Accord overall because, if the United States backed out of the accord, it would set a precedent for other countries to do the same (Obama 2017). On December 31, 2017, President Donald Trump announced that the United States would withdraw from the Paris Climate Accord (Shabaud 2017).

The closure of the Navajo Generating Station is largely attributed to economic forces—specifically, the dropping prices of natural gas production, which coal can no longer compete against (Thompson 2017). Many western utility companies supplied by the Navajo Generating Station, including NV Energy, PacifiCorp, and California's independent grid operators, have teamed up to form an energy imbalance market that allows the utilities to share electricity generators, which are increasingly from renewable sources (Thompson 2017). In fact, California recently enacted legislation committing it to achieving a 100 percent renewable energy supply by 2045 (California Public Utilities Code n.d.).

THE BARRIERS TO IMPLEMENTING RENEWABLE ENERGY INFRASTRUCTURE ON TRIBAL LAND

According to the National Renewable Energy Laboratory, there are approximately 17,600 billion kilowatt hours/year of solar energy potential and 535 billion kilowatt hours/year of wind energy potential in the Indian Country in the lower forty-eight states (Jones and Necefer 2016). Particularly in the southwestern United States, there is potential for tribes to invest in community-scale solar panels. Specifically, photovoltaic solar panel projects are well-suited for development in arid, rural areas because they require only minimal water for system batteries for routine operation. Approximately 83 of the 326 Indian reservations in the United States could benefit economically from concentrated solar power generation, but few tribes have made the attempt (White Hawk 2016). A few tribes, however, including the Navajo Nation, have built smaller-scale solar facilities to bring electricity to some communities or areas of their reservations and save money (Misbrener 2018), while others are undertaking studies to examine the possibility of creating renewable energy plants that will contribute to economic development for their tribes (Cowan 2018; Institute for Tribal Environmental Professionals 2015).

There are many factors that may influence whether a tribe chooses to implement a renewable energy project. Despite the widespread need for better access to electricity in Indian Country and the damaging legacy of extractive industries and dirty energy production on tribal lands, many tribes face common barriers to the implementation of renewable energy projects when the opportunity arises. These barriers include cultural considerations (Jones and Necefer 2016) and obstacles rooted in federal law and policy (Jones and Necefer 2016; Sullivan 2010).

The cost of developing infrastructure or conducting an Environmental Assessment or Environmental Impact Statement pursuant to the National Environmental Policy Act may be an initial barrier, as tribes are often located in rural and remote areas and may lack the necessary funds (Jones and Necefer 2016; White Hawk 2016). Congress has recognized the need for and responsibility of the federal government to assist with implementation of energy infrastructure in Indian Country, passing the Indian Tribal Energy Development and Self-Determination Act in 2005 (Sullivan 2010; Title 25 of the Energy Policy Act of 2005). The vast majority of projects proposed pursuant to this act have been for renewable energy development. Although this act mandates that the Department of Energy provide both technical and financial assistance to tribes pursuing energy development projects, few projects initiated with the Department of Energy are actually constructed and developed after initial feasibility studies, in part due to the high construction costs (Sullivan 2010).

Tribal norms, customs, histories, and politics may also play a role in the development of renewable energy projects. For example, a large offshore wind farm in Massachusetts was vehemently rejected by the Wampanoag tribes whose culture and traditions require an unobstructed view of the rising sun to hold certain ceremonies (Lehmann 2009). There, the shafts of the turbines would extend eighty feet into the seafloor, disturbing an ancient burial site that the Wampanoag's oral history document as being covered by the ocean thousands of years ago. Joining several environmental groups, the tribes sued under the National Historic Preservation Act in the case *Public Employees for Environmental Responsibility v. Beaudreau* (2014), asserting that the United States Bureau of Ocean Energy Management improperly consulted with them and that the Nantucket Sound should be classified as a traditional cultural property, thereby preventing the construction of the wind farm (Lehmann 2009). Although the court ruled against the tribes in that case, the project was officially canceled in 2017 due to the ongoing costs of legal and regulatory challenges posed by widespread opposition by the tribes, environmental groups, and private landowners (Seelye 2017).

In a similar conflict, in *Quechan Tribe v. U.S. Department of the Interior* (2010), the U.S. district court for the Southern District of California granted injunctive relief to the tribe to stop the construction of a concentrated solar project (White Hawk 2016). The proposed site of 30,000 solar collectors was located on an area of great cultural and religious import to the Quechan tribe, as it contained hundreds of individual ancestral burial sites and ancient trails. There, the court held that the federal government failed to adequately consult with the tribe before approving the project. Challenges to implementing renewable energy projects on tribal land may be overcome by improved communication with the federal government and by approaching development in a manner consistent with tribal cultural values (Jones and Necefer 2016).

In contrast to the *Quechan Tribe* ruling, the Moapa Band of Paiutes recently completed a project with First Solar Inc. to develop a solar farm on the 72,000-acre Moapa River Indian reservation about thirty miles north of Las Vegas (*Indian Country Today* 2017). This is the first ever utility-scale solar power plant to be built in Indian Country, and the tribe hopes to serve as an example to others. This solar power plant has the capacity to power approximately 111,000 homes as a part of the City of Los Angeles's goal of obtaining 50 percent of its energy from renewable sources by 2025. Although none of this electricity will be used on-reservation, it will benefit the tribe by creating about 115 jobs and generating income through the land leased to First Solar, all without negative impacts to the environment and human health (*Indian Country Today* 2017).

Similarly, the Rosebud Sioux tribe is soon to complete the largest wind farm on tribal lands in the county (Oceti Sakowin Power Authority n.d.). It had been pursuing this renewable energy project, the Owl Feather War Bonnet Wind Farm, since the 1990s. Recognizing that it lacked the necessary capital to implement the project on its own, the tribe made the decision to seek out a private investor, whom the tribe agreed would have the sole ownership interest in the project for the first ten years, including all profits from electricity sales, after which the tribe will assume full ownership (Sullivan 2010). Although this agreement was not ideal, it allowed the Rosebud Sioux to overcome the financial barriers that often prevent renewable energy projects from coming to fruition. The Rosebud Sioux also established an intertribal power authority to oversee the project. The wind farm is expected to be fully operational in 2021 (Oceti Sakowin Power Authority n. d.).

These case studies suggest that renewable energy projects in Indian Country are most successful when the tribe has some level of ownership over the project, as in the cases of the Moapa Band of Paiutes and the Rosebud Sioux, and when external corporate or governmental entities engage in open communication with the tribe. In cases where a tribe is not adequately consulted before a renewable energy project is proposed or where the implementation is being entirely driven by an external entity, as in the cases of the Quechan tribe and the Wampanoag tribes, then projects are more likely to be opposed by a tribe. Tribes may have more control over the implementation of a project located on their own reservations than projects proposed off the reservation on culturally and historically significant sites. All tribes have unique and individual economic, cultural, and environmental landscapes, and the development of renewable energy projects should reflect those individual needs and differences; ideally, these efforts should be led by tribes, for tribes.

THE NEXUS

A FUTURE OF CLIMATE CHANGE

The perpetuation of climate change—as one by-product of the water–energy nexus—and the impacts that it will likely have on water resources in the Southwest may prove to be an existential threat for the tribes, like the Navajo Nation, that are already grappling with environmental degradation in the region. According to the Colorado River Basin study, the Colorado River and its tributaries provide water to approximately forty million people in addition to the water rights of twenty-two federally recognized tribes, Navajo and Hopi included (DOI 2012). In the face of the worst drought in the last century and projections of increased water demand coupled with decreased supply due to climate change, increased water use efficiency is a key factor in securing long-term water reliability in the Colorado River Basin (DOI 2012). The National Climate Assessment reports that the Southwest region of the United States is expected to experience a decline in water supplies due to prolonged periods of drought, characterized by a decrease in snowpack and streamflow. This will also lead to an increase in the frequency and intensity of wildfires (National Climate Assessment 2018).

For Indigenous Peoples, climate change is an EJ issue because they are among the most vulnerable populations to the impacts of climate change, yet contribute very little to the problem (Tsosie 2007; Warner 2017). There are many factors that may influence a particular tribe's vulnerability to climate change, including socioeconomic factors, spiritual and cultural factors, ecosystem services and land use factors, infrastructural factors, and political factors, in addition to changes to the climate, hydrology, and ecosystems where a tribe resides (Cozzetto et al. 2013). Because the cultures, languages, and histories of tribal peoples are linked to a particular landscape, in addition to often being legally tied to a particular reservation, tribes cannot migrate to avoid ecological degradation caused by climate change (Warner 2017). Leaving traditional lands may well prove genocidal for tribes, who would lose their cultural and political status if forced to relocate (Tsosie 2007).

Regarding tribal water resources, climate change is expected to impact the water supply and management of tribes, the aquatic species important for culture and subsistence, ranching and agriculture, tribal sovereignty, and rights associated with water resources—including fishing, hunting, and gathering, and soil quality—which may be degraded by extended drought. Already, Navajo and Hopi lands have experienced an increase in the formation of sand dunes due to a decrease in water resources, and approximately 25 to 40 percent of residents on the Navajo Nation are already hauling in water from an average distance of fourteen miles away because they do not have running water in their homes (Cozzetto et al. 2013). Increased sand dune formation and movement in the future may destabilize housing and transportation on the Navajo nation, worsen air quality, and further endanger human health (Hiza-Reedsteer et al. 2011). Climate change will continue to negatively impact the standard of living on the Navajo Nation if nothing is changed.

Given the projected impacts of climate change in addition to the impacts associated with energy generation, the closure of the Navajo Generating Station offers the Navajo Nation the opportunity to regain regulatory control over their land and uphold their right to environmental self-determination. This right encompasses the "need for tribes to decide their own priorities for economic development and to assume authority as sovereigns over the reservation environment" (Tsosie 2007, 1631). Ultimately, because the closure of one generating station cannot change the course of climate change on a global scale, the Navajo Nation will have to decide if the benefits of closure outweigh the heavy economic costs.

While tribal communities are often disproportionately impacted by climate change impacts because the industries emitting greenhouse gases are typically not within the control of tribal governments (Tsosie 2007), here the Navajo Nation can take steps to fill the energy void left by the closure of the Navajo Generating Station with renewable energy in a manner that is consistent with tribal cultural values. In fact, some renewable energy companies are already exploring the possibility of using the existing power lines for a renewable energy project (Randazzo 2017).

RESTORING ENVIRONMENTAL JUSTICE IN THE WATER–ENERGY NEXUS

The Navajo people have a history of activism opposing extractive industries and environmental hazards in their homeland (Needham 2014). The Indigenous Environmental Network (IEN), an international coalition of grassroots IEJ organizations, began with a struggle against a toxic waste incinerator on the Navajo Nation in the 1980s (Cole and Foster 2001). In 2003 Diné activists, primarily women and elders, led a successful campaign to stop the Desert Rock Energy Project—a proposed 1,500 megawatt coal-fired power plant in the northeastern corner of the Navajo reservation (Powell 2018). This project was supported jointly by the Navajo Nation and Sith Global Power, but the Diné Power Authority was ultimately unsuccessful in acquiring the required federal air quality permission to move the project forward, in part due to the pressure generated by Diné activists and EJ organizations (Powell 2018). Activism by the inhabitants of Black Mesa is ongoing (Kelley and Francis 1994).

As growing awareness of disproportionate environmental harms and demand for changes coincide with the closure of the Navajo Generation Station, now may be the time that the Navajo Nation reassesses the benefits of the current framework of energy politics (Powell 2018). By implementing a renewable energy project in a manner consistent with tribal history, culture, and values, the Navajo Nation could exercise its tribal sovereignty and self-determination while recovering from the economic loss inflicted by the closure of the Navajo Generating Station. The Navajo Nation is already taking some steps to do so, with a solar energy project in Kayenta (Navajo Tribal Utility Authority 2015). Income generated by a tribally owned renewable energy project could even contribute to funding water infrastructure projects, allowing the Navajo Nation to utilize its senior water rights.

Once the Navajo Generating Station was created, it perpetuated an environmentally racist paradigm, where all of the costs of a coal-fired power plant, including harm to the environment and human health, are borne by tribal communities, while the majority of benefits are exported to nontribal communities. For the Navajo Nation, the water–energy nexus drives this continued environmental injustice. Although demand for water and electricity in the Southwest are unlikely to dissipate, the development of its own renewable energy resources may enable the Navajo Nation to pursue economic development on its own terms, in a manner that both honors its cultural values and promotes environmental justice.

CONCLUSION

The United States is reliant on tribal natural resources to support its energy needs. The history of this relationship has largely been exploitative, with the benefits of energy production being exported to nontribal communities while the costs to environmental quality and human health are borne by tribal communities. For tribes like the Navajo Nation, achieving EJ means exercising tribal sovereignty over decisions concerning the use of natural resources on tribal lands.

The development of renewable energy sources is likely going to continue and become more widespread as prices become increasingly competitive with traditional energy sources. For the Navajo Nation, overcoming the cultural and financial barriers to implementing renewable energy projects in the wake of the closure of the Navajo Generating Station provides an opportunity for the tribe to protect its natural resources and communities, pursue carbon-free economic growth, and begin to recover from the damage inflicted by extractive industries and corporate energy production.

REFERENCES

Burton, Lloyd. 1991. *American Indian Water Rights and the Limits of Law.* Tucson: University of Arizona Press.

Cole, Luke W., and Sheila R. Foster. 2001. *From the Ground Up: Environmental Racism and the Rise of the Environmental Justice Movement.* New York: New York University Press.

Cowan, Emery. 2018. "Navajo Utility Proposes Solar Project Near Cameron." *Arizona Daily Sun.* July 21, 2018. https://azdailysun.com/news/local/navajo-utility-proposes -solar-project-near-cameron/article_361b8a26-0eb8-5619-b6bc-cd3407334bdb.html.

Cozzetto, K., K. Chief, K. Dittmer, M. Brubaker, R. Gough, K. Souza, F. Ettawageshik, S. Wotkyns, S. Optiz-Stapleton, S. Duren, and P. Chaven. 2013. "Climatic Change Impacts on the Water Resources of American Indians and Alaska Natives in the U.S." *Climate Change* 120 (3): 569–84. https://doi.org/10 .1007/s10584-013-0852-y.

DOI (U.S. Department of the Interior). 2012. *Executive Summary: The Colorado River Basin Study.* https://www.usbr.gov/lc/region/programs/crbstudy/finalreport/ Executive%20Summary/CRBS_Executive_Summary_FINAL.pdf.

Fischer, Howard. 2019. "Drought: Arizona Lawmaker Vows to Press on Despite Tribe's Threat." *Verde Independent.* February 16, 2019. https://www.verdenews .com/news/2019/feb/16/drought-arizona-lawmaker-vows-press-despite-tribes/.

Fleck, John. 2013. "Judge Approves Navajo Water Rights Settlement." *Albuquerque Journal* August 16, 2013. https://www.abqjournal.com/248780/judge-approves -navajo-water-rights-settlement.html.

Gerke, S. 2008. "Hopi Reservation." GRCA History. http://grcahistory.org/sites/ beyond-park-boundaries/hopi-reservation/.

Getches, David H., Charles F. Wilkinson, Robert A. Williams Jr., and Matthew I. M. Fletcher. 2011. *Cases and Materials on Federal Indian Law.* 6th ed. Eagan, Minn.: West.

Glennon, Robert Jerome. 1995. Coattails of the Past: Using and Financing the Central Arizona Project. *Arizona State Law Journal* 27:677–756.

Goffman, Ethan. 2016. "Surrounded by Coal Plants, Navajo Nation Fights for a Clean Future." Earth Law Center. January 3, 2016. https://www.earthlawcenter

.org/newsfeed/2017/1/surrounded-by-coal-plants-navajo-nation-fights-for-a
-clean-future.

Grijalva, James M. 2008. *Closing the Circle: Environmental Justice in Indian Country*. Durham, N.C.: Carolina Academic Press.

Hiza-Reedsteer, Margaret, Rian C. Bogle, and John M. Vogel. 2011. *Monitoring
and Analysis of Sand Dune Movement and Growth on the Navajo Nation, Southwestern United States*. United States Geological Survey. https://pubs.usgs.gov/
fs/2011/3085/fs2011-3085.pdf.

Hughes, Richard W. 1988. "Indian Law." *New Mexico Law Review* 18:403–66.

Indian Country Today. 2017. "Moapa Band a Front-Runner in Clean Energy: First
Utility-Scale Solar Plant on Tribal Land." March 20, 2017. https://newsmaven
.io/indiancountrytoday/archive/moapa-band-a-front-runner-in-clean-energy
-2wPGfMM9BoCaeE8aSxZYbw/.

Jones, Thomas, and Len Necefer. 2016. *Identifying Barriers and Pathways for Success
for Renewable Energy Development on American Indian Lands (Sandia Report)*.
Albuquerque, N.M.: Sandia National Laboratories.

Kelley, Klara B., and Harry Francis. 1994. *Navajo Sacred Places*. 1st ed. Blooming-
ton: Indiana University Press.

Kennedy, Merrit. 2016. "Hundreds of U.S. Businesses Urge Trump to Uphold
Paris Climate Deal." *National Public Radio*. November 17, 2016. http://www
.npr.org/sections/thetwoway/2016/11/17/502425711/hundreds-of-u-s-businesses
-urge-trump-to-uphold-paris-climate-deal.

Lehmann, Evan. 2009. "Pioneering Wind Farm Faces Another Delay, This Time
over Indian Sites." *New York Times*. October 5, 2009. http://www.nytimes.com/
cwire/2009/10/05/05climatewire-pioneering-wind-farm-faces-another-delay
-thi-73053.html?pagewanted=all.

McCool, Daniel. 1994. *Command of the Waters: Iron Triangles, Federal Water Development, and Indian Water*. Tucson: University of Arizona Press.

McCool, Daniel. 2006. *Native Waters: Contemporary Indian Water Settlements and
the Second Treaty Era*. Tucson: University of Arizona Press.

Minard, Anne. 2016. "Let the Water Flow! Navajo in Utah Closer to Water
Rights Settlement." *Indian Country Today*. July 26, 2016. https://newsmaven
.io/indiancountrytoday/archive/let-the-water-flow-navajo-in-utah-closer-to
-water-rights-settlement-F1d72tmNiUG-9Cosyp_-5A/.

Misbrener, Kelsey. 2018. "Department of Energy Funds $9 Million in Tribal
Energy Projects, Includes Solar." *Solar Power World*. August 15, 2018. https://
www.solarpowerworldonline.com/2018/08/department-of-energy-funds
-tribal-solar-energy/.

National Climate Assessment. 2018. *The National Climate Assessment: Southwest*.
https://nca2018.globalchange.gov/chapter/25/.

Navajo Nation. 2011. "History, Navajo Nation Government." http://www.navajo-nsn.gov/history.htm.

Navajo Tribal Utility Authority. 2015. "NTUA's Kayenta Solar Farm Project." Presentation to the Tribal Solar Working Group. Northern Arizona University. June 23 and 24, 2015.

Needham, Andrew. 2014. *Power Lines: Phoenix and the Making of the Modern Southwest.* Princeton: Princeton University Press.

Obama, Barack. 2017. "The Irreversible Momentum of Clean Energy." *Science.* January 9, 2017.https://science.sciencemag.org/content/355/6321/126.

Oceti Sakowin Power Authority. n.d. "The Oceti Sakowin Power Project." Accessed February 2, 2019. http://ospower.org/the-project/.

Osborn, Rachael P. 2013. "Native American Winters Doctrine and Stevens Treaty Water Rights: Recognition, Quantification, Management." *American Indian Law Journal* 2 (1): 76–113.

Pasqualetti, Martin J., Thomas E. Jones, Len Necefer, Christopher A. Scott, and Benedict Colombi. 2016. "A Paradox of Plenty: Renewable Energy on Navajo Nation Lands." *Society and Natural Resources* 29 (8): 1–15. doi.org/10.1080/08941920.2015.1107794.

Powell, Dana E. 2018. *Landscapes of Power: Politics of Energy in the Navajo Nation.* Durham, N.C.: Duke University Press.

Randazzo, Ryan. 2017. "Navajo Generating Station's Power Lines Could Benefit Solar and Wind Development, Energy Experts Say." *Arizona Republic.* April 26, 2017. http://www.azcentral.com/story/money/business/energy/2017/04/26/navajo-generating-stations-power-lines-could-benefit-solar-and-wind-development-energy-experts-say/100861896/.

Rechtschaffen, Clifford, Eileen Gauna, and Catherine A. O'Neill. 2009. *Environmental Justice: Law, Policy, and Regulation.* 2nd ed. Durham, N.C.: Carolina Academic Press.

Roffman, S. 2012. "The Navajo-Hopi Water Rights Settlement Act of 2012." *Green Fire Times.* July 31, 2012. http://greenfiretimes.com/2012/08/the-navajo-hopi-water-rights-settlement-act-of-2012/#.Uqol5mRDt9U.

Ross, Anne E. 2013. "Water Rights: Aboriginal Water Use and Water Law in the Southwestern United States: Why the Reserved Rights Doctrine Was Inappropriate." *American Indian Law Review* 9 (1): 195–209.

Rowe, Claudia. 2013. "Coal Mining on Navajo Nation in Arizona Takes Heavy Toll." *Huffington Post.* June 6, 2013. http://www.huffingtonpost.com/2013/06/06/coal-mining-navajo-nation_n_3397118.html.

Scott, C. A., S. A. Pierce, M. J. Pasqualetti, A. L. Jones, B. E. Montz, and J. H. Hoover. 2011. "Policy and Institutional Dimensions of the Water–Energy Nexus." *Energy Policy* 39 (10): 6622–30. https://doi.org/10.1016/J.ENPOL.2011.08.013.

Seelye, Katharine Q. 2017. "After 16 Years, Hopes for Cape Cod Wind Farm Float Away." *New York Times*. December 19, 2017. https://www.nytimes.com/2017/12/19/us/offshore-cape-wind-farm.html.

Shabaud, Rebecca. 2017. "Trump Pulls Out of Climate Deal." *CBS News*. December 31, 2017. https://www.cbsnews.com/news/trump-paris-agreement-withdraws-announcement/.

Sherry, John W. 2002. *Land, Wind, and Hard Words: A Story of Navajo Activism.* Albuquerque: University of New Mexico Press.

Stein, Jay F. 1988. "The McCarran Amendment and the Administration of Tribal Reserved Water Rights." Santa Fe, N.M.: Simms and Stein.

Sullivan, Bethany C. 2010. "Changing Winds: Reconfiguring the Legal Framework for Renewable-Energy Development in Indian Country." *Arizona Law Review* 52:823–52.

Thompson, Barton H., Jr., John D. Leshy, and Robert H. Abrams. 2013. *Legal Control of Water Resources.* 5th ed. Eagan, Minn.: West.

Thompson, Jonathan. 2017. "The West's Coal Giant Is Going Down." *High Country News*. February 14, 2017. https://www.hcn.org/articles/the-wests-coal-giant-is-going-down.

Tsosie, Rebecca. 2007. "Indigenous People and Environmental Justice: The Impact of Climate Change." *University of Colorado Law Review* 78:1625–77.

Warner, Elizabeth K. W. 2017. "Environmental Justice: A Necessary Lens to Effectively View Environmental Threats to Indigenous Survival." *Transnational Law and Contemporary Problems* 26:343–69.

White Hawk, Racheal M. 2016. "Community-Scale Solar: Watt's in It for Indian Country?" *Environs Environmental Law and Policy Journal* 40:1–37.

Yale Law Review. 1979. "Indian Reserved Water Rights: The Winters of Our Discontent." *Yale Law Journal* 88:1689–712.

LEGAL RESOURCES

Arizona House Bill 2476 (Surface water forfeiture; repeal) (2019)

California Public Utilities Code § 454.53

Doctrine of Discovery

Energy Policy Act. Title XXVI, 42 U.S.C. §§ 16001, 7144e, and 25 U.S.C. §§ 3501–3506 (2005)

Indian Tribal Energy Development and Self-Determination Act. Public Law 115–325 (2005)

Johnson v. M'Intosh. 21 U.S. 543–605 (1823)

McCarren Amendment. 43 U.S.C. § 666 (1952)

National Environmental Protection Act. 83 Stat. 852 (1969)

National Historic Preservation Act. 54 U.S.C. 300101 et seq (1966)

Navajo Treaty (1868)

Navajo-Hopi Little Colorado River Water Rights Settlement Act. S. 2109, 112th Cong. (2012)

Paris Climate Accord (2016)

Prior Appropriations Doctrine

Public Employees for Environmental Responsibility v. Beaudreau. 25 F. Supp. 3d 67–130 D.D.C. (2014)

Quechan Tribe of Fort Yuma Indian Reservation v. U.S. Dept. of Interior. 755 F. Supp. 2d 1104–1122 S.D. Cal. (2010)

State of Arizona v. State of California. 373 U.S. 546–646 (1963)

UN Declaration on the Rights of Indigenous Peoples (2007)

Winters v. United States. 207 U.S. 564–577 (1908)

7

NOT IN OUR LANDS

A Canadian Comparative Case Study of Indigenous
Resistance Strategies to Natural Resource Development
in British Columbia and the Arctic

T. TIMOTHY CASEY

To study politics, at this date, is to study strategy.
—CHALOUPKA, 2003

HISTORICALLY, ENVIRONMENTAL advocacy has often been driven by a concern for broad theories applied to specific environmental issues rather than the seemingly more mundane aspects of political strategizing; however, such strategizing is a necessary component of the transformation from theory into concrete action (Magnusson 2003). There seems to be a rift in environmental advocacy between theory and tactics. The First Nations peoples of Canada are facing a similar challenge. At the level of theory, most environmentalists and the First Nations agree that preserving "nature" is the driving force behind their campaigns, whether in the coastal forests of British Columbia or the Arctic plains of the far north. While the theory might unite them in their advocacy, often they diverge on what tactics are best utilized to achieve their "lofty" objectives (Chaloupka 2003). The study of tactics and strategy is essential for the achievement of these goals. As such, it is important to consider not only the goals of Indigenous rights and ecological advocacy but the strategies for obtaining these goals.

In the case of British Columbia (B.C.), Native people have been a vital part of the resistance to developing timber resources in the fragile

Great Bear Rainforest along the Pacific coast, as well as the efforts to resist the development of the Enbridge Northern Pipeline project across B.C. and the development of natural resources in the area known as the Sacred Headwaters. Strategies and tactics used by the First Nations of B.C. have been remarkably successful in their fight for environmental justice (EJ). The threats to the Canadian Arctic and the First Nations living there have come from a much larger scale due to global climate change and its magnified effects in the region. These changes in the Arctic environment, especially massive sea ice loss, have created an opportunity for new access to the development of natural resources and tourism in the area. As such, Native peoples have had to deploy different strategies of resistance aimed at consolidating their voice and power through international forums and semi-autonomous modes of sovereignty over the area. These cases make clear that different settings and threats require different approaches to resistance and environmental advocacy in order to be effective. A careful study of the strategies and tactics used by First Nations in B.C. and the Canadian Arctic to resist natural resource development on their traditional homelands will offer insight into the ways other Indigenous Peoples might use their position to advocate for Indigenous and environmental justice.

Strategic thinking in the political realm involves utilizing the tools and options you have available to you (Chaloupka 2003). This type of strategy is impossible if one remains at a theoretical level. Every situation is different, and the successful resource development resistance or environmental advocacy movement must artistically combine all of the available resources to develop a compelling narrative, a broad coalition network, a favorable framing of the issue, and raise issue salience so that their "story" is adopted as the dominant understanding of the issue placed high on the public agenda. To do so, they must first understand the multifaceted dimensions of their situation and exploit fissures in the dominant resource consumptive paradigm.

Fundamentally, there are two approaches available to advocates for EJ. They can either try to control the story (discourse), or control the landscape (sovereignty); ideally they would try to have an effect on both. Controlling the story entails having an impact on shaping what gets discussed in policy circles and how it discussed. At a minimum, Indigenous Peoples push to ensure that their perspective is heard in policy conversations about natural resource development in their traditional homelands. They are most effective when their perspective is heard and when it shapes the conversation. The discourse surrounding any issue shapes what is perceived as possible in terms of policy action. One can see the Great Bear Rainforest as either an economic opportunity full of millions of board feet of timber or as a living landscape essential to support the flora and fauna that live there, including the people who have developed a relationship with that landscape that is integral to their very identity. Depending on which of these discourses prevails, one can imagine very different policy outcomes for the same "objective" reality of the rainforest in B.C. While this dichotomy oversimplifies the discourse and choices available in this case study, it should illustrate the importance of controlling the discourse. In order to control the landscape, a group must exercise some legal authority over a given territorial space or landscape. At a minimum this would include the right to be consulted on policies that affect a specific landscape where one has some claim to rights related to the space; but the legal right to actually make the policy decisions about a specific landscape is at the heart of the concept of sovereignty.

In each of these cases (B.C. and the Arctic), the Canadian First Nations have successfully employed both of these approaches, controlling part of the story and the landscape. Because they cannot control either completely, the combination has been necessary to leverage their symbolic and legal position into effective resistance to the natural resource development efforts in their homelands. Either approach on its own would be unlikely to achieve the same outcome. These Canadian case studies of resistance by First Nations and Inuit people to resource development on their traditional homelands will enhance our understanding of how Indigenous people can protect their land, rights, and identity through a strategic use of the discursive and legal context available to them.

THE CASES: BRITISH COLUMBIA AND THE ARCTIC

The Canadian province of British Columbia is the traditional homeland of 203 First Nations, which accounts for about one-third of all First Nations in Canada. The status of these First Nations in Canadian constitutional law is rather unique because the majority of B.C. First Nations never signed any treaties with the Canadian government ceding sovereignty to the national government (INAC 2017). As a result of this status, the First Nations of B.C. remain sovereign over their traditional homelands and reserve the right of consultation for any development of resources on those lands or in the coastal waters. While there are limitations to this sovereignty, it provides the First Nations with a strong voice on any matters that affect the landscape they have been connected to for millennia. The B.C. First Nations have effectively used their "nontreaty" status to advocate for EJ in a number of campaigns against timber, oil, and mineral resource development in recent years.

There are three recent or current campaigns against resource development in B.C. that are worth noting for what can be learned from the strategy and tactics employed on these campaigns. In the late 1990s, several First Nations of British Columbia, borrowing on successful tactics earlier developed in the Clayoquot Sound campaign, formed a coalition with Greenpeace and other environmental advocacy groups to successfully block timber production in the boreal rainforest along the Pacific coast. Their success can be contributed to certain tactics, including physically occupying the landscape and controlling the discourse. Tactics have included the appeal to a charismatic megafauna (CMF) that are found only in that particular B.C. zone. "Charismatic megafauna" is a term used to describe large wildlife, generally mammals or birds, that have a particular appeal to humans, such as the Kermode bear, known as the spirit bear and found in the B.C. rain forest, and B.C. salmon, or the caribou and polar bear in the Arctic. Once again, the dual approach of controlling the story and the landscape proved a winning tactical combination to protect an area of B.C. larger than many nation-states. On February 6, 2006, the B.C. government announced they had developed a plan to implement a landmark agreement that had been reached five years earlier with environmentalists, the timber industry, several First Nation tribes, and other interested actors, to preserve nearly five million acres of land on the province's central coast to be known as the "Great Bear Rainforest" (British Columbia Office of the Premier 2006).

In the last ten years, new threats to Indigenous homelands have emerged and continue to emerge from a globally powerful oil market. Geographically, B.C. is located next to the province of Alberta, which has recently experienced an unprecedented oil boom from the development of oil (tar) sands in and around the northern town of Fort McMurray, although as global oil prices have declined the boom has temporarily slowed down. Alberta is clearly Canada's largest producer of oil and natural gas, accounting for 70 percent of the Canadian total production of these resources. It has the largest oil sands deposits in the world, thought to rival Saudi Arabia in total reserves with a potential of as much as 315 billion barrels of conventional oil from the deposits (Brownsey 2005). The problem for Alberta is transporting all of this oil to a global market. A variety of proposed pipelines would transit the oil across Indigenous homelands in B.C., destined for a larger global market.

Recognizing the strength in unity, the First Nations declared their opposition to these efforts through the Save the Frasier Declaration in 2010 that was signed by seventy First Nations initially (that number has now grown to over one hundred). Through the Frasier Declaration, the B.C. First Nations claim sovereignty over the Fraser River watershed and the headwaters area of the Skeena, Naas, and Stikine Rivers, long considered sacred by local Indigenous populations.

The final campaign of note is also an effort to save the Sacred Headwaters region of B.C., this time from mining efforts around the headwaters of these three major rivers. The recent effort, started by the Tahltan First Nation near Iskut, B.C., is aimed at resisting the efforts by Fortune Minerals to open a large open-pit anthracite coal mine in the region. The Indigenous resistance operating under the name of the Klabona Keepers has employed a variety of previously successful tactics, such as occupying the roadways, networking with other groups, and operating an international media campaign (Sacred Headwaters 2017). As of 2018 it is still too early to gauge their success; but they have learned from and adopted tactics from previously successful Indigenous resistance campaigns in the province, which could act as a model for future Indigenous resistance for EJ around the world.

The Arctic is another site of resistance. It has been a homeland for the Inuit, the Saami, and others who have called this area their land for millennia. Far from being an isolated and ice-filled wasteland, it was a delicate ecosystem in which they used traditional knowledge to survive and thrive through hunting and gathering in an interactive relationship with the frozen landscape. They developed cultures uniquely situated to the landscape of land, sea, and ice, and cultures protected in their isolation from the rest of the world by the ice and distance (Loukacheva 2009). Significant changes in technology and in the planetary climate are rapidly transforming these relationships to the Arctic region in the last half century. Rapid technological change made it possible not only to enhance transportation (icebreakers and large cargo and cruise ships, as well as military vessels) but to map resources (oil and gas deposits and the seabed), extract those resources (offshore drilling rigs and modern pipeline construction, as well as mining technologies), and survive in the harsh climate (clothing, snowmobiles, and building structure). The global demand for the resources found in large supply in the Arctic, such as oil, gas, and minerals (zinc, nickel, palladium, gold, copper, iron ore, etc.), as well as fishing resources, has grown significantly in recent decades. Combined with the scarcity of these resources in other parts of the world-system due to overproduction and resource collapse, this demand is a significant driver in the growing interest in the region and efforts to settle sovereignty disputes over the rights to those resources (Brigham 2010).

There is a great deal of controversy regarding the discourse of sovereignty as it is applied to the Arctic waters and lands surrounding the Arctic Ocean. First Nations groups and the Inuit themselves are trying to offer a counterdiscourse that will recast the question of sovereignty claims by the Government of Canada and other groups (Weber and Shields 2011). Officially, the Arctic and Nunavut policy is driven by the overall values and principles embodied in Canada's "Northern Strategy," which includes an emphasis on devolution of power to the Indigenous populations. The landmark 1993 Nunavut Land Claims Agreement (NLCA) was highlighted as a model for future devolution of power to Indigenous people of the region. That agreement allows Inuit people to control much of the domestic agenda in the province but left foreign policy (including policy in the Arctic, which becomes foreign policy by virtue of the international activities in waters off the coast) to the federal government in Ottawa. In exchange, Ottawa gained Aboriginal title to the North that it uses to prove long-term occupancy necessary to make sovereignty claims in the region (Loukacheva 2009). The NLCA specifically mentions that "Canada's sovereignty over waters of the Arctic archipelago is supported by Inuit use and occupancy" (Byers 2009, 112). It is noteworthy that Canada's Northern Strategy addresses the Indigenous population so prominently in its four priorities, as this differs significantly from the

Arctic policies of the other littoral states and the European Union policy on the Arctic (Heinenen and Nicol 2007). While these others all mention the Indigenous populations, they do not prioritize them in the same way.

Canada has been critiqued for using the Inuit when it serves their purpose and ignoring them in the "high politics" of international relations and human rights concerns (Hohmann 2009). Nevertheless, a unique opportunity exists for Inuit Indigenous resistance to natural resource development through participation in the adjudication process built into the agreement.

STRATEGIES: CONTROL THE STORY (DISCOURSE)

The discourse surrounding an issue is the way a community talks about the issue based primarily in the language used to describe it, which, in turn, shapes the reality of the issue as we perceive and understand it. Discourse consists of linguistic shortcuts—such as metaphors, analogies, narratives, symbolic speech, and even visual references—that help us to organize the information we receive. These shortcuts help us to determine what is intelligible about a phenomenon as they connect that phenomenon to ideas and images we already have. A specific discourse shapes what we can conceptualize as a policy response to the phenomenon. Some policies seem believable; others do not. Any discourse surrounding an issue is subject to change, so strategically if one wants to affect policies surrounding an issue, one would do well to control some or all of the discourse around that issue. For First Nations on the frontlines of resistance to resource development in their traditional homelands and resistance to environmental injustice, controlling the story around those landscapes, or at least influencing it, has been essential to their strategy of resistance. Such an approach has proven effective in achieving their goal to halt or alter the resource development. One can have an influence on the discourse by achieving a variety of goals, such as increasing the salience (or importance) of the issue to different audiences, participating in the framing or reframing of the issue from a different perspective, and offering compelling storylines or narratives that people can relate to and support. If the story is believable, important, and properly framed, the public will demand policy action. Once the goals of controlling the story (discourse) are understood in the context of these case studies, we can turn our attention to the tactics employed by Canadian First Nations to realize these goals.

We owe a debt of gratitude to the field of public policy for elaborating on the process by which an idea is transformed into policy action. According to these practitioners, the key to successful policy advocacy lies in the process of agenda setting (Kingdon 1984). According to this theory, there are many possible issues that a government must consider at any given time. The success of any issue at becoming policy starts with obtaining a place on the official agenda. This can be accomplished in a variety of ways. Some issues are of such large impact or have consequences on such a wide variety of actors in the system that they "naturally" receive a "place at the table." National security issues and domestic issues such as health care come readily to mind in this regard. Other issues require "policy entrepreneurs" to steer the issues to the top of the agenda. These entrepreneurs can achieve this by broadening the issue to encompass more constituencies, engaging in mass campaigns to inform the public of a problem, or changing the way in which the issue is perceived or "framed" (Pralle 2006). Environmental issues have the potential to affect large constituencies and draw the public into the problem, but they are less obvious in their impact on the population. Indigenous issues seem to affect smaller numbers of people, although their goals would have a positive effect on a much larger population, human and others; thus the role of policy entrepreneurs and transnational advocacy networks is heightened in environmental issues (Keck and Sikkink 1998).

Ultimately, whether an issue becomes part of the political agenda or not relies on the importance of the issue to those who influence the decision-makers. This phenomenon is referred to as an issue's salience, which indicates how broadly and deeply the public cares about the issue— that is, whether it is enough to demand action. Issue salience is affected by a variety of factors, including the pervasiveness of the issue, the size and commitment of its advocacy networks, the timing of the issue relative to other issues, the proximity of issues to the public, and the latency time-line between cause and effect in the issue area. Issues with short latency periods, such as crime or war, enjoy a high degree of salience, whereas issues with a long latency period between cause and effect, such as climate change and deforestation, often suffer from a low degree of issue salience. The public might care about environmental issues, but they do not see them to be as pressing as other issues on the political agenda. Similarly, if the issue advocacy network is limited in size, as is the case with organized environmental advocacy in Canada, even a vital issue can suffer from low salience due to the inability to convince the public of its importance (McKenzie 2002). The good news for environmental advocates is that this challenge of issue salience, like all political problems, is dynamic and subject to change, given a "winning" strategy to increase issue salience.

A related issue to agenda setting entails how the issue is framed—that is, how the public and major actors perceive the nature of the issue. Indigenous environmental advocates often perceive their issues in radically different ways from the general population, thus there is a need to develop strategies for changing the way the issue is framed. This can be done in a variety of ways, and the creativity of issue framing is an ongoing dynamic process in most environmental issues (Magnusson and Shaw 2003). Often an issue such as habitat preservation must rely on a variety of strategies, such as the use of simulacra and differentiated value systems, to change the way in which the issue is framed (Sandilands 2003). If Indigenous and environmental advocates can successfully change the issue framing, they will open up the possibility of different actions and the incorporation of previously marginalized groups. These new groups and alternative actions can dramatically change the process of policy formation, leading to more environmentally acceptable outcomes. This type of strategy, for example, led to a transformation of the logging of old-growth forests in the Clayoquot Sound region of B.C. in the 1990s (Shaw 2003).

One of the ways to ensure that an issue is placed on the public agenda is to "tell a good story." Narratives move an issue from abstraction to appeal and thus increase the likelihood of its place on the political agenda (Schram and Neisser 1997). A narrative needs characters that the public can identify and empathize with. The greater the public sympathy for the characters of an issue narrative, the more likely they are to insist that the issue be placed on the public agenda. While this is not a new insight for marketers of film and literature, it is often overlooked by policy advocates.

To achieve these goals of agenda setting, issue framing, and narrative telling, the First Nations engaged in a variety of strategies and tactics during their resistance campaigns. These approaches were successful at changing the discourse by impacting what we pay attention to through their proclamations and direct actions, such as roadblocks and hunger strikes, to raise awareness of the issues. The First Nations influenced what we know by offering their traditional knowledges of the areas that have been developed over generations of relationship with the landscape and its inhabitants. This is an especially effective tactic in Canada, where First Nations have a protected status regarding consultation. In 2004 the Supreme Court of Canada ruled in *Haida Nation v British Columbia* that whenever actions of a government might infringe on Aboriginal rights and claims, the government has an obligation to consult with Aboriginal peoples (Gregory, Failing, and Harstone 2008). The First Nations also affect who is involved in the issue by drawing an ever-increasing coalition of domestic and international partners in their resistance to resource development, often creating pressure on the timber and oil companies that they might not have otherwise had if they didn't nurture these coalitions. The Indigenous Peoples were able to shape how others think about the story by offering compelling narratives with characters (human and animal) that engaged the larger audiences through an emotional connection. This was particularly true when they wove that narrative around charismatic megafauna. Finally, they were able to control the spaces that the discourse takes place in through the use of websites, social media, and other alternative venues for adjudicating their concerns. These new forms of communication are particularly effective nodes of power that shape public perceptions in a profound way (Castells 2013).

Because of their long-standing and symbolic connection to the landscape as well as their traditional ecological knowledges, First Nations are in a unique position to speak truth to power through formal statements such as the Save the Frasier Declaration that was signed in 2012 by 130 First Nations in order to prohibit tar sands exports across Indigenous lands. The declaration "bans tar sands pipelines and tankers, as a matter of indigenous law, from First Nation territories forming an unbroken chain from the US border to the Arctic Ocean and spanning the entire length of B.C. from north to south" (Rabble Staff 2012). Proclamations are an important part of the Inuit strategy in the Arctic case as evidenced by the statements of the Inuit Circumpolar Council (ICC) regarding resource development in the Arctic and the ICC-Canada Statement to Crown Partnership Declaration that specifically identifies the unique role of Indigenous voices in the management of the Arctic. "The Arctic Council remains the most important venue for Inuit and for Canada in ensuring Inuit voices are heard and the Arctic issues and policy decisions are evidenced based and built on both indigenous and scientific knowledge" (Nakimayak 2017). Part of the nature of sovereignty is that people can speak with their own voice and authority on matters that are relevant to them. Clearly these declarations are an act of sovereign discourse by the First Nations and Inuit to reclaim their story for the landscape.

Even though proclamations are an important part of shaping and controlling the discourse, they may not be enough on their own to bring about the desired change. Sometimes people must put their bodies on the line through the use of direct actions such as blocks, rallies, and hunger strikes in order to push an issue onto the public policy agenda. This symbolic speech has been an effective tool in Indigenous resistance movements to resource exploitation and other issues of concern to Native Peoples in Canada. For example, after the Harper government voted in the United Nations against the Declaration on the Rights of Indigenous People (Wilson 2013), Chief Teresa Spense, in 2013, engaged in a hunger strike until Prime Minister Stephen Harper agreed to meet with the leaders of the First Nations to discuss Aboriginal rights, including the passage of omnibus bill C-45 that disregarded such rights. The number of witnesses to her hunger strike were magnified through the use of social media with the birth of the #IdleNoMore movement. While this example started as a protest of official public policy regarding Indigenous rights, the #IdleNoMore movement has since joined forces with the First Nations resistance movements in B.C., the Arctic, and across Canada to act as a magnifier of the voices of the Indigenous standing up for EJ. Other efforts to resist resource development on traditional homelands include rallies such as the annual Tar Sands Healing Walk in Alberta. In August 2012 more than 250 participants, including First Nations people from all over Canada and concerned citizens from the United Kingdom and the United States, walked in solidarity with victims of public health damage from the tar sands project (Wong 2012). These direct action tactics were used in the B.C. case of resistance to pipeline development when Grand Chief Stewart Phillip of the Union of B.C. Indian Chiefs indicated that they were willing to use all tactics, including "linking arms" on the front lines, to block the Enbridge pipeline project in B.C. (Rabble Staff 2012). As another example, road blocks are being used by the Klabona Keepers in their resistance efforts to stop Fortune Mining Company from developing resources in the Sacred Headwaters region (Sacred Headwaters 2017).

The direct action strategy has not been employed often in the Arctic case study. This is likely due to the remote environment in which it is difficult to develop the visual press coverage needed to enhance such efforts. The old adage, "If the tree falls in the forest, and no one hears it, does it make a sound?" could be modified here to ask, "If an Inuit protests above the Arctic Circle and no one sees it, is it an effective protest?" Direct actions are often most effective when they are employed as part of an overall strategy that also includes partnering with other groups who share the concern for EJ both at home and abroad.

The literature on social movements stresses the need for successful coalition building when forming advocacy networks (Keck and Sikkink 1998). The environmental movement is often critiqued for remaining too parochial in its advocacy. Members simply preach to the choir of other environmentalists and miss the opportunities to broaden the issue by incorporating other groups who share similar goals, such as First Nations groups, minorities disproportionately affected by environmental destruction, natural resource workers, and international consumers of natural resources (Shellenberger and Nordhaus 2004). To be successful, environmental advocates must actively engage in coalition building with "unlikely" allies in order to get their issue on the political agenda (Pralle 2006). Successful coalition-building strategies often depend on seeking common ground between these groups and changing the way the issue is framed to allow participation by groups who previously thought the issue was not their concern. Often the salience of an issue and the chance of it being placed on the public agenda are directly related to the size and the commitment of these advocacy networks. This is especially true if the advocates run into initial resistance at the local decision-making level and thus broaden their coalition to the national or international level (Keck and Sikkink 1998). An example of this successful broadening of a coalition from the local environmentalists to the international community can be seen in the strategy employed by advocates in the Great Bear Rainforest Campaign in B.C. In recent campaigns the First Nations have been effectively using new social media networks to create a transnational issue network on Indigenous rights and land protection (Carleton 2012).

While the transnational issue advocacy networks have been an important element in this discursive campaign of resistance, they cannot replace the importance of First Nations standing united in their efforts to resist resource development in their traditional homelands. One of the first actions of these timber and pipeline resistance campaigns was to unite the First Nations of B.C. to address environmental negotiations. Eighty percent of First Nations in British Columbia joined the coalition to stop the Enbridge-Gateway Northern pipeline project (Sterritt 2012). The ICC is an effort to magnify the voice of Indigenous people in the Arctic through a show of unity that crosses international boundaries.

While a similar worldview and connection to a common landscape have been helpful in developing these Indigenous coalitions of resistance, it is often difficult to develop as strong a bond across cultural divides. Clash of discourses among coalition partners in the Great Bear Rainforest coalition is documented in an article by Lynne Davis (2011), where she goes on to describe the "ecological Indian" problem that haunts the relationship between environmentalists and First Nations that might share a similar end desire, but motivations and understanding of the value of the end result differ dramatically in this potentially unstable coalition (Davis 2011). Differences arise particularly in conceptualizations of nature, the value of development, and other ontological matters; however, both sides have strong reasons to stay in these coalitions despite the cultural differences that give rise to coalition tension. "It is also increasingly difficult, if not impossible, for environmentalists to pursue campaigns focused on resource use or management without the support of affected First Nations" (Low and Shaw 2011, 14). These coalitions can also include other partners beyond First Nations and environmentalists. Sometimes they can successfully partner with businesses, as evidenced in the broad coalition to protect the Great Bear Rainforest (Sterritt 2012).

There are perhaps no more than a few hundred spirit bears in the entire world, and all of them inhabit the area known as the Great Bear Rainforest along the west coast of B.C. (Russell 1994). The rareness of the spirit bear lends itself to appeal as a charismatic megafauna (CMF) for the region. This attraction has been quantified and substantiated in such survey instruments as the Wildlife Attitudes and Values Survey developed by researchers at Cornell University (Gray 1993). The ability of CMFs to raise the salience of an issue such as species protection has been clearly documented in the United States and Canada (Petersen 2002; McKenzie 2002). CMF are photogenic and create a nuanced emotional appeal. Images of the rare white spirit bear in the coastal B.C. rainforests or the polar bear personified in modern films such as *Arctic Tale* (Latifah 2007) provide the public an opportunity to be inspired to action in order to preserve such beauty and majesty. CMF seem to be ideal "spokes-species" for habitat preservation, and the modern media of film provides the venue for reaching a broader audience. This appeal is also enhanced due to the use of narrative regarding the spiritual quality of the bear in the First Nation stories of the region. The act of appropriation of this Native spirituality is itself not without colonizing implications (Rossiter 2004). Nevertheless, its unique role in the spirituality of the local First Nations helped to transform the spirit bear into a CMF superstar and was actively used to increase the issue salience of habitat preservation (Birch 2002). This appeal to First Nations spirituality drew in not only previously disinterested coalition partners around the world but also the First Nations themselves into the advocacy network. The concern for Aboriginal rights in the area became a central part of the policy discussion, and the First Nations representatives were a critical component of the agreement to establish the Great Bear Rainforest (British Columbia Office of the Premier 2006). With the support of the international community and their new First Nations partners, environmental advocates were able to change the terms of the debate and successfully negotiate protections in the area.

By reaching out to a larger global audience and forming coalitions across political jurisdictions, the B.C. First Nations were able to have their concerns received more favorably. Likewise, the Inuit First Nations in the Canadian Arctic realized that the threats to their ecosystem were beyond Canada's exclusive control, thus they engaged in larger venues, such as the ICC, the Arctic Council, and the UN. In these venues they were able to more effectively advocate against the threats to their homeland.

STRATEGIES: CONTROL THE LANDSCAPE (SOVEREIGNTY)

First Nations in Canada have a rather unique constitutional status and rights that suggest the possibility of a different strategy of resistance to natural resource development on their traditional homelands that is often not available to Indigenous Peoples in other countries. The Canadian Constitution and subsequent court cases have established certain group rights for the First Nations regarding any activity on their traditional homelands. They must, at a minimum be consulted in any proposed changes to their landscapes. These rights differ depending on whether the First Nation has signed a treaty with the Canadian government or not. Nontreaty peoples, the majority in B.C., have special status because they have not ceded their sovereign claim to their homelands. In 1867 when Canada became independent, B.C. did not recognize any Aboriginal rights, so the issue became a federal matter. Since 2005, B.C. has developed a consultation approach called "the New Relationship Agreement." A government-to-government forum was established to work out the shared responsibility of plan implementation. One of the ways the federal government has embraced this responsibility is through the creation of comanagement councils with the First Nations (Gregory, Failing, and Harstone 2008). These councils are an institutional means for First Nations to preserve and transmit their traditional knowledges regarding the landscape and thus preserve some measure of sovereignty over the areas most important to them.

Other Indigenous people in Canada, such as the Inuit in the Arctic, have gained more direct sovereignty over their homelands by the creation of a territory, Nunavut, which is almost entirely made up of Indigenous populations. They have a major role to play in the regional government. While the original acquisition of tribal lands did not go well for the Indigenous Peoples already inhabiting those places, recent government action and court rulings have established a right to consult for First Nations when anything impacts their traditional lands, such as resource development. Court cases that established Indigenous title to lands in B.C. include the 1967 *Calder* case, which stated there was Aboriginal title in British Columbia; the *Delgamuukw* case, which indicated what that title is; and the *Haida* Case, which established the right to consultation on those lands (Sterritt 2012). The Canadian Constitution, Article 39, and subsequent court cases established a Crown duty to consult in addition to other Crown responsibilities, such as fiduciary and treaty obligations (Sanderson, Bergner, and Jones 2012). Historically, Indigenous resistance movements have been helped by efforts such as the stonewalling of the

Meech Lake Accord in parliament by Cree Manitoba MLA (member of the Legislative Assembly) Elijah Harper. These efforts remind the Canadian federal government of their legal obligation to take seriously the concerns of the First Nations when taking action that affects their traditional homelands.

Canada's Indigenous population has utilized not only their domestic constitutional status but also their participation in international forums to advocate for EJ. One of the most important forums in this regard is their participation in the Arctic Council through the Inuit Circumpolar Conference and its formal consultative status in that intergovernmental organization. The Arctic Council is the international governing body in the Arctic region. It is made up of the five littoral states (United States, Canada, Russia, Denmark/Greenland, and Norway); they are joined by three other Arctic states (Sweden, Finland, and Iceland), as well as representation from six Indigenous groups, including the Inuit Circumpolar Council (Heinenen and Nicol 2007). In keeping with the international custom that only sovereign nation-states are given voting status in intergovernmental organizations, the Indigenous representatives are given observer status. It is worth noting that even granting such a status to the Indigenous populations makes the Arctic Council rather unique in the Westphalian international system that has been dominated by nation-states and sovereign government entities for 450 years. The Arctic Council largely coordinates research efforts in the Arctic at this point without any ability to enforce regulations; however, as a representative authoritative body, it is well-positioned to shape the agenda and frame the issues confronting the region.

CONCLUSION

Through their efforts to control the story (discourse) and the landscape (sovereignty), the First Nations of B.C. and the Arctic provide an excellent set of case studies to better understand the strategies and tactics available to those Indigenous populations who are on the front lines of the fight for EJ in their traditional homelands and around the world. In these cases the first stewards of the land have effectively offered resistance to natural resource development by speaking with an authority embedded in traditional knowledges and long-standing relationships with the landscape and all of its inhabitants. Although their legal status in Canada might be a unique tool available to these First Nations, other strategies such as agenda setting, issue framing, changing venues, transnational advocacy networks, coalition building, narrative devices (like the use of charismatic megafauna), and direct actions are available to Indigenous populations around the world who want to offer effective resistance to the threats they see to the landscapes they care for.

REFERENCES

Birch, Simon. 2002. "Saving a Spiritual Home: The Success of the Campaign to Save Canada's Great Bear Rainforest Is Being Heralded as a Model Solution for Conserving the World's Remaining Ancient Forests." *Geographical* 74 (4): 14–19.

Brigham, Lawson. 2010. "Think Again: The Arctic." *Foreign Policy* 181:70–74.

British Columbia Office of the Premier. 2006. "Backgrounder: Province Announces a New Vision for Coastal B.C." *Ministry of Agriculture and Lands.* February 7, 2006. https://archive.news.gov.bc.ca/releases/news releases 2005 -2009/2006AL0002-000066.htm.

Brownsey, Keith 2005. "Alberta's Oil and Gas Industry in the Era of the Kyoto Protocol." In *Canadian Energy Policy and the Struggle for Sustainable Development,* edited by G. B. Doern, 200–222. Toronto, Ont.: University of Toronto Press.

Byers, Michael. 2009. *Who Owns the Arctic? Understanding Sovereignty Disputes in the North.* Madeira Park, B.C.: Douglas and McIntyre.

Carleton, Sean. 2012. "Decolonizing in the Empire State: A View of #IdleNoMore Solidarity from Abroad." December 31, 2012. http://rabble.ca/news/2012/12/decolonizing-empire-state-view-idlenomore-solidarity-abroad.

Castells, Manuel. 2013. *Communication Power.* Oxford: Oxford University Press.

Chaloupka, William. 2003. "There Must Be Some Way Out of Here: Strategy, Ethics and Environmental Politics." In *A Political Space: Reading the Global through Clayoquot Sound,* edited by Warren Magnusson and Karena Shaw, 67–90. Minneapolis: University of Minnesota Press.

Davis, Lynne. 2011. "Home or Global Treasure?: Understanding Relationships between the Heiltsuk Nation and Environmentalists." *BC Studies* 171:9–36.

Gray, Gary G. 1993. *Wildlife and People: The Human Dimensions of Wildlife Ecology.* Chicago: University of Illinois Press.

Gregory, Robin, Lee Failing, and Michael Harstone. 2008. "Meaningful Resource Consultations with First Peoples: Notes from British Columbia." *Environment* 50 (1): 34–45.

Heinenen, Lassi, and Heather Nicol. 2007. "The Importance of Northern Dimension Foreign Policies in the Geopolitics of the Circumpolar North." *Geopolitics* 12:133–65.

Hohmann, Jessie. 2009. "Igloo as Icon: A Human Rights Approach to Climate Change for the Inuit." *Transnational Law and Contemporary Problems* 18 (2): 296–315.

INAC (Indigenous and Northern Affairs Canada). 2017. "About British Columbian First Nations." https://www.aadnc-aandc.gc.ca/eng/1100100021009/1314809450456.

Keck, Margaret E., and Kathryn Sikkink. 1998. *Activists Beyond Borders: Advocacy Networks in International Politics.* Ithaca, N.Y.: Cornell University Press.

Kingdon, John W. 1984. *Agendas, Alternatives, and Public Policies.* Boston, Mass.: Little, Brown.

Latifah, Queen. 2007. Performance in *Arctic Tale.* 2007. Directed by Adam Ravetch and Sarah Robertson. Paramount Pictures.

Loukacheva, Natalia. 2009. "Nunavut and Canadian Arctic Sovereignty." *Journal of Canadian Studies* 43 (2): 82–108.

Low, Margaret, and Karena Shaw. 2011. "First Nations Rights and Environmental Governance: Lessons from the Great Bear Rainforest." *BC Studies* 172:9–31.

Magnusson, Warren. 2003. "Introduction: The Puzzle of the Political." In *A Political Space: Reading the Global Through Clayoquot Sound,* edited by Warren Magnusson and Karena Shaw, 1–20. Minneapolis: University of Minnesota Press.

Magnusson, Warren, and Karena Shaw. 2003. *A Political Space: Reading the Global Through Clayoquot Sound.* Minneapolis: University of Minnesota Press.

McKenzie, Judith I. 2002. *Environmental Politics in Canada: Managing the Commons into the Twenty-First Century.* Toronto: Ont.: Oxford University Press.

Nakimayak, Herbert. 2017. "Inuit Circumpolar Council-Canada." February 9, 2017. https://www.inuitcircumpolar.com/press-releases/inuit-to-crown-partnership-declararion-herbert-nakimayak-vice-president/.

Petersen, Shannon. 2002. *Acting for Endangered Species: The Statutory Ark.* Lawrence: University Press of Kansas.

Pralle, Sarah B. 2006. *Branching Out, Digging In: Environmental Advocacy and Agenda Setting.* Washington, D.C.: Georgetown University Press.

Rabble Staff. 2012. "'Wall of Opposition' to Tar Sands Pipeline in B.C. Grows Stronger." December 14, 2012. http://rabble.ca/news/2012/12/wall-opposition-tar-sands-pipelines-bc-grows-stronger.

Rossiter, David. 2004. "The Nature of Protest: Constructing the Spaces of British Columbia's Rainforests." *Cultural Geographies* 11:139–64.

Russell, Charles. 1994. *Spirit Bear: Encounters with the White Bear of the Western Rainforest.* Toronto, Ont.: Key Porter Books.

Sacred Headwaters. 2017. *Sacred Headwaters Campaign*. www.sacredheadwaters .com.

Sanderson, Chris W., Keith Bergner, and Michelle Jones. 2012. "The Crown's Duty to Consult Aboriginal Peoples." *Alberta Law Review* 49 (4): 821–53.

Sandilands, Catriona. 2003. "Between the Local and the Global: Clayoquot Sound and Simulacral Politics." In *A Political Space: Reading the Global Through Clayoquot Sound*, edited by Warren Magnusson and Karena Shaw, 139–68. Minneapolis: University of Minnesota Press.

Schram, Sanford F., and Phillip T. Neisser. 1997. *Tales of the State: Narrative in Contemporary US Politics and Public Policy*. Lanham, MD: Rowman and Littlefield.

Shaw, Karena. 2003. "Encountering Clayoquot, Reading the Political." In *A Political Space: Reading the Global Through Clayoquot Sound*, edited by Warren Magnusson and Karena Shaw, 25–66. Minneapolis: University of Minnesota Press.

Shellenberger, Michael, and Ted Nordhaus. 2004. "The Death of Environmentalism: Global Warming Politics in a Post-Environmental World." http://grist .org/article/doe-reprint/.

Sterritt, Art. 2012. "Standing Up to Big Oil: How Coastal First Nations Built Tar Sands Pipeline Resistance." December 11, 2012. http://rabble.ca/news/ 2012/12/standing-big-oil-how-coastal-first-nations-built-tar-sands-pipeline -resistance.

Weber, Barret, and Rob Shields. 2011. "The Virtual North: On the Boundaries of Sovereignty." *Ethnic and Racial Studies* 34 (1): 103–20.

Wilson, Daniel. 2013. "Stephen Harper Prepares to Fail His Biggest Test as PM." January 9, 2013. http://rabble.ca/blogs/bloggers/daniel-wilson/2013/01/stephen -harper-prepares-fail-his-biggest-test-pm.

Wong, Rita. 2012. "Ethical Waters: Healing Walk in the Tar Sands Grows Year by Year." August 8, 2012. http://rabble.ca/news/2012/08/ethical-waters-healing -walk-tar-sands-grows-year-year.

LEGAL RESOURCES

Calder et al. v. Attorney General of British Columbia. S.C.R. 313 (1973)

Canadian Constitution, Article 39

Delgamuukw v. British Columbia. 3 S.C.R. 1010 (1997)

Haida Nation v. British Columbia (Minister of Forests). 3 S.C.R. 511 (2004)

Meech Lake Accord (1987)

Nunavut Land Claims Agreement (1993)

United Nations Declaration on the Rights of Indigenous People (2007)

8

URBAN NATIVE AMERICAN WOMEN AS ENVIRONMENTAL JUSTICE LEADERS

ANNE LUNA-GORDINIER

We can create a healing for the people that are here. Not just the Ohlone people but all people that exist on this land.
—CORRINA GOULD, FOUNDER OF INDIAN PEOPLE ORGANIZING FOR CHANGE

RESEARCH ON urban Indian communities offers insight into cultural transformation and continuance, gender and identity politics, and social action and resistance. This chapter addresses the rise of Native American women's environmental justice (EJ) leadership in urban areas and the role Native women play in generating and sustaining urban Indian community life. The chapter opens with examinations of patriarchy and decolonizing approaches to the subject. Next it addresses historical materialism and how it can be applied to Indigenous women's experiences. Finally, it presents an analysis of Native women's EJ leadership in urban centers.

Researchers of oppressed people tend to view social groups or identities as fixed units of analysis, which is problematic as groups experience multiple layers of identity. Although speaking of Native American women as a monolithic group may be convenient, it is deeply problematic. As Seidman (1993, 134) argues, "Identity is a site of on-going social regulation and contestation rather than a quasi-natural substance or an accomplished social fact." Native women experience and embody many intersecting constructions involving identity and the self. Researchers have noted that groups are internally differentiated, yet it is difficult to utilize such differentiations within research design and implementation. That is, "we need to know more about how these different aspects of identities work, separately and together as well as in relation to particular contexts" (Orellano and Bowman 2003, 26).

In the United States, urbanization has affected everyone, but the experience of Native peoples has been one of forced and induced urban migration through the Indian Relocation Acts (Fixico 2000). American Indians, like other ethnic groups, found ways to fit into urban areas while maintaining their cultures. Urban Indian centers contribute to the organization of communities, cultural activities, and pan-Indian identity. This urban experience and pan-Indian movement has enhanced Native women's leadership.

THE IMPORTANCE OF PLACE

There is no established definition of the American Indian population. While official tribal membership criteria is determined by individual tribal governments, people have the right to self-identify as Native American for the purpose of the United States Census and other large surveys (Rindfuss, Sandefur, and Cohen 1997). Since American Indian identity has no concrete definition, researchers who collect data that represents the group as a whole (or of subpopulations) usually establish an operational definition of their own.

Lobo (1998) notes that urban Indian identity often revolves around cultural activities connected with an Indian center rather than a particular neighborhood. Regarding tribal homelands, a major source of identity is rooted in the land as articulated by songs and stories connecting personal reality to time and space, while in urban Indian communities, the main land base is associated with community organization buildings. Given that Indigenous Peoples are scattered through cities, resulting in a lack of geographic concentration, urban Indian populations are often invisible to the general public. Although the majority of Natives live in urban areas, this does not separate them from their homelands. Even third- and fourth-generation urban people maintain a feeling of connection to their land of origin.

Urban communities are structured differently from tribes, but share many similarities. Urban community centers lend a sense of belonging along with a social obligation to contribute to the well-being of members. The "urban tribe" also offers an opportunity for those who have been adopted out as children to reestablish their Indianness in adulthood (Lobo 1998, 96). These communities continue to grow and become increasingly diverse and complex as a proliferation of organizations serve a multigenerational and multitribal community. This links the urban community to geographically distant places and people with not only increased economic and class diversity but an urban history that creates a framework for modern Native identity.

Urban Indigenous communities have different criteria for membership from that of tribes. There are no traditional roles like there are on reservations; instead, identity is fluid and promotes a shared understanding of participation and informal consensus. Aspects defining urban Native identity include ancestry, appearance, cultural elements, and community participation. Native women who fill leadership roles in urban programs and cultural activities are thus able to find a sense of place and belonging that ties them to the urban Indian community.

NATIVE AMERICAN WOMEN, COLONIALISM, AND FEMINISM

Issues of class, ethnicity, regional location, and light-skin privilege affect the realities of all women of color in America. Making blanket statements about Native American women has the potential to whitewash the experiences of these women. A theoretical approach to the study of these peoples can help to ground a researcher's perspective. It should be understood, however, that Native American theoretical approaches to the study of women and gender issues vary greatly.

Although there are multiple epistemologies and perspectives within feminism, Stephanie A. Sellers recommends "moving from a western theoretical and terminological approach and practices in Women's Studies to a Native one" (2008, 50). This is because most Native women are not simply fighting to end oppression for themselves but also for their families and communities. "They do not fight for women's rights, but for communal rights, and community means Mother Earth and all her creatures" (54). Indigenous societies are based on gender complementarity, not on gender conflict. Gender conflict is a facet of western culture, so it is only logical to use feminist theory within that context (Luna-Gordinier 2014).

Some Native American women scholars argue that women of color should take responsibility for fighting the pervasive racism in the women's movement; it should not be left to white women to address the problem. Lee Maracle (1996, 137) argues: "White women of North America are racist and that they define the movement in accordance with their own narrow perspective should not surprise us. White people define everything in terms of their own people, and then very magnanimously open the door to a select number of others." Maracle (138) believes that women of color should "leave the door closed" until white women own up to the racism in our society and work to defeat it.

The reality is that most Native women today live in a settler society under colonial and patriarchal oppression. Although Native women do now suffer from gender and racial oppression, their work is not only to advance the place of women. "Indigenous women seek to restore gender balance to their nations to reconnect with their traditions, which is the cultural strength of their people" (Sellers 2008, 55). Indeed, they seek to improve conditions for all of their people. Andrea Smith (2005b, 118) argues that "Native women activists' theories about feminism, about the struggle against sexism both within Native communities and the society at large and about the importance of working in coalition with non-Native women, are complex and varied."

Some Native women scholars are working toward creating a unique Aboriginal/ Indigenous/Native feminism. Shari M. Huhndorf and Cheryl Suzack (2010, 2) state that "Indigenous feminism remains an important site of gender struggle that engages the crucial issues of cultural identity, nationalism, and decolonization particular to Indigenous contexts." Smith (2005b, 104) also points out that Native American feminist theory has an important impact on feminist politics because it questions the "legitimacy of the United States specifically and the nation-state generally as the appropriate form of governance." Regardless of where a Native American woman's theoretical alignment may be, there is no one authoritative voice for these women and no one theory can encapsulate all Native American women's experiences.

Smith argues that heteropatriarchy is the building block of U.S. empire and the basis of the modern nation-state (2006, 71). In order to colonize peoples whose communities are not based on hierarchy, colonizers had to first normalize hierarchy through the institutionalization of patriarchy. In fact, "Patriarchy rests on a gender binary system in which only two genders exist, one dominating the other" (72). The colonial world is based on heteronormativity. "Just as the patriarchs rule the family, the elites of the nation-state rule their citizens. Any liberation struggle that does not challenge heteronormativity cannot substantially challenge colonialism or white supremacy" (72). Although Native American societies may not have been patriarchal to begin with, they are subjected to white patriarchy within the modern American context. Therefore it is reasonable to apply the concept of heteropatriarchy to the analysis of modern problems such as EJ within the white American framework, but this does not necessarily mean that it is appropriate for the analysis of situations within all Native communities.

Maile Arvin, Eve Tuck, and Angie Morrill (2013) argue that by examining settler colonialism within a context of women's and gender studies, scholars can reveal the ongoing structure of settler colonialism and its powerful effects on people in our society. "Because the United States is balanced upon notions of white supremacy and heteropatriarchy, everyone living in the country is not only racialized and gendered, but also has a relationship to settler colonialism" (9). Developments in Native feminist theory create new ways of thinking about how settler colonialism has impacted communities and also offer new possibilities for building alliances across communities. For example, rather than ignoring issues of tribal affiliation and land in order to create solidarity across groups of women, differences should be celebrated and relationships to settler colonialism should be examined (19). This issue is central to working for social justice in urban areas with many stakeholders.

Relatedly, the EJ movement focuses on the material places where community members live, work, and play. One problematic "consequence of colonialism is the flattening of land with property, a process that contains Indigenous bodies and land into colonial categorizations" (Aikau et al. 2015, 96). Objectifying people and the land on which they live is one way continue to dominate and exploit them. In defiance of this, many EJ leaders focus on their own backyards. "When Indigeneity is placed at the center, when we turn our attentions in a material rather than a metaphorical way to the lands upon which we stand, to 'āina, then we are able to challenge the fundamental legitimacy of the nation-state structure" (85). Approaching the study of Native American women as EJ leaders within the context of these theoretical approaches is useful, as they acknowledge the ongoing impacts of settler colonialism, race, and gender in analyzing issues pertinent to Native women. These approaches offer us a way forward.

THE LONG ROAD TO URBANIZATION

This section illustrates how the exercise of government power has oppressed Native American people with forced migration to urban areas. This shared experience fueled a broader pan-Indian identity that led to the formation of the Red Power movement. Finally, it addresses how this and other human rights movements paved the way for the Native women's EJ leadership in urban Indian centers.

For this part of the discussion, a basic understanding of federal Indian law and policy is necessary as it illustrates the dispossession and relocation that resulted in urban Native communities. Indian law, a reflection of federal Indian policy, has evolved through myriad shifts over the course of history. During some periods, the dominant view was that tribes are enduring independent bodies for whom the geographic base should be protected. During other periods the disruption of tribes was the goal, with the hope that their members would be assimilated into the majority society. These two opposing views have worked together to form a patchwork of policies that is complicated to navigate. These laws have worked to oppress Native peoples in the United States.

After the War of Independence, the government wished to prevent wars between state citizens and tribal nations. Congress chose to address this issue under the Articles of Confederation, and gave the administrative branch the power to deal with tribes with the consent of the Senate. They set the pattern of federal Indian law through a series of Trade and Intercourse Acts passed between 1790 and 1834. The policy subjected all interactions to federal control, minimized contact between Indians and non-Indians, and established the boundaries of Indian Country.

Conflicts escalated as non-Indian pressure for land intensified. The solution pushed in the early nineteenth century by Presidents Monroe and

Adams was to remove tribes west. President Jackson called for removal in his 1829 State of the Union Address. Simultaneously, the Supreme Court built legal doctrines that influenced Indian law for generations to come. These decisions underlined the primacy of the federal government to entreat tribes who had inherent Aboriginal title to their lands but gave the federal government power to extinguish that title—that is, in *Johnson v. McIntosh* (1823).

In the 1820s Georgia carved up Indian lands among its counties, invalidated all Cherokee laws, applied state law to all Cherokee lands, and made it illegal for the Cherokee Nation to act as a government. The Cherokee Nation turned to the United States Supreme Court for assistance wherein the Court held that tribes are domestic dependent nations (*Cherokee Nation v. Georgia* 1831). This terminology was a mixed blessing. It laid the groundwork for protection of tribal sovereignty, but it also opened up the opportunity for courts to determine the limits of tribal sovereignty inherent in the status.

In another case, Chief Justice John Marshall ruled that state law could have no force over Indian tribes (*Worcester v. Georgia* 1832). In the end, however, Jackson removed most of the tribes in the south to Indian territory through the Removal Act in 1830, a policy that was voluntary in name, but coerced in reality (Indian Removal Act 1830). In 1838, after much resistance, the Cherokees were forced to walk the Trail of Tears over 1,200 miles to designated Indian territory. Thousands of Cherokee people died along the way.

As population pressures from incoming colonizers continued, the federal government restricted tribes to specific reservations. Most of this was done through treaties wherein tribes would cede most of their land to reserve title to a smaller portion. Some tribes were moved to reservations far from their homelands. Reservations were intended to help keep the peace by creating space between Indians and non-Indians (Getches Wilkinson, and Williams Jr. 2005, 140–41). Eventually they came to be viewed as tools for "civilizing" Native Americans.

THE ALLOTMENT ERA

As Canby (2004) asserts, each reservation was placed under the control of an Indian agent whose role was to supervise their adaptation to non-Indian ways. When reservation schools were first set up in 1865, they were directed by religious organizations with the goal of Christianizing

Indians. In 1878 off-reservation boarding schools were established to remove Indian children from their tribal environments. These schools forced conformity while undermining the roles of women who were taught to be docile domestic workers and often were sexually abused by school administrators.

In the 1870s and 1880s, federal circles felt increasing dissatisfaction with reservation policy. People friendly to the Indians knew that tribal economies were a mess, individuals were living in extreme poverty, and no progress was being made to overcome these problems (Indian Rights Association 1885). Those who were not fond of Indians resented the fact that reservation lands were not open to white settlement (Canby 2004). These two positions led to the most disastrous piece of Indian legislation in history: the General Allotment Act of 1887, also known as the Dawes Act (1887).

The government believed that if Indians were given plots of land for cultivation, they would assimilate into the dominant culture and prosper like middle-class American farmers (Getches, Wilkinson, and Williams Jr. 2005, 168). They viewed the tribal structure as an obstacle to the economic and cultural development of Indians, and sought to end to this structure. The Dawes Act authorized the president to allot reservation land to individual Indians without the consent of tribes or individual Indians.

The primary effect of the act was a decrease in the amount of Indian-held land from 138 million acres in 1887 to 48 million in 1934 (Canby 2004, 22). Another impact of the legislation was that it undermined women's traditional roles in horticulture. Instead, the land and tools were given to male heads of household and women were relegated to the role of homemaker. In effect, the law divested Indians of their land and traditional roles.

THE INDIAN REORGANIZATION ERA

In 1924 Congress passed a law conferring citizenship to all Indians born in the United States (Indian Citizenship Act). In 1928 the Meriam Report documented the failure of the Allotment program and provided the impetus for a change in federal policy, which was embodied in the Indian Reorganization Act (IRA) of 1934. The IRA helped tribes establish legal structures necessary for self-government and protected their remaining lands. It ended allotment and extended the trust period for allotments still held in trust. The act authorized the secretary of the Interior to restore remaining surplus lands to tribal ownership, acquire new lands and water rights for tribes, and create new reservations. Unfortunately, the damage had been already been done to women's and men's statuses in tribal societies. They had been divested of their traditional roles, and when tribes were reorganized, American patriarchal structures were already in place.

The IRA authorized tribes to organize and adopt constitutions and by-laws subject to ratification by tribal members and the secretary of Interior (Canby 2004). The tribal constitutions suggested by federal authorities followed non-Indian patterns and were often inappropriate for tribal needs and conditions. They were modeled on capitalist notions of democracy and proved problematic because most of the tribes implementing them were unable to tailor them to fit their traditional modes of governance. Although women had historically served in tribal leadership, they were not acknowledged by agents assisting with tribal reorganization.

By the mid-twentieth century, federal Indian policy shifted again with the congressional adoption of a policy of "termination" in 1953 (Canby 2004, 26). The purpose was to, "as rapidly as possible . . . end [Indian's] status as wards of the United States" (26). The United States Congress passed several termination acts on a tribe-by-tribe basis. Congress determined that some tribes no longer needed federal protection, and asserted that conditions on the reservation would improve if they were not subject to BIA supervision. From a tribal standpoint, the purpose of this program was to break up tribal culture that has always been rooted in the land and assimilate Natives into the United States economy and culture as quickly as possible. In 1973 their relationship with the federal government was restored and remaining lands were put back into trust. By the end of the termination period, 109 tribes, Rancherias, and bands were stripped of their sovereign status, and 1,369,000 acres of Indian trust land was removed from trust status by the federal government (Fixico 1986, 183). Estimates of land lost are as high as 2,500,000 acres, once subsequent sales of land to non-Indians are taken into account.

THE ERA OF TERMINATION AND RELOCATION

The Bureau of Indian Affairs (BIA) encouraged Natives to leave the reservation under its Voluntary Relocation Program in order to hasten termination (Wunder 1994, 105). This policy was intended to dispossess American Indians of their reservation homelands and relocate them to urban areas where they could join the wage-labor system. Couched as a response to high unemployment rates on the reservation, the BIA offered grants and other incentives to Indians who would leave the reservation to seek work in specific metropolitan areas.

Tribal members were offered a one-way bus or train ticket, and upon arrival, a BIA relocation representative provided them with a check for clothing, groceries, one month's rent, housing recommendations, and a job (Wunder 1994, 106). That was the extent of the assistance. Many Natives were misled by promises of skilled permanent jobs, paid vacations, health benefits, union membership, and pension plans. Some were successful in securing employment in the urban economy, but most of the jobs were unskilled, and only limited training was available.

Vocational training for men was largely concentrated in semiskilled industrial realms as well as low-level business work, such as bookkeeping (Rosenthal 2012, 57–58). Women who relocated to cities were sometimes provided with vocational training, including clerical, beautician, and medical-assistant skills, but if they were single mothers or had already attended boarding schools, they were often denied training and placed in positions as domestic servants (Rosenthal 2012, 56–57). Women who attempted to attain training that fell into the realm of men's work were prevented from participating in those programs (58). They would be denied job training all together or placed in programs deemed appropriate for women under the patriarchal standards of United States government agents (Luna-Gordinier 2014).

The program created a population of unemployed American Indians in major relocation cities, including Los Angeles, Oakland, San Francisco, San Jose, Denver, Chicago Cleveland, Oklahoma City, Tulsa, Dallas, and Seattle. Housing was substandard and often worse than on the reservation. Urban Indian ghettos emerged from the concentration of unemployed American Indians. They suffered the problems of the urban poor with the added trauma of cultural dislocation. From this contrived diaspora emerged urban Indian community centers that helped relocated Indians and assisted in meeting basic needs and finding a sense of belonging far from their homelands.

By 1957 almost twenty-five thousand American Indians had relocated to urban areas, and ten years later, almost half of all Indians in the United States were living in relocation cities (Wunder 1994, 106). Some people called it a new extermination program: "Youngsters were enticed to the city to die, while the old starved on the reservation" (106). A major impact of relocation was the loss of federal services: once they left the reservation they were no longer eligible for healthcare, housing, food, or education. Cities and states had to provide for a huge refugee population but were not provided the funds to do so. In fact, the governmental constituencies most hit by relocation were the ones who eventually forced the BIA to suspend the relocation program.

THE SELF-DETERMINATION ERA

By the late 1960s, the assimilationist ideal was fading. Although there was a turn in policy toward self-determination for tribes, the assimilationist policies had already wreaked havoc on American Indian life. Many urban Indians no longer identified with their tribes or land of origin and instead identified with a growing pan-Indian identity. It is with this history in mind that this chapter seeks to illuminate how urban Indian communities fostered a pan-Indian identity that helped to reinforce the roles of women in urban centers, including in the area of environmental leadership.

Terry Straus and Debra Valentino (2001, 85–94) stipulate that Natives in the 1970s were concerned that the intertribal nature of urban environments would lead Indian people to become merely racially identified rather than bearers of their tribal knowledge and connections. They address this concern by illustrating the evolution of pan-Indian identity alongside the continuation of tribal identity. The first intertribal Indian organization in Chicago, the Indian Council Fire, was established in 1923 to accommodate all of the new urban Indians who were relocating after World War I (87). Though pan-Indian movements are not a new phenomenon, they accelerated due to contact with whites.

The American Indian Movement (AIM) and other Red Power (American Indian rights) groups arose out of urban settings where young people had only distant reservation experience but acted to strengthen their intertribal connections within urban areas and into reservations. AIM arose in Minneapolis in 1968 but quickly spread to other cities like Cleveland, Denver, and Milwaukee (88). Although the 1972 Trail of Broken Treaties, a cross-country protest, initially magnified strains between urban and reservation Indians, it eventually strengthened their connections. Red Power protests shifted from short-term urban actions to longer events, often on or near reservations, turning the primarily urban movement into one rooted in reservation communities. The result of the urban-initiated intertribal political action was increased federal funding, expanded programs, and enhanced self-determination on the reservations.

The Great Society Office of Economic Opportunity programs also aided urban intertribal communities via enhanced services for urban Indian residents (Straus and Valentino 2001). As a result, communities became conscious of their unique intertribal urban identity by creating a sense of place. Although a cleavage existed between urban Indian communities and reservations, growing urban populations motivated tribes to establish offices in cities where they had large memberships. Over time, cooperation between the groups evolved; for example, many urban centers work with tribes to enroll members dwelling in urban areas (Strauss and Valentino 2001).

During the relocation era, Native people grappled with creating community in urban areas while downplaying cultural differences. Since third and fourth generations have been born in urban areas, tribal affiliation is respected and pan-Indian identity is shared through community participation. In addition, intermarriage in urban areas has led to multifaceted heritages. Today pan-Indian and tribal specific identities are jointly conceived and represented by Native people. These developments have created urban spaces where Indigenous women may flourish.

According to Donald Fixico (2000, 124), "'Group' emphasis or 'community' represented the way of life for Indian people, and this outlook has extended noticeably into urban Indian communities since World War II, when Indian people left reservations to join the armed services." At crucial times in history, pan-Indianism, social relations (like political circumstances during war), and kinship bonds during ceremonies brought people from different tribes together. Historically, reasons for pan-Indian relations arose from social, political, and economic concerns. In the modern era, these reasons have also led to the formation of urban Indian identities.

In a basic sense, Indian people have benefited from being with each other, especially in the wake of termination and relocation. For generations, many Indians had been converted to Christianity and viewed themselves not according to tribal norms, but as sinful people who needed to be saved (Fixico 2000, 124). Conversion to Christianity had been used as a tool for mainstreaming Indians and reculturalizing them. In urban areas, churches became important places for Indians to gather as well, but the focus was on finding a sense of belonging far away from home reservations.

By the end of the 1960s, there were about forty Indian-operated urban Indian centers. In December 1969 the Office of Indian Affairs began examining the needs of urban Indians and developing a proposal for funding Indian centers. The Native Americans Program Act of 1974 aimed to "provide technical assistance, training, and financial support to help Native Americans achieve economic and social independence by enabling them to identify their own needs; establish their own priorities; conduct their own programs to meet those needs; and control the institution and programs that affect their daily lives" (131). Although defunded during the Reagan era, the programs continue to provide services to their communities.

Indian centers became pivotal to Indian socialization and helped create a sense of belonging for urban Indian people. These organizations united with each other to secure federal funding and create greater intertribal unity. Through pan-Indianism in cities, urban Indians were tasked with retaining their Native traditions while participating in urban activities that changed their lives permanently. This new pan-Indianness created a feeling in which all Native people could belong. Youth who may have previously lacked successful role models are exposed to greater opportunities through urban Indian centers. The centers have helped urban Indians achieve higher levels of education and economic success and have lifted up an urban Indian middle class.

The effective destruction of social safety nets, such as cuts to Medicare, social security, welfare, and other federal funding, in the early part of the twenty-first century put increased pressure on community centers to provide much-needed resources for urban Indians. The urban Indian organization model evolved with the help of Indigenous women's leadership, and they will be instrumental in serving the needs of their communities as we enter this new period of capitalist crisis.

NATIVE WOMEN'S LEADERSHIP AND INDIGENOUS ENVIRONMENTAL JUSTICE

Native women were traditionally seen as valuable members of society who made important contributions to their communities. As stated earlier, Christian Europeans sought to undermine many aspects of Native cultures. Historically, the majority culture has emphasized rigid gender roles for the purpose of procreation and to reinforce patriarchy. To settlers of North America, women needed to be put in their proper place.

Andrea Smith (2005a) discusses the role of violence as a tool of patriarchy and colonialism. Quoting a Dominican cleric: "Their marriages are not sacrament but a sacrilege. They are idolatrous, libidinous, and commit sodomy. Their chief desire is to eat, drink, worship heathen idols, and commit bestial obscenities" (10). The view of Native peoples as heathens and their practices as subhuman was a justification for colonization. As a result of the vast colonial violence that occurred, many Native people today have internalized patriarchy and racism.

The colonial relationship, as noted earlier, also reinforces heterosexist ideology (14). Smith points out that prior to colonization, Native societies were not male-dominated, which is a stark contrast to the patriarchal nature of European societies. "Patriarchal gender violence is the process by which colonizers inscribe hierarchy and domination on the bodies of the colonized" (23). Violent victimization of Native women was the most forceful tool colonizers could use to undermine tribal societies, which, in turn, forced Native women's conformity to American subservient roles of wife and mother.

In Native societies motherhood is a sacred role. According to Paula Gunn-Allen (1986, 209), "Naming your own mother . . . enables people to place you precisely within the universal web of your life, in each of its dimensions: cultural, spiritual, personal, and historical." Unlike European colonizers, the roles of mothers in Native societies were not limited to the private sphere. Traditional American Indian systems relied on complementarity and all facets of tribal life were organized as such. Everyone had a role in the private sphere, although some ritual knowledge was shared only between specific clan members or initiates to ritual societies. Some of these societies were gender specific and some were open to any gender. Most, however, were dominated by a particular gender but allowed helping roles to be filled by other genders (31–32). This separation of roles by gender was not seen as divisive but rather emphasized the complementarity of roles within harmonious tribal society (82).

In many ways Native American emphasis on cultural continuity runs counter to contemporary American ideals. Native communities value members who maintain traditions, "even after centuries of concerted and brutal effort on the part of the American government, the churches, and the corporate system to break the connection between individuals and their tribal world" (210). If Americans followed Native traditions, women's contributions would be honored, and the necessities of life would be distributed based on need. If people turn to Native traditions we may find escape from an exploitative patriarchal system. Even early European socialists saw women's liberation as an important aspect of revolution. "Indeed, the basic ideas of socialism, the egalitarian distribution of goods and power, the peaceful ordering of society, and the right of every member of society to participate in the work and benefits of that society, are ideas that pervade American Indian thought and action" (220).

Explorers' accounts often depicted female leaders as holding considerable influence and power. According to Mankiller and Wallis (1993, 19), "Prior to European contact and the influence of the whites on our culture, women played a prominent role in the social, political, and cultural life of the Cherokees." Mankiller and Wallis (1993) point out that Cherokee women leaders were expected to be present in meetings where decisions affecting the tribe were made. Colonists were critical of Cherokee women's involvement in governance, stating, "The Cherokees have a petticoat government" (19).

Due to patriarchal gender role stereotypes, in the past it was hard for women, and especially women of color, to ascend to leadership roles. They did have influence, however. In Chicago in the 1950s, men held public positions of authority in the American Indian Center (Straus and Valentino 2003, 527). Women's input was considered important, however, and they sanctioned men's public positions. Indian women were involved with organizing community events, developing contacts, and providing essential support to newcomers. "They served on committees, went to meetings, and advised the men. They recruited members and participants in the center's events, and pushed for children's activities" (527).

Throughout the country, influenced in part by the civil rights movement, Red Power movements began to develop, with the occupation of
Alcatraz in 1969 as a turning point. Numerous women participated in
the occupation of Alcatraz, including Wilma Mankiller (529). On reservations and in urban communities, women were more likely to complete
high school and attend college. Activism in Native communities led to
the establishment of new organizations and opportunities for women to
serve in official positions of leadership. According to Straus and Valentino
(2003), the 1970s through the early 1980s showed a balance of men and
women on the boards and staffs of community organizations in Chicago.
"By 1990 every one of the more than fifteen existing organizations . . .
was run by a woman" (530). The American Indian Women's Leadership
Development Project worked to solidify Native American women's community leadership. "A growing number of women's voices was needed to
bring back accountability and quality services within our organizations
and close attention to the needs of our Indian community. The need for
women to step into these roles of leadership became apparent" (530).

The concentration of women in community work is not unique to
Indian Country. Given that community work is family focused, many
women become involved in an effort to improve life for their children.
Much of the work done in Indian community centers is voluntary, which
brings women leaders into occupying informal leadership positions in
their communities through grassroots organizing, which eventually leads
to formal leadership positions (Prindeville 2002, 78). Many Native women
leaders are still reluctant to take on the title of "leader," and instead refer
to themselves as organizers, facilitators, or problem solvers in many areas,
including EJ (Prindeville 2002). Their vision of their role in urban Indian
centers was not severable from the work of other community members.
This stands in stark contrast to patriarchal standards of leadership for
personal gain or economic security (Luna-Gordinier 2014). Many of these
women are concerned with community health, environmental preservation, and the well-being of future generations.

Researchers have found that many women in leadership roles today
must work harder than men (Prindeville 2002, 70). This is largely an effect
of patriarchy, in that their work is not valued because of sexism. They must
also perform more work, since domestic duties fall on them. Prindeville
found that Native American and Hispanic women leaders, like most

women, are more successful when their spouses, friends, and community support them.

NATIVE WOMEN'S UNIQUE PERCEPTION OF "LEADERSHIP" AND ENVIRONMENTAL JUSTICE

Most Native women in leadership perceive their role as helping to empower others in their communities. They are motivated to lead because of the interconnectedness of all things, the value of inclusivity, and their drive to improve the world for all living beings. They are stimulated "by a desire to achieve fundamental changes in existing social, political, and economic systems in order to make these more egalitarian and equitable for children, women, and racial/ethnic minority groups" (Prindeville 2002, 87). Leadership is a cooperative undertaking for Native people. Mentoring, advising, and supporting future leaders "through the use of a traditional American Indian worldview that involves collectivism, collaboration, compassion, and courage" develops effective Native leadership (Portman and Garrett 2005, 287).

Native women leaders and organizers share the experience of being on the frontline of the immediate educational, employment, health, and social needs of Native people in the city. Most of these community centers only seek to address structural issues in society, rather than systemic ones. This is partially due to the fact that during the twentieth century, while Native people were migrating to cities, capitalism in the United States was still expanding. The social safety net was intact and the state was still motivated to make concessions to workers and community groups. Things have changed, however. After the influx of robotics into production, for example, unemployment rates in manufacturing went sky high. Manufacturing-related employment numbers will not be rising any time soon, as the market no longer has much use for manual labor. What remains are service jobs for the few who can secure them. These provide the context for the Native women's leadership. Just as Native people were dispossessed of their lands, so have many urban Natives lost access to their means of economic survival in the twenty-first century. We are at a critical turning point where we must choose between a system driven toward ecological destruction and one based on responsible stewardship of the earth's resources (see, for example, Wildcat 2009).

Native women are in a unique position to lead their communities for collective and collaborative action for a just society. Native women are often at the forefront of Indigenous environmental justice issues. Whether they are in urban areas or living on traditional homelands, "Indigenous feminist movements are often the first to identify the intersections of violence, colonization, poverty, and environmental injustice" (Begay and Goldtooth 2018, n.p.). Indigenous women are involved in direct action concerning Indigenous environmental justice issues involving the impacts of climate change on Indigenous Peoples; the intersection of Indigenous women, EJ, and reproductive justice; and more (Lorenzo 2016; Begay and Goldtooth 2018; Hoover 2018).

CORRINA GOULD: A VOICE FOR THE OHLONE PEOPLE

Born and raised in Oakland, California, the territory of Huichuin, Corrina Gould is the spokesperson for the Confederated Villages of Lisjan/ Ohlone. She has dedicated her life to cultural and sacred sites preservation. She has worked at the nexus of many communities in the San Francisco Bay Area to nurture partnerships with stakeholders to envision and create a sustainable future for everyone. One of her key issues is to raise awareness about the Ohlone people so that they will not continue to be invisible on their homelands (Creating Freedom Movements n.d.).

As a cofounder and lead organizer for the Native-run grassroots organization called Indian People Organizing for Change, she sponsored the Shellmound Peace Walk between 2005 and 2009. The purpose was to raise awareness about the desecration of sacred cultural sites in the Bay Area. With the organization, she hosts the Shellmound gathering every year where an ancient site was desecrated by the development of the Emeryville Mall. The organization is also working to block new development in West Berkeley on the oldest inhabited Oholne site in the Bay Area. Archaeological evidence demonstrates that there was at least one shellmound, a cemetery, and a large ceremonial house, along with sacred objects such as charmstones and bird-bone whistles at the site (Indian People Organizing for Change n.d.).

In April 2011 Gould, along with a committee of Indigenous organizers, established an occupation and prayer vigil at Sogorea Te in Vallejo, California. The group occupied a fifteen-acre sacred site located along the Carquinez Straits for 109 days. The result was a cultural easement between

the City of Vallejo, the Greater Vallejo Recreation District, and two federally recognized tribes. This triumphant struggle set a precedent in Indigenous environmental justice organizing for sacred sites protections within
city limits in the state of California (Creating Freedom Movements n. d.).

Corrina Gould also cofounded the Native-women-led Sogorea Te'
Land Trust. The community organization works to facilitate Indigenous
stewardship of Chochenyo and Karkin Ohlone lands in the Bay Area.
The organization builds bridges between people living in the Bay Area
so they may collaborate to reenvision what it means to live in Ohlone
territory. "Guided by the belief that land is the foundation that can bring
us together, Sogorea Te' calls on us all to heal from the legacies of colonialism and genocide, to remember different ways of living, and to do
the work that our ancestors and future generations are calling us to do"
(Sogorea n.d.-a). In consultation with Sogorea Te', individuals living on
colonized Chochenyo and Karkin Ohlone land created the Shuumi Land
Tax. The voluntary annual financial contribution was created to support
the work of Sogorea Te' to reclaim an Ohlone land base in the East Bay.
The tax will be used to obtain and preserve land, create a cemetery to
reinter stolen Ohlone ancestral remains, and build community centers,
urban gardens, and sacred arbors. The goal is to help current and future
generations of Native people so that they may flourish in the Bay Area
(Sogorea n.d.-b). In collaboration with Michelle Steinberg, Gould also
created a film entitled *Beyond Recognition*, which focuses on the land trust.
The film won the Green Award at the 2015 San Francisco Green Film
Festival. Corrina Gould is just one example of how Native women have
come to the forefront of EJ movements in order to protect their land
and communities. Through her leadership, many Native and non-Native
people have reestablished their connection to the land in the Bay Area.

REFLECTIONS ON WOMEN'S INDIGENOUS ENVIRONMENTAL LEADERSHIP IN URBAN INDIAN CENTERS

The work of Native American women scholars and activists has been
central to creating alternative theories based on holistic understandings.
They have drawn on their experiences with American oppression and
exploitation to develop perspectives that empower their communities.

By challenging majoritarian theoretical approaches, Native women have stimulated a rich dialogue about the underlying assumptions of feminism and Western modes of thought. In doing so, these activists and scholars have helped to generate a deeper understanding of the diverse issues facing Native Americans.

Native women have been central to building and sustaining urban Indian communities. This is due to their direct participation in social movements, as well as through the roles they play in the organization of family, the maintenance of culture, and securing the material necessities of life (Luna-Gordinier 2014). Native women have provided the foundation for the organizations that are the backbones of urban Indian communities. Their experiences of urban migration provide insights into the power dynamics of class, gender, and race politics.

Women have been instrumental in maintaining the connection with traditions that contribute to binding the urban-Indian community together. These leaders have helped the Native community maintain a sense of belonging and have created a forum in which to address issues facing American Indians, such as environmental justice. Native women have played key roles in the development of pan-Indian identity and a sense of urban social consciousness. As such, Native women are in a particularly powerful place to lift up the screen of capitalist and white supremacist ideology and expose the history of domination that still works to oppress the majority of American society. They have the power to set an example to other peoples and organizations by creating and reinforcing ideology that is inclusive of broader worldviews and lifeways. Native American women leaders, who historically held respected positions in their communities, can help modern American people understand alternative modes of being and thinking. This development is the first major step down a long road to create true equality and freedom in America.

REFERENCES

Aikau, Hokulani K., Maile Arvin, Mishuana Goeman, and Scott Morgensen. 2015. "Indigenous Feminisms Roundtable." *Frontiers: A Journal of Women Studies* 36 (3): 84–106.

Arvin, Maile, Eve Tuck, and Angie Morrill. 2013. "Decolonizing Feminism: Challenging Connections Between Settler Colonialism and Heteropatriarchy." *Feminist Formations* 25 (1): 8–34.

Begay, Jade, and Dallas Goldtooth. 2018. "Sierra Club: Letter from Indigenous Activists." Sierra Club. October, 2018. https://www.sierraclub.org/sierra/letter-indigenous-activists.

Canby, William C., Jr. 2004. *American Indian Law in a Nutshell.* 4th ed. St Paul, Minn.: Thompson West.

Creating Freedom Movements. n.d. "Corrina Gould." Accessed June 12, 2019. http://www.creatingfreedommovements.org/corrina-gould.html.

Fixico, Donald. 1986. *Termination and Relocation: Federal Indian Policy, 1945–1960.* Albuquerque: University of New Mexico Press.

Fixico, Donald L. 2000. *The Urban Indian Experience in America.* Albuquerque: University of New Mexico Press.

Getches, David H., Charles F. Wilkinson, and Robert A. Williams Jr. 2005. *Cases and Materials on Federal Indian Law.* 5th ed. St Paul, Minn.: Thompson West.

Gunn-Allen, P. 1986. *The Sacred Hoop: Recovering the Feminine in American Indian Traditions.* Boston, Mass.: Beacon Press.

Hoover, Elizabeth. 2018. "Environmental Reproductive Justice: Intersections in an American Indian Community Impacted by Environmental Contamination." *Environmental Sociology* 4 (1): 8–21.

Huhndorf, Shari M., and Cheryl Suzack. 2010. "Indigenous Feminism: Theorizing the Issues." In *Indigenous Women and Feminism: Politics, Action, Culture,* edited by Cheryl Suzack et al., 1–17. Vancouver: University of British Columbia Press.

Indian People Organizing For Change. n.d. "We Need Your Help to Save the West Berkeley Shellmound/Village Site." Accessed on June 12, 2019. http://ipocshellmoundwalk.homestead.com/West-Berkeley-Shellmound.html.

Indian Rights Association. 1885. *The Second Annual Report of the Executive Committee of the Indian Rights Association.* Philadelphia, Pa.: Office of Indian Rights Association.

Lobo, Susan. 1998. "Is Urban a Person or a Place? Characteristics of Urban Indian Country." *American Indian Culture and Research Journal* 22 (4): 89–102.

Lorenzo, Rachel. 2016. "At Standing Rock, Reproductive Justice Is Environmental Justice." *Rewire.news.* October 20, 2016. https://rewire.news/article/2016/09/20/standing-rock-environmental-justice-reproductive-justice/.

Luna-Gordinier, Anne. 2014. "Organized Resistance to Dispossession: Urban Indian Centers and Women's Leadership." PhD diss., Howard University.

Mankiller, Wilma, and M. Wallis. 1993. *Mankiller: A Chief and Her People.* New York: St. Martin's Press.

Maracle, Lee. 1996. *I Am Woman: A Native Perspective on Sociology and Feminism.* Vancouver, B.C.: Press Gang.

Meriam, Lewis. 1928. *The Problem of Indian Administration* [Meriam Report]. Baltimore, Md.: Johns Hopkins University Press.

Orellano, M. F., and P. Bowman. 2003. "Cultural Diversity Research on Learning and Development: Conceptual, Methodological and Strategic Considerations." *Educational Researcher* 32 (5): 26–32.

Portman, T. A. A., and M. T. Garrett. 2005. "Beloved Women: Nurturing the Sacred Fire of Leadership from an American Indian Perspective." *Journal of Counseling and Development* 83:284–91.

Prindeville, D. M. 2002. "A Comparative Study of Native American and Hispanic Women in Grassroots and Electoral Politics." *Frontier* 23 (1): 67–89.

Rindfuss, R. R., G. D. Sandefur, and B. Cohen. 1997. "Demography of American Indians and Alaska Natives." *Population Research and Policy Review* 16:1–10.

Rosenthal, N. G. 2012. *Reimagining Indian Country: Native American Migration and Identity in Twentieth-Century Los Angeles.* Chapel Hill, N.C.: University of North Carolina Press.

Seidman, S. 1993. "Identity and Politics in a 'Postmodern' Gay Culture: Some Historical and Conceptual Notes." In *Fear of a Queer Planet: Queer Politics and Social Theory,* edited by M. Warner, 105–42. Minneapolis, Minn.: University of Minnesota Press.

Sellers, Stephanie A. 2008. *Native American Women's Studies: A Primer.* New York: Peter Lang.

Smith, Andrea. 2005a. *Conquest: Sexual Violence and American Indian Genocide.* Cambridge, Mass.: South End Press.

Smith, Andrea. 2005b. "Native American Feminism, Sovereignty, and Social Change." *Feminist Studies* 31 (1):116–32.

Smith, Andrea. 2006. "Heteropatriarchy and the Three Pillars of White Supremacy: Rethinking Women of Color Organizing." In *Color of Violence: The INCITE! Anthology,* edited by Incite! Women of Color Against Violence, 66–74. Cambridge, Mass.: South End Press.

Sogorea Te Land Trust. n.d.-a. "HorSe Tuuxi (Good day)." Accessed June 12, 2019. https://sogoreate-landtrust.com/.

Sogorea Te Land Trust. n.d.-b. "Shuumi Land Tax." Accessed June 12, 2019. https://sogoreate-landtrust.com/shuumi-land-tax/.

Straus, Terry, and Debra Valentino. 2001. "Retribalization in Urban Indian Communities." In *American Indians and the Urban Experience,* edited by Susan Lobo and Kurt Peters, 85–94. Walnut Creek, Calif.: Altamira Press.

Straus, Terry, and Debra Valentino. 2003. "Gender and Community Organization
   Leadership in the Chicago Indian Community." *American Indian Quarterly* 27
   (3–4): 523–32.
Wildcat, Daniel R. 2009. *Red Alert: Saving the Planet with Indigenous Knowledge.*
   Golden, Colo.: Fulcrum.
Wunder, J. R. 1994. *Retained by The People: A History of American Indians and the
   Bill of Rights.* New York: Oxford University Press.

LEGAL RESOURCES

Cherokee Nation v. Georgia. 30 U.S. 1 (1831)
General Allotment Act [Dawes Act]. 25 U.S.C.A. 331 (1887)
Indian Citizenship Act. 43 U.S. Stat. 253 (1924)
Indian Removal Act. 4 Stat. 411 (1830)
Indian Reorganization Act. 25 U.S.C. 461 (1934)
Johnson v. M'Intosh. 21 U.S. 543 (1823)
Native Americans Program Act. 42 U.S.C. 2991(1974)
Trade and Intercourse Acts. 25 U.S.C. 177 (1790–1834)
Worcester v. Georgia. 31 U.S. 515 (1832)

CONCLUSION

KAREN JARRATT-SNIDER AND
MARIANNE O. NIELSEN

INDIGENOUS ENVIRONMENTAL justice issues for Native peoples are numerous and vary widely. In some cases, Native peoples are working to protect their culturally significant, or sacred, sites, while in other cases the fight is for their very lives against toxins poisoning their water, land, and air. From 2001 to 2009, deaths from all forms of cancer went down for white men and women (see also Robyn's chapter). During the same period, deaths went up for American Indian men and women (CDC n.d.). According to the U.S. Centers for Disease Control these deaths are most likely due to social, behavioral, and *environmental factors* (CDC n.d.). Contamination also exists in foods used for subsistence and cultural gatherings, such as uranium deposits in the meat from Navajo sheep and elevated levels of contaminants in fish eaten in Alaska, the Pacific Northwest, and Wisconsin (Ingram n.d.; EPA 2002). Uranium from contaminated soil and water and plants consumed by sheep can concentrate in various parts of their bodies (Ingram n.d.). Many non-Indigenous Peoples do not have to worry about the safety of their daily food supplies, but too often, Indigenous Peoples do. Environmental contamination is so widespread, as Robyn mentions, that over five hundred Superfund sites are either located on or affect the lands and people of Native American tribes in the United States. As the headline reads in reference to these Superfund sites: "Kill the Land, Kill the People" (Hansen 2014). If not remediated, environmental contamination may do just that; as the cases of

Tar Creek and uranium on Navajo lands show, cleanup of environmental sites often takes decades. In the case of the Navajo, as Robyn has shown, it is taking generations. The issue is not a hidden one. Judy Pasternak (2010) wrote a New York Times best seller, *Yellow Dirt*, telling the story of the poisoning of Navajo lands. Today any public outcry the book evoked has died away, and Navajo people continue to suffer the effects of uranium contamination.

Corporate entities are not the only groups responsible for social harms resulting from environmental degradation. Federal agencies play a huge role by sometimes facilitating corporate exploitation of Indigenous lands and resources, like the Bureau of Indian Affairs did with Tar Creek. Federal agencies can either facilitate corporate activities that lead to environmental injustice for Indigenous Peoples, or, alternatively, they can act to fulfill the meaning of the Executive Order on Environmental Justice (Executive Order 12898) and the Executive Order on Consultation and Coordination with Indian Tribal Governments (Executive Order 13175). This means federal agencies can and should work to ensure fairness in environmental decision-making, as was the case with the power line project mentioned in Jarratt-Snider's chapter. Either way, federal agencies play a significant role in environmental justice or *in*justice.

For Native peoples, their deep spiritual connections to their homelands, which also define their cultural identity, mean impacts on their homelands are, in fact, Indigenous environmental justice (IEJ) issues. Unlike others whose land becomes contaminated or is taken from them, Native peoples cannot simply pack up, leave, and find new homelands. There is no substitute. Connections to their homelands mean, in turn, that any issues affecting those lands have a disproportionate impact on that group of Indigenous people. Whether the issue is sacred sites now on public lands or environmental devastation to their lands, the impact is automatically disproportionate.

Claims of spiritual connection to homelands as a right to free exercise of religion have failed over and over in the courts, and this seems unlikely to change in the future. The record of success using an environmental justice approach, though, is somewhat different. The power line case on the Carson National Forest offers the possibility of a strategy for success in protecting Native peoples' sacred places, at least in the United States (Jarratt-Ziemski 2006). Those cases also underscore the necessity of using the right legal tools, as discussed earlier in several chapters, and not relying only on one tool or strategy. For example, combining Executive Order 13175 on Consultation and Coordination with Executive Order 12898 on Environmental Justice means that federal agencies must offer opportunities for meaningful participation to satisfy the requirements of both executive orders. Additionally, regulations promulgated by federal agencies to implement Executive Order 12898 often have detailed examples of the type of outreach and opportunities for meaningful participation that agencies must engage in with environmental justice (EJ) populations. For example, the U.S. Department of Agriculture (USDA 1997) created regulation 5600–2 on Environmental Justice to guide agencies in its departments, including the USDA Forest Service, on how to include EJ in their work. As many Native nations' lands are adjacent to national forests and many traditional homelands and cultural sites are now within national forests, agency-specific regulations on EJ may be a useful tool for effecting just solutions to IEJ issues. Combining such legal tools to find strategies that fit the situation at hand may offer success in protecting and accessing sacred sites, where religious freedom claims have failed.

Similarly, the human rights of Indigenous Peoples, while protected under international law, have yet to be successful in the United States as a method to assure environmental justice solutions for Native peoples. As Timothy Casey writes in chapter 7, sometimes an issue needs to be reframed. Reframing religious freedom claims as the EJ issues they are may facilitate protection of culturally significant sites in times when tribes are unlikely to find relief in the courts. In one author's experience, it is not uncommon to encounter agency staff unaware of their own agency's EJ regulations and/or how Native culturally significant sites are indeed EJ issues (Personal Observation). Similarly, some staff members within federal agencies take both C's in Executive Order 13175 on Consultation and Coordination seriously, and go beyond formal consultation activities to focus on ways of coordinating with tribal nations, thus providing meaningful participation opportunities for Native nations. Procedural justice activities will not guarantee just outcomes for environmental issues for Native people, but without equal participation in the process, tribal nations have little hope of finding justice in environmental decision-making.

Resilience of Indigenous Peoples is shown in many ways throughout this volume, including the investment some have made in renewable resources that may help reduce environmental impacts from fossil fuels on their lands. An Indigenous environmental justice issue not discussed at length in this volume is one that is and will continue to affect Indigenous Peoples worldwide—climate change. Climate change is already affecting tribal nations in the Arctic and coastal areas (UN-Indigenous Peoples n.d.; U.S. Geological Survey n.d.; Tsosie 2007, 2009, 2013). For example, uncharacteristically strong storms led to the Houma in Louisiana literally losing a great deal of their lands. Chapters on Indigenous environmental justice issues resulting from climate change alone could fill an entire volume (Abate and Warner 2013; Maldonado, Colombi, and Pandya 2014; Tsosie 2007, 2009, 2013), but additional research in this area describing impacts on specific Native nations and Indigenous communities needs to be done, as effects of climate change continue to cause harm to Native communities.

Finally, as noted in the introduction, de facto sovereignty and self-determination are an important piece of community responses and Indigenous resilience. In the case of Indigenous environmental justice, de facto sovereignty may offer EJ solutions for more tribal nations, as seen in some of the chapters in this volume. Too much has been written about the "dependency" of American Indian tribes, as if those Native nations are welfare cases (see, generally, White 1988; Porter 2005). The—in our view—mistaken idea that American Indians are economically dependent leads the discussion away from the political and legal sovereignty of Native nations and at times compares the services, programs, and funding tribal nations receive to welfare (Claiborne 1998; St. Clair 2000). Although states receive similar services and funding from the federal government—albeit based on different legal origins—one doesn't hear people remarking that states are dependent entities. Such statements mistakenly take attention away from the legal and political statuses of Native nations. Speaking about Native nations in the way that recognizes their inherent sovereignty throughout the world has become a continuous struggle (Deloria 1992). Those discussions also lead to a dangerous road where policy-makers can seek to treat Indian tribes as welfare recipients and means test them, presumably with the long-term goal of ending the (U.S.) government's fiduciary obligations to Native nations and possibly even permanently abrogating treaty rights (Johansen 2004). Here we present a different approach to the challenges facing Native peoples—this time in the environmental justice arena. The resilience of Indigenous Peoples and communities shine through in those chapters where Native nations have found solutions through their own ingenuity, environmental technical capacity, and/or political engagement. As we have said elsewhere in this volume, as well as in the first volume in the series (Nielsen and Jarratt-Snider 2018)—and it merits reiterating—the cases where just solutions for Indigenous Peoples have been or are being achieved due to their own persistence and ingenuity can offer important road maps for others in similar situations. Those cases are further examples of de facto sovereignty. To echo the words of a Native elder as told to noted Indigenous scholar Taiaiake Alfred (1999, 110): "*Tewatatotie*'—we take care of ourselves."

REFERENCES

Abate, Randall S., and Elisabeth A. K. Warner, eds. 2013. *Climate Change and Indigenous Peoples: The Search for Legal Remedies*. Cheltenham, UK: Edward Elgar.

Alfred, Gerald Taiaiake. 1999. *Peace Power and Righteousness: An Indigenous Manifesto*. Don Mills, Ont.: Oxford University Press.

CDC (U.S. Centers for Disease Control). n.d. "Cancer Among American Indians and Alaska Natives." Accessed June 18, 2019. https://www.cdc.gov/cancer/healthdisparities/what_cdc_is_doing/aian.htm.

Claiborne, William. 1998. "At Indian Affairs, a Tough Act to Balance." *Washington Post*. November 17, 1998. https://www.washingtonpost.com/archive/politics/1998/11/17/at-indian-affairs-a-tough-act-to-balance/2f3c7575-8b54-421c-9891-0032a8ca20b6/?noredirect=on&utm_term=.1e61029aa2e0.

Deloria, Vine, Jr., ed. 1992. *American Indian Policy in the Twentieth Century*. Norman: University of Oklahoma Press.

EPA (Environmental Protection Agency). 2002. *Fish Consumption and Environmental Justice: A Report Developed from the National Environmental Justice Advisory Council of December 3–6, 2001*. https://www.epa.gov/sites/production/files/2015-02/documents/fish-consump-report_1102.pdf.

Hansen, Terri. 2014. "Kill the Land, Kill the People: There Are 532 Superfund Sites in Indian Country!" *Indian Country Today Media Network*. June 17, 2014. https://newsmaven.io/indiancountrytoday/archive/kill-the-land-kill-the-people-there-are-532-superfund-sites-in-indian-country-LpCDfEqzlkGEnzyFxHYnJA/.

Ingram, Jani C. n.d. "Cancer Risk to Exposure from Uranium Among the Navajo." Presentation to the Partnership for Native American Cancer Prevention. https://www.niehs.nih.gov/news/events/pastmtg/assets/docs_c_e/cancer_risk _from_exposure_to_uranium_among_the_navajo_508.pdf.

Jarratt-Ziemski, Karen. 2006. "Meaningful Participation in Environmental Justice: Policy Designs and Implications for Re-envisioning, Reinstating, and Reinforcing Tribal Sovereignty." PhD diss., Northern Arizona University.

Johansen, Bruce Elliot. 2004. "The New Terminators." In *Enduring Legacies, Native American Treaties and Contemporary Controversies*, edited by Bruce Elliot Johansen, 305–32. Westport, Conn.: Praeger.

Maldonado, Julie K., Benedict Colombi, and Rajul Pandya, eds. 2014. *Climate Change and Indigenous Peoples in the U.S.: Impacts, Experiences, and Actions.* New York: Springer International.

Nielsen, Marianne O., and Karen Jarratt-Snider. 2018. *Crime and Social Justice in Indian Country.* Tucson: University of Arizona Press.

Pasternak, Judy. 2010. *Yellow Dirt: A Poisoned Land and the Betrayal of the Navajos.* New York: Simon and Schuster.

Porter, Robert Odawi. 2005. *Sovereignty, Colonialism, and the Indigenous Nations: A Reader.* Durham, N.C.: Carolina Academic Press.

St. Clair, Jeffrey. 2000. "The Last Indian Fighter: Slade Gorton Is American Indians' Public Enemy No. 1." October 2, 2000. *InTheseTimes.com.* https:// inthesetimes.com/issue/24/22/stclair2422.html.

Tsosie, Rebecca. 2007. "Indigenous Peoples and Environmental Justice: The Impact of Climate Change." *Climate of Environmental Justice: Taking Stock.* March 16–17, 2007. http://scholar.law.colorado.edu/climate-of-environmental -justice/8.

Tsosie, Rebecca. 2009. "Climate Change, Sustainability, and Globalization: Charting the Future of Indigenous Self-Determination." *Environment and Energy Law and Policy Journal* 4 (2): 188–255.

Tsosie, Rebecca. 2013. "Climate Change and Indigenous Peoples: Comparative Models of Sovereignty." *Tulane Environmental Law Journal* 26 (2): 239–57.

UN-Indigenous Peoples. n.d. "Climate Change." Accessed June 18, 2019. https:// www.un.org/development/desa/indigenouspeoples/climate-change.html.

U.S. Geological Survey. n.d. "Climate Change, Coastal Tribes and Indigenous Communities." Accessed June 18, 2019. https://www.usgs.gov/news/climate -change-coastal-tribes-and-indigenous-communities.

USDA (U.S. Department of Agriculture). 1997. "Regulation 5600–2: Program Initiatives Within USDA Related to Environmental Justice." Washington, D.C. December 15, 1997.

White, Richard. 1988. *The Roots of Dependency: Subsistence, Environment, and Social Change Among the Choctaws, Pawnees, and Navajos*. Lincoln: University of Nebraska Press.

LEGAL RESOURCES

Executive Order 12898. "Environmental Justice" (1994)

Executive Order 13175. "Consultation and Coordination with Indian Tribes" (2000)

CONTRIBUTORS

T. Timothy Casey is professor of political science at Colorado Mesa University in Grand Junction, Colorado. He is also the director of the Natural Resource Center at Colorado Mesa. He teaches a wide variety of courses on political theory and public policy with an emphasis on environmental and Indigenous politics. His research interests include public lands and democratic participation in public land planning. He has also written and presented extensively in the field of Canadian studies.

Mia Montoya Hammersley (Tigua and Yaqui descendant) grew up in Flagstaff, Arizona. She received a BA in environmental studies from Franklin University in Lugano, Switzerland; an MS in water, society, and policy from the University of Arizona; and a JD, specializing in environmental law, science, and policy and Indigenous Peoples law and policy, also from the University of Arizona. In law school, she served as the secretary of the Native American Law Students Association and editor-in-chief of the *Arizona Journal of Environmental Law and Policy*. She has worked for a variety of environmental and public interest law organizations, including as the Healthy Communities Law Fellow for Earthjustice, working on behalf of communities that bear a disproportionate share of environmental health harms. She is the author of a number of publications on climate change, social-ecological systems, and the impact of dams on the environment. Her research interests are environmental law, watershed management, and Native American natural resources.

Karen Jarratt-Snider (Choctaw descent) is associate professor and chair of the Department of Applied Indigenous Studies at Northern Arizona University. She is co-editor with Marianne O. Nielsen of *Crime and Social Justice in Indian Country* and *Traditional, National and International Law and Indigenous Communities*. Her expertise is in the areas of Indigenous environmental justice, federal Indian policy, tribal administration, and tribal environmental management. She has over fifteen years of experience working with tribal nations' projects in applied, community-based research. Her work engages three critical areas for Indigenous Peoples: environmental management and policy, policy and administration, and sustainable economic development—all of which coalesce around the overall topic of Indigenous sovereignty and self-determination. She teaches Indigenous environmental justice and federal Indian policy and law, as well as tribal environmental management.

Lomayumtewa K. Ishii (Hopi) is an artist from the village of Sichomovi, First Mesa, on the Hopi Reservation in northern Arizona. He is of the Rabbit/Tobacco clan and is a Hopi practitioner of religious activities and Hopi dry-farming agriculture. He has recently completed an artist fellowship at the School of Advanced Research in Santa Fe, New Mexico. He is the cover artist for the first two books in the series, *Crime and Social Justice in Indian Country* and *Traditional, National and International Law and Indigenous Communities* as well as this volume.

Anne Luna-Gordinier (Choctaw and Cherokee) is assistant professor at California State University, Sacramento. She earned a a law degree and MA in American Indian studies from the University of Arizona in 2004 and a PhD in sociology from Howard University in 2014. She teaches on social theory, social inequality, gender, environmental justice, and social movements. Her research in Native American sociology focuses on radical criminology, environmental justice, urban Indians, and women's leadership. She is also a contributor to the first book in this series, *Crime and Social Justice in Indian Country*.

Marianne O. Nielsen is a professor in the Department of Criminology and Criminal Justice at Northern Arizona University. Her expertise is in justice issues affecting world Indigenous populations. She has worked for

Native organizations and has done research in Indigenous communities. She is co-author with Linda M. Robyn of *Colonialism Is Crime*; co-editor with Karen Jarratt-Snider of *Crime and Social Justice in Indian Country* and *Traditional, National and International Law and Indigenous Communities*; co-editor with Robert Silverman of *Aboriginal Peoples and Canadian Criminal Justice*, *Native Americans, Crime and Criminal Justice*, and *Criminal Justice in Native America*; and co-editor with James W. Zion of *Navajo Peacemaking: Living Traditional Justice*. She is also the co-author with Barbara Heather of several articles about Quakers and American Indians.

Linda M. Robyn (Anishinabe descent) received her doctorate from Western Michigan University in 1998. She is a professor in the Department of Criminology and Criminal Justice at Northern Arizona University in Flagstaff. She is co-author with Marianne O. Nielsen of *Colonialism Is Crime* and numerous articles and book chapters on Indigenous justice issues. Her current research interests include American Indians and the criminal justice system, sterilization of American Indian women, environmental justice (including uranium and coal mining resource acquisition), and the effects of state-corporate crime on American Indian nations. She is also a contributor to the first book in this series, *Crime and Social Justice in Indian Country*.

Richard M. Wheelock (Oneida Nation, Wisconsin) is associate professor emeritus of Native American and Indigenous Studies at Fort Lewis College, having retired in 2012 after nearly thirty years of teaching and service there. His writings have been inspired by his experience as editor of his tribe's newspaper, the *Kalihwisaks*, in the early 1980s, and interactions with thinkers like Vine Deloria Jr., Robert K. Thomas, and N. Scott Momaday, who were among his teachers, and many other Native authors and friends over the years. Publications include the following book chapters: "The 'Ideal Tribe' and 'Mass Society' in Tribal Communications Research," in *A Good Cherokee, A Good Anthropologist*; "The American Story: Impact of Myth on American Indian Policy," in *Destroying Dogma: Vine Deloria, Jr. and His Influence on American Society*; "Native People in American Mythology and Popular Culture," in *American Indians and Popular Culture*; and "Reconsidering America's Errand: Wilderness and Indians in Cinema," in *Critical Perspectives on Hollywood's Indians*.

INDEX

#IdleNoMore, 170
#NoDAPL. *See* Dakota Access Pipeline

activism, 12, 153, 194. *See also* entries for
    resistance and direct action
assimilation, 37–38, 126–28, 145, 189
allotment, 37–38, 126–30, 185–86
American Indian Women's Leadership
    Development Project, 194
American Indian and First Nations
    Peoples and Nations: Alaska Natives,
    43, 116, 119–25; Aleut, 44; Apache, 10,
    48–50; Cherokee, 185, 193; Chippewa,
    31; Choctaw, 10; Diné, 10, 13, 41, 74,
    81, 140, 153. *See also* separate entry
    for Navajo; Eskimo, 44; Hopi, 10,
    60–73, 84–86, 103, 137, 142, 146, 151–52;
    Iñupiat, 120–125, 132–33; Inuit, 162–75;
    Karok, 46; Lakota, 18, 61, 95, 106,
    109–110; Lummi, 32; Makah, 32;
    Native Hawaiian, 43–44; Native Vil-
    lage of Barrow (NAB), 119–139; Nez
    Perce, 10; Ojibwe, 31–32; Oneida, 32;

Paiutes, 150–51; Quapaw, 94, 106, 119,
    126–33; Quechan, 150–51; Saami, 164;
    San Carlos Apache, 48; Spokane, 10;
    Talowa, 46; Taos Pueblo, 51; Sioux, 8,
    18, 26, 92, 95–98, 106, 110, 150–51; Ute,
    63, Yurok, 46; Zuni, 49–51, 54, 73
American Indian Self-Determination
    Policy, 6, 39, 46
Arctic Circle, the, 121, 171
Arctic Council, the, 169, 173, 175
Arctic Ocean, the, 165, 169
Arizona Department of Environmental
    Quality (ADEQ), 79–80
Arthur, Chester A., 64–66
Atencio, Ernest, 7

Bennet Land Freeze, 70–73, 78, 86
Bennett, Robert L., 70–71
bioregionalism, 23, 32
Black Hills, 18, 95
Black Lives Matter movement, 36
Black Mesa, 62, 69, 84, 86, 137–38, 141–42,
    153

Boasberg, James, 96

Boyden, John Sterling, 67- 69

Bullard, Robert, 5, 8

Bureau of Indian Affairs (BIA), 38, 68, 70, 127–31, 187–89, 204

Bureau of Land Management (BLM), 42

cadmium, 3, 94

cancer, 3, 61, 74–77, 99, 203

Carson, Kit, 63, 140

Carson National Forest (CNF), 51–53, 204

Catholic Church, 38, 128, 131

Central Arizona Project (CAP), 137, 139, 140–41

Centers for Disease Control (CDC), 94, 203

charismatic megafauna (CMF), 163, 169, 172–73, 176

Christianity, 10, 37–38, 191

cities (United States): Cameron, Arizona, 80; Detroit, Michigan, 100–101; Flagstaff, Arizona, 80; Flint, Michigan, 92, 99–110; Las Vegas, Nevada, 67, 137, 150; Los Angeles, California, 67, 137, 150, 188; Moab, Utah, 80; Oakland, California, 188, 196; Phoenix, Arizona, 47, 50, 67, 137, 139; Salt Lake City, Utah, 67; San Francisco, California, 196–97; Taos, New Mexico, 51; Utqiavik, AK (Barrow, AK), 119–34

climate change, 21, 138–39, 151–161, 165, 167, 196, 206

Clinton, Bill, 6, 40, 44

coal: 60, 69, 95, 98, 102, 147–48, 164; and state-corporate crime, 84, 86, 89; mining, 59, 61–62, 109; on the Navajo Nation, 136–139, 141–42, 154

coalition building, 109, 171, 176

Cold War, 30, 73–74, 121

community resilience, 3–13, 36–55, 119–33, 160–76, 203–207

companies: Belle Fourche(United States), 97–98; Cyprus Amax Minerals (United States), 83; Energy Transfer Partners (United States), 98; Fortune Mining (Canada), 164, 171; Freeport McMoRan (United States), 83; General Motors (United States), 94, 108; Gulf Oil (United States), 76; Peabody Coal (United States), 69, 84, 141; Resolution Copper (United States) , 48; Western Nuclear Inc. (United States), 83

corrective justice, 7, 104–105, 132

court decisions (Canada): *Calder v. British Columbia* (1973), 174; *Delgamuukw v. British Columbia* (1997), 174; *Haida Nation v. British Columbia* (2004), 169, 174

court decisions (United States): *Cherokee v. Georgia* (1831), 9, 185; *Healing v. Jones* (1959), 63–65, 69, 70; *Johnson v. M'Intosh* (1823), 39, 144, 185 ; *Lyng v. Northwest Indian Cemetery Protective Association* (1988), 46–47, 50, 54; *Navajo Nation v. U.S. Forest Service (2008)*, 54; *Oliphant v. Suquamish Indian Tribe* (1978), 54; *Public Employees for Environmental Responsibility v. Beaudreau* (2014), 149; *Quechan Tribe v. U.S. Department of Interior* (2010), 150; *Save the Peaks Coalition v. US Forest Service* (2012), 54; *State of Arizona v. California* (1963), 145; *Tee Hit Ton Indians v. United States* (1955), 122–123; *United States v. Navajo Nation* (2009), 84; *US v. Wong Van Ark* (1898), 37; *US on Behalf of the Zuni Tribe of New Mexico v. Platt* (1990), 50; *Worchester v. Georgia*

(1832), 9, 185; *Winters v. United States* (1908), 143, 145;

Dakota Access Pipeline (DAPL), 8, 12, 96–99, 101, 106, 110
deep ecology, 17, 21–32
Department of Defense (DOD), 125–26, 131
Devil's Tower, the, 45
direct action, 12, 170, 17, 176, 196
discourse: as a means of garnering public support, 161–175 of assimilation, 145. *See also* assimilation
distributive justice, 7
Doctrine of Discovery, 18, 39, 55, 144

Environmental Impact Statement (EIS), 46, 48, 51 149
environmental racism, 4–5, 100–111, 136, 138
Environmental Protection Agency (EPA), 4, 6, 39–41, 72, 77, 95, 102, 129–132

feminism, 181–82, 198
First Amendment, 36–37, 42–53
First National People of Color Environmental Summit, 5
Fixico, Donald, 105, 180, 187, 190–91
Flake, Jeff, 48
Formerly Used Defense Sites (FUDS), 119, 124, 132

Gaia, 24
gender, 179, 181–84, 192–93, 198
Gould, Corina, 196–97
Great Bear Rainforest, 162–63, 171–73
Greenpeace, 163
Gunn-Allen, Paula, 192

habitat preservation, 168, 173
Hammoud, Fadwa, 104–5

Harper, Elijah, 175
Healing, Dewey, 63
Helmes, Kathy, 70–71
human rights, 3–13, 17–19, 115–17, 203–207

identity: and intersectionality, 179–80, 182; land as the basis of, 8, 10, 41, 121, 162, 181; loss of, 18, 121; pan-Indian, 184, 189–90, 198
Imoda, J.C., 38
Indian Health Service (IHS), 77, 129
Indigenous Environmental Network (IEN), 153
indigenous values, 3–13, 21–33, 36–55
indigenous women as leaders of Indian Environmental Justice, 179–98
Inter-Agency Working Group (IWG), 6, 40
Inuit Circumpolar council, 169, 172–73

Jones, Paul, 63

Klabona Keepers, 164, 170
Kuehn, Robert, 7, 103, 132

LaDuke, Winona, 10, 32
Lake Powell, 138–39, 142
legal statutes: Alaska National Interest Lands Conservation Act (ANILCA) (1980), 123–24; Alaska Native Claims Settlement Act (ANCSA) (1971), 123–24; American Antiquities Act (1906), 42; American Indian Religious Freedom Act (AIRFA) (1978), 42–44 ; Archeological Resources Protection Act (ARPA) (1979), 42; Clean Air Act (1970), 4; Clean Water Act (1972), 4, 79, 100; Comprehensive Environmental Response, Compensation and Liability Act (CERCLA) (1980), 93, 109; Dawes Act

(1887), 186; Dine Natural Resource Protection Act (2005), 81; Executive Order 12898 (1994), 6, 40–41, 52–54, 204–205; Executive Order 13007 (1996), 42; Executive Order 13175 (2000), 42; Executive Order (1882), 64–66; Fort Laramie Treaty (1868), 18, 95; General Mining Law (1872), 78–79; Groundwater Management Act (1980), 139; Homestead Act of 1868, 95; Indian Removal Act (1834), 42, 185; Indian Reorganization Act (1934), 65–66, 120, 180, 186–187; Indian Tribal Energy and Self Determination Act (2005), 149; National Environmental Policy Act (1969), 4, 51, 79, 149; National Historic Preservation Act (NHPA) (1996), 42, 149; Native American Graves Protection and Repatriation Act (NAGPRA) (1979), 42–43; Radiation Exposure Compensation Act (RECA) (1990), 82; Religious Freedom Restoration Act (RFRA) (1993), 42; Safe Drinking Water Act (1974), 4; Territorial Organic Act (1884), 22; Treaty of Guadalupe Hidalgo (1848), 63; Treaty of Cession from Russia (1867), 122; Tribal Forest Protection Act (2004), 42

logging, 46, 55, 168
Long Walk, the, 63, 140
Lovelock, James, 23
Lytle, Clifford, 29

mass society, 22–33
McCain, John, 48, 146
Meech Lake Accord (1987), 175
mining, 59–86, 119–33, 136–55, 160–76
missionaries, 37–38
Missouri River, 95–98, 106, 110

Naess, Arne, 22–25
National Park Service (NPS), 42–43, 45–46
Native American Lands Environmental Mitigation Program (NALEMP), 125
Navajo: and mining, 73–83; Nation, 13, 59, 61–72, 84, 86, 92–93, 95, 99–103, 106, 109, 110, 136–54, 203–4; people, 18, 41, 85
Navajo Generating Station, 137–42, 146, 148, 153
Navajo-Hopi Land Dispute, 63–64, 69–71, 86
Naval Arctic Research Laboratory (NARL), 121
Nunavut Land Claims Agreement (NLCA) (1993), 165

Oak Flat, 46–48
Obama, Barack, 73, 147, 148

Paris Climate Accord, 147–48
patriarchy, 179, 183, 192, 194
procedural justice, 7, 132, 137, 205
provinces (Canada): Alberta, 163–64, 170, 176; British Columbia (B.C.), 116, 160–64, 168–69, 171–75
public lands, 36–55, 160–76

radiation. See uranium
Red Power, 189, 190, 194.
relatedness, 21–22, 26, 32, 105
religion: Judeo Christian, 10
religious freedom: and Indigenous environmental justice, 11–13, 36–58, 205
removal policy, 37, 63, 69, 77, 86, 109, 185. See also, sub-entry Indian Removal Act under legal statutes
resistance, 8, 12, 84, 97, 160–76
resource extraction, 4, 12, 18, 61–62, 66, 84. See also, mining
Russia, 122, 175

sacred sites, 3–13, 36–55
San Francisco Peaks, 54–55
Save the Frasier Declaration (2010), 164, 169
self-determination: 124, and environmental justice, 5–6, 104, 131, 136, 153–54 de facto, 12, 126, 206; era of, 39, 46, 189–90,
Sellers, Stephanie A., 181–82
Session, George, 22–25
settler colonialism, 54, 104–105, 110, 132, 183–84
Shoot the Last Arrow Ceremony, the, 127
Smith, Andrea, 182, 192
Snyder, Rick, 100
social justice, 7, 12, 110, 183
solar energy, 147–48, 150, 154
sovereignty, de facto, 12, 117, 126, 131, 206–207
spirituality, Indigenous, 10, 11, 24–25, 27, 38, 136, 173, 192, 204
Stewart, Phillip, 170
Superfund sites: and the EPA, 102, 109, 129–32; in Indian Country, 93–94, 99, 119, 203; on the Navajo Nation, 13, 103, 110

Tar Creek, 12, 116, 119, 126, 129–32, 204
Tar Sands Healing Walk, 170
timber, 123, 160–63, 169, 172
tribal councils, 66–67, 141, 174
tribal sovereignty, 160–76
Trump, Donald J., 79, 96, 98, 147–48
Trust Doctrine, 9

Udall, Stewart, 64–66, 74, 78
Universal Declaration on Human Rights (1948), 6

United Nations Declaration on the Rights of Indigenous Peoples (2007), 6, 11, 15, 30, 111, 116, 170
uranium, 4, 60, 67; mining, 11, 13, 18, 59, 69, 71, 98; poisoning, 72, 74–86, 93–95, 99, 102, 203–204
urban: ghettos, 103; Indian identity, 115–16; Indian leadership in, 12, 179–98; reliance on tribal resources, 136, 139, renewal, 43. See also, cities
Urban Indian Health Commission (UIHC), 116,
U.S. Army Corp of Engineers, 96
U.S. Department of Agriculture Forest Service (USDA Forest Service), 42, 46–49, 52–53, 123
U.S. Department of Health (USDH), 97–98, 103

water, 59–86, 92–111, 136–55, 160–76
Water Protectors, The, 99
water rights: 136, 143–47, 151–52; American Indian reserved water rights, 138, 143–46
Weber, Francis, 38
White Earth Land Recovery Project, The, 31
Wilderness, 4, 25
World Bank, 29
World Trade Organization, 29
World War II, 67, 73, 83, 121, 139, 190

zinc, 3, 94, 128, 165
Zuni Heaven, 49–50, 54